MW00561779

Modern Middle Eastern
Jewish Thought

PUBLICATION OF THIS BOOK
IS SUPPORTED BY A GRANT FROM
Jewish Federation of Greater Hartford

THE TAUBER INSTITUTE SERIES FOR
THE STUDY OF EUROPEAN JEWRY
Jehuda Reinharz, General Editor
Sylvia Fuks Fried, Associate Editor
Eugene R. Sheppard, Associate Editor

THE BRANDEIS LIBRARY OF MODERN JEWISH THOUGHT
Eugene R. Sheppard and Samuel Moyn, Editors

This library aims to redefine the canon of modern Jewish thought by publishing
primary source readings from individual Jewish thinkers or groups of thinkers in reliable
English translations. Designed for courses in modern Jewish philosophy, thought, and
intellectual history, each volume features a general introduction and annotations to each
source with the instructor and student in mind.

Modern Middle Eastern Jewish Thought: Writings on Identity, Politics, and Culture, 1893–1958
Moshe Behar and Zvi Ben-Dor Benite, editors
Jews and Diaspora Nationalism: Writings on Jewish Peoplehood in Europe and the United States
Simon Rabinovitch, editor
Moses Mendelssohn: Writings on Judaism, Christianity, and the Bible
Michah Gottlieb, editor
Jews and Race: Writings on Identity and Difference, 1880–1940
Mitchell B. Hart, editor

FOR THE COMPLETE LIST OF BOOKS THAT ARE FORTHCOMING IN
THE SERIES, PLEASE SEE HTTP://WWW.BRANDEIS.EDU/TAUBER

Modern Middle Eastern Jewish Thought

Edited by
Moshe Behar and
Zvi Ben-Dor Benite

WRITINGS ON IDENTITY, POLITICS, AND CULTURE, 1893–1958

Brandeis University Press

Waltham, Massachusetts

American Hebrew Academy Library

BRANDEIS UNIVERSITY PRESS

An imprint of University Press of New England

www.upne.com

© 2013 Brandeis University

All rights reserved

Manufactured in the United States of America

Designed by Eric M. Brooks

Typeset in Albertina and Verlag by

Passumpsic Publishing

University Press of New England is a member of the
Green Press Initiative. The paper used in this book meets
their minimum requirement for recycled paper.

For permission to reproduce any of the material in this book,
contact Permissions, University Press of New England, One Court
Street, Suite 250, Lebanon NH 03766; or visit www.upne.com

Library of Congress Cataloging-in-Publication Data
Modern Middle Eastern Jewish thought: writings on identity,
politics, and culture, 1893–1958 / edited by Moshe Behar and
Zvi Ben-Dor Benite.—1st ed.
    pages ; cm. — (The Brandeis library of modern Jewish thought)
(The Tauber Institute for the Study of European Jewry series)
Includes index.
ISBN 978-1-58465-884-9 (cloth: alk. paper)—
ISBN 978-1-58465-885-6 (pbk.: alk. paper)—
ISBN 978-1-61168-386-8 (ebook)
1. Jews—Middle East—Identity. 2. Arabs—Middle East—Ethnic
identity. 3. Jews—Middle East—Intellectual life—20th century.
4. Arabs—Middle East—Intellectual life—20th century.
5. Jewish nationalism—Middle East. 6. Arab Nationalism—
Middle East. 7. Zionism—Palestine—History—20th century.
8. Israel—Ethnic relations. I. Behar, Moshe, editor. II. Ben-Dor
Benite, Zvi, editor.
DS143.M62   2012
305.892'4—dc23   2012030327

5 4 3 2 1

To our parents,

Nina Vivante, of blessed memory, and Albert Behar;

and David Aziz and Tikva Bushra Ben-Dor,

who taught us that Middle Eastern boundaries could

be crossed and crossed again, if one so chooses

Contents

Foreword

It is with great enthusiasm that we present a volume of the Brandeis Library of Modern Jewish Thought devoted to a heterogeneous set of intellectuals who stood at the intersection of Jewish and Arab identities. These Jews from the Arab East, some of whom identified themselves as Mizrahim, wrestled with questions of religious difference and national aspirations in Arabic, Hebrew, and French publications since the confluence of *haskala* and nahda intellectual movements at the close of the nineteenth century. Moshe Behar and Zvi Ben-Dor Benite open a window onto the vibrant visions for Jewish culture and politics within overlapping Arabic, Islamic, and colonial contexts. The rise of secular nationalist movements, the disintegration of the Ottoman Empire, and the Zionist call for Jewish settlement in Palestine dramatically changed the landscape that Middle Eastern Jews inhabited. After 1948 there would be a whole new set of responses to integration within the State of Israel, a polity and society dominated by elites from Europe or their descendants. Within one decade of statehood, Israel became the regional center for Middle Eastern Jewry. Thus would begin a new era of intellectual ferment, one that would be decisively conditioned by Israel's cultural and political coordinates. In this sense, this volume traces the largely unacknowledged origins of the reconstituted Mizrahi intellectual of subsequent generations.

Eugene R. Sheppard and Samuel Moyn, Editors
The Brandeis Library of Modern Jewish Thought

Acknowledgments

In retrospect, the inception of this anthology probably dates back to 1990 when we met in Jerusalem as undergraduate students and realized that we were both reading and distributing the now legendary Mizrahi semi-*samizdat* publication *Iton Aher* (The other paper). Our friendship is an outgrowth of that one precious Jerusalemite afternoon.

Ammiel Alcalay, to whom we owe a two-decade-long intellectual aspiration, has always maintained that writing Middle Eastern Jewish intellectual history should be a collective effort, and this anthology is precisely that. Locating some of the documents included in this collection was made possible because fellow scholars and friends shared our belief in both its importance and the need for it, and thus helped us to obtain them. Ziad Fahmi was kind enough to share with us texts by Ya'qub Sannu'; Lital Levy shared with us both essays by Esther Moyal; Amos Noy shared with us Avraham Elmaleh's essay (in addition to his forthcoming article on Elmaleh); and Abigail Jacobson saved us time, money, and energy by kindly giving us, on a particularly humid day in Tel Aviv, a more readable copy of Nissim Malul's article than the one we had. It is a pleasure and a duty to recognize the important work that these four scholars have been producing in the field, work that informs this anthology in many ways. Bryan Roby responded positively when we asked him to photocopy in the Givat Haviva Institute Sami Michael's essay in *al-Jadid*; Mansoor A. Mirza was kind enough to photocopy for us at the London School of Economics Elie (Eliyahu) Eliacher's testimony before the Palestine Royal Commission (the Peel Commission). We also thank Nissim Rejwan, Shimon Ballas, Sasson Somekh, and Reuven Snir, all of whom offered us kind advice on Iraqi Jewish intellectuals. For their help in finding other documents, we are grateful to the staffs of the Princeton University Library, Brandeis University Library, International Institute for Social History in Amsterdam, the Public Record Office in London, and, in Jerusalem, the Ben Zvi Institute, Central Zionist Archive, and Israel's National Library.

We would also like to thank Eugene Sheppard, Samuel Moyn, and Sylvia Fuks Fried for supporting from the very beginning the idea of assembling an anthology such as this. Phyllis D. Deutsch, editor in chief at the University Press of New England, was kind and diligent in guiding us through the production process. As editors of the Brandeis Library of Modern Jewish Thought, Eugene Sheppard and Sam Moyn were continuously helpful and ready to offer advice throughout. We would also like to thank Jonathan Decter and the anonymous reviewers for their comments and suggestions on both the proposal and first draft of this anthology.

We were also aided by skillful translators. Fuad Saleh carefully translated the Arabic texts by Ya'qub Sannu', Esther Moyal, Murād Farag, Marsil Shirizi, and Yusuf Harun Zilkha. Atef Alshaer translated Sami Michael's essay from the Arabic. Alistair Ligertwood translated the French texts by Ya'qub Sannu', Joseph Aslan Cattaui Pacha, and Henri Curiel. We thank them for their care, diligence, and rigor. Lucy Mair and Lee Manneberg graciously helped us revise, translate, and edit texts from Hebrew. Jeanne Ferris carefully edited the entire manuscript, identifying and weeding out many problems that still hid in the text. For scholarly, linguistic, and communication considerations, we edited and sometimes emended all the translations in this book; if errors remain, they are ours alone and not those of the translators.

The Tauber Institute generously provided funds for the translations, and we thank Miriam Hoffman and Sylvia Fuks Fried for their constant support and care in managing those funds. Thanks also go to Golan Moskowitz for carefully managing numerous drafts of the manuscript. A grant from New York University's Humanities Initiative Grants-in-Aid fund and a grant from the Pears Foundation's support for the University of Manchester's library arrived at a crucial moment and facilitated the completion of this project.

Conversations with friends and scholars over the last two decades helped us imagine and conceptualize this project. Although they are too many to be mentioned here, some of these friends and colleagues appear in the introduction to this volume as well as in our suggestions for further reading. It was thrilling to realize how much work they have accomplished over the years.

This anthology, however, teaches us that there is a great deal more work to be done on the modern history, sociology, and political science of Middle Eastern Jewry. We are therefore hopeful that many other—older and younger—colleagues and students alike will be able to use this book and expand this collective endeavor. We consider this project as important as a monograph because it lays a foundation for the rethinking and reconceptualization of modern Middle Eastern and Jewish thought in historical, sociological, and political terms.

Without Lucy Mair's and Katherine Fleming's support, patience, and advice, we would not have been able to find the time and energy to produce the anthology. Our daughters, Sophia, Eliya, Lulu, Camile-Nina, and Cora-Louise—who live their lives between the Middle East, Europe, and the United States—always remind us of the international dimensions of Middle Eastern Jewish writing. Our parents, Albert Behar, Nina Vivante (of blessed memory), David Aziz, and Tikva Bushra Ben-Dor, remain a constant inspiration. They crossed the borders of the Middle East on their way to Israel, but they taught us that borders can be crossed again and again. They lived through parts of the history unfolded in the pages of this book, and we dedicate it to them.

Moshe Behar
Zvi Ben-Dor Benite

Editors' Note

In translating the texts for this volume, we strove to produce versions in smooth English that would be accessible to the widest readership possible. Thus transliterated Hebrew and Arabic words are rendered in the standard simplified Romanization system, with minimal diacritical markings. However, where names or words appear in the original texts in Latin characters, we preserved that spelling even if it does not conform with current Romanization systems. Therefore in some cases the reader will find Koran instead of Qur'an, Mugrabi instead of Maghrebi, Mohammed rather than Muhammad, and the prefix Abou instead of Abu. In one case, we opted to transliterate the name Farag as it sounds in Egyptian Arabic and not as it should be according to literary Arabic (Faraj). Farag himself transliterated his name when writing Hebrew in this way.

Annotations that explain terminology or provide information about individuals and events are presented in square brackets to distinguish them from notes that appear in the original texts. In a few instances the *original* editors of a text intervened; we identify these interventions clearly. When the words "the editors" appear in a text, they are part of the original text and do not refer to us.

Certain words, particularly in the Hebrew texts included in this volume, presented us with different challenges. For instance, the term "Aretz" appears in many different contexts that require different interpretations: land, country, Palestine, and the Land of Israel. We have translated this word according to the context. Certain words, such as "aliya" (immigration of Jews to the Land of Israel) and "kibbutz," have become part of the English language. The same is true for the less familiar "Yishuv" (the Jewish residents in Palestine before the creation of the State of Israel) and "Histadrut" (the full name in English would be General Federation of Laborers in the Land of Israel), which we kept in the original.

"Mizrah" (meaning East or Orient), which appears in this volume numerous times, is a special case. In recent years, "Mizrah" and the derivative "Mizrahi" (Easterner or Oriental) and its plural, "Mizrahim," have become common in academic jargon—as in "Mizrahi studies," or "the invention of the Mizrahim." We therefore use these words in our introduction, prefatory notes to the texts, and annotations as an English neologism, just like other Hebrew words that have become common in English. We avoid using the name "Adot Ha-Mizrah"

(Communities of the East), which was the official label for Mizrahim in Israel and in Hebrew until the late 1980s. We similarly avoid using the term "Oriental Jews," which was in use for a while. Depending on the context, the word "Mizrah" is rendered sometimes as East and sometimes as Orient. "Mizrah," as many authors imply or explicitly say, is not limited to the East as a geographical category, referring to Asia. In many cases it refers to the East writ large—including both the North African Maghreb and the Balkans. Readers should take note that in many cases authors used the terms "Sephardi" or "Sephardic" and "Mizrah" or "Mizrahi" interchangeably.

Suggested further readings are listed following the selections.

Introduction
Mizrahi and Modern Middle Eastern Thought: Present and Past

Mizrahi Conversations and the East

A significant development in the world of Jewish thought during the past two decades is evident in the rise of a discourse—better yet, conversations—explicitly concerned with Mizrahim, or Jews of non-Ashkenazi descent whose origins lie in the East outside Europe. At first, the collective name "Mizrahim" simply denoted Jews of Asian and North African origin who lived in Israel after the 1950s. More recently, however, the name is often applied to all Jews of Middle Eastern descent, whether they live in Israel or elsewhere. Simultaneously there has been a surge of publications of all sorts concerned with Mizrahim, first in Israel and later also in the United States and other countries. Mizrahi experiences, identities, and histories are presented, assessed, and debated in scholarly articles and monographs, political statements, personal testimonies and memoirs, poetry and fiction, and music and cinema, as well as on websites and blogs.[1] These often passionate conversations take place in a variety of locations—in the "Jewish street," in political and social organizations, and in academia.[2] Perhaps the best indication that something new is happening is the emergence of a body of knowledge that is sometimes called Mizrahi studies, separate from what used to be called "Sephardi studies."[3] At the same time, the word "Mizrahi" is increasingly replacing terms such as "Oriental Jews" or "Middle Eastern Jews," thereby signaling the importance of the specifically Israeli or Hebrew context within which many of these conversations have emerged in recent years.[4] In any case, geography—physical and, more important, cultural and political—plays a key role, as the term "Mizrah" (East) keeps reminding us. If we can be allowed one overarching generalization about these conversations, then it is that the relationship with and the linkage to the East, however defined, and the condition of "being an Eastern Jew," again however defined, are key elements in all of these conversations. Briefly put, Mizrahi conversations are built on the consciousness of "being in"—and/or "being from"—the East.

Nonetheless, although there seems to be a consensus today about the existence of a distinct collectivity known as Mizrahim, and although the term is common in contemporary Israeli speech as well as in English academic jargon, agreement about its boundaries, origins, and characteristics remains elusive. The one possible exception is the notion that Mizrahim are non-Ashkenazi Jews who originated in Asia or Africa. One of the core issues of Mizrahi conversations in the current phase is the problem of Mizrahi difference from the "mainstream" Israeli Ashkenazi society that repeatedly gives rise to heated debates about the possibility and the necessity of Mizrahi "assimilation" within that society. Indeed, the question of Mizrahi identity—particularly its distinctive place within Israeli society, politics, and culture—is crucial for contemporary Mizrahi intellectuals. The sociologist Yitzhak Dahan, a Mizrahi scholar himself, has recently attempted to classify the major trends among Mizrahi intellectuals between 1970 and 2005. Dahan identifies several major orientations. At one end of the spectrum he finds radical criticism of Zionism and intense resistance to assimilation within Israeli society and an emphasis on "traditional Mizrahi roots and refusal to detach from them." At the other end he finds a constant struggle to "harmonize" the "three elements of [Mizrahi] identity: the Jewish, the Zionist, and the Mizrahi," in order to make space for Mizrahim within the political and cultural mainstream in Israel.[5] All orientations, it should be noted, assume a distinct Mizrahi identity. A recent collection of studies on Mizrahim suggests that "Mizrahim" is "a descriptive term—a category, designation, or name—used to distinguish between classes of persons or groups," as well as a term that "connotes identity, relating to a sense of self, to self-image, to how individuals and groups define themselves and their place in their world, to what is distinctive to them and at the same time separates themselves from others."[6] Furthermore, it goes almost without saying that just as there is little agreement on what the term "Mizrahim" connotes, there is even less agreement about the scope of its history. For instance, the questions of what is Mizrahi history and what is its relationship to Jewish history in general—and to the history of Jews in the Middle East before the establishment of the State of Israel—are among the most hotly debated topics emerging in the wake of the appearance of both Mizrahi studies and Mizrahi conversations.[7] In fact, these conversations, and the conflicts they reflect, are reshaping the ways in which the more traditional historiographies of Middle Eastern Jewries both before and after 1948 are viewed and framed.[8]

These issues have immense significance today, when it is becoming increasingly clear that what we call "Jewish history" and "Jewish historiography" has been shaped and framed almost exclusively by European Jewish experiences of the past 200 years—an intensely turbulent trajectory culminating with the

Shoah and the creation of the State of Israel. The impact of modern European Jewish history and experience on the way in which scholars view modern Jewish history in general is predictably immense. Jewish modernity writ large and the modern Jewish historical trajectory are not only seen as coming out of European experiences, but those experiences also serve as the quintessential yardstick according to which all other Jewish histories are measured and assessed.

As we shall see, we must not superimpose this historical trajectory on Jewish history as a whole. This insight is relevant to non-European Jewish experience as a whole and especially, we contend, to non-European Jewish reflections on this experience. Thus, we must ponder the place of non-European, modern Middle Eastern Jewish thinking and writing in modern Jewish intellectual history. To begin with, is it "modern" at all? Is it simply a derivative of European Jewish thought? Furthermore, the seemingly rapid emergence of such a huge body of knowledge raises other serious questions. For example, where does this knowledge come from? Does it have a history? And when, where, and how did the issues and topics that concern intellectuals who define themselves as Mizrahi originate and take shape? In other words, can we speak of a different historical trajectory in which Middle Eastern Jews—now also known as Mizrahim—engaged questions pertaining to their identity, experiences, and place in both Jewish and Arab history? Can we also speak of a considerably longer historical trajectory, one that begins before the creation of the State of Israel and the mass Mizrahi immigrations of the 1950s?

These and other such questions inform this anthology of modern Middle Eastern Jewish writings produced by intellectuals who formed a distinguishable historical strand within the larger context of modern Jewish thought. They were embedded in, shaped by, and reacted to, complex historical contexts. In many cases these people knew each other or read each other's works, and they related to one another as belonging to the same, or related, strands of thought. They certainly did not think of themselves as mere isolated voices, as some scholars would describe them today. It is the combination of the affinities with the Middle East and the sense of dialogue with European Jewish history and culture that creates the space for Middle Eastern Jewish thought within the broader context of modern Jewish thought. Indeed, it is this combination of features that in our view render the authors whose works we present here modern Middle Eastern Jewish intellectuals. Of course, these features shaped or informed the thought of various members of this group of intellectuals in different ways and played different roles in the writings of various authors. This phenomenon that we term "modern Middle Eastern Jewish thought" is by no means homogeneous—it never has been. Yet its basic platform has long been the same: a dual interest in the affinity between Jewishness and the Middle Eastern context, on the one hand, and a sense of juxtaposition to the European Jewish context, on the other hand.

This anthology demonstrates that Mizrahi intellectuals have been active for many decades, and in any event well before the rise of contemporary Mizrahi conversations. Just like today's intellectuals, their predecessors addressed—albeit in different terms—the key issues that render Mizrahi writing Mizrahi, most important of which are the relationship with, and the linkage to, the East, however defined; and the condition of being an Eastern Jew. In a speech delivered at an annual meeting of Sephardi and Mizrahi Jews in 1939, Rabbi Ben-Zion Hai Meir Uziel declared: "Sephardim are not only those who came from Spain. 'Sephardim' are those who adopted Spanish influences. All those who are based in eastern countries, and adopted the Spanish influence, are called in the respectable name: the Sephardi tribe."[9] We might see things differently. But Rabbi Uziel's words serve us well by forcefully reminding us that, much like today's intellectuals, the authors in this anthology tended to see all Eastern Jews as a distinct group within world Jewry but at the same time debated how to define it. Moreover, much like their modern successors, these authors were not contending with these questions in a vacuum but in a world—a Jewish world—in which Europe and the West, however defined, played a dominant role. This anthology points to the possibility that what we might wish to term "Mizrahi thought" has had a considerably longer history than is commonly known or understood. This is a history of an emerging sense that the Eastern Jewish existence has a distinct meaning in a modern world dominated by Europe and Europeans. It is a history that can be characterized by numerous different attempts to articulate this consciousness. And like Jewish thought in general, Mizrahi thought is a diverse and heterogeneous body of knowledge.

Interest in Middle Eastern Jewish intellectuals exists but has yet to produce substantial scholarly attention. The obscurity and inaccessibility of many of these past intellectuals and their writings prevent many modern readers from reaching and engaging them. Affinities forged today between contemporary Mizrahi intellectuals and their predecessors raise a host of historical questions about the concreteness, validity, and meaning of these affinities. Interest in Middle Eastern Jewish writing has produced a few fresh studies in Israel, Europe, and the United States. They shed light on the social, intellectual, and political contexts out of which the intellectuals whose works we gather here emerged. Interestingly enough, most of the studies that focus specifically on intellectual histories of Jews in the Middle East have thus far been produced by literary scholars rather than by historians or comparative social scientists.[10] This anthology has two purposes in this regard. The first is to render at least some of these past intellectuals more accessible and better known. The second is to lay a solid foundation for a meaningful dialogue with them by drawing attention to the more explicitly political and social aspects of their works—thus bringing their writings closer to other academic disciplines. Therefore, in this anthology we purposefully chose to include nonfiction, sociopolitical writings, which are much harder to access than literary texts.

Scholars have occasionally noted the presence of Middle Eastern Jewish writing in modern Jewish intellectual history. Yet few systematically treat the writers' broader historical and intellectual contexts or the themes that Middle Eastern intellectuals addressed.[11] Histories of modern Jewish intellectuals usually focus almost exclusively on European and American contexts.[12] Arab and other Middle Eastern intellectuals tend to overlook or avoid the role of Jews in the intellectual histories of various Middle Eastern countries. This may be why even serious studies that mention Middle Eastern Jewish intellectuals tend to speak of them as "voices"—as if they come out of the wilderness instead of solid historical contexts.[13]

It is tempting to attribute this ignorance to dismissive attitudes that European Jews might have toward Middle Eastern Jews, or to nationalist Arab approaches that sometimes prefer to ignore Jewish aspects of Arab history in light of Israel's post-1948 triumph. In many cases, these interpretations would be accurate. But one must also bear in mind that in comparison to European Jewry, Middle Eastern Jews have made up less than 10 percent of the Jewish people worldwide. They were also a tiny minority community in the region. The number of Jews in the Arab Middle East in the middle of the twentieth century was roughly 750,000, and they were divided into ten different minority communities. It follows that the absolute number of Middle Eastern Jewish intellectuals was small. It must be also noted that since the mid-1970s, Middle Eastern intellectual history has been pushed to the sidelines of Middle Eastern studies and has tended to "lag behind and remain ghettoized."[14] It is therefore no surprise that thus far there have been very few attempts to engage Middle Eastern Jewish intellectual history comprehensively. In fact, it is even hard to find any references to Middle Eastern Jewish intellectual history. The reason is that terms such as "modern Jewish political thought" and "Jewish intellectual" relate almost exclusively to phenomena and figures within the realm of European history. Educated readers can commonly outline the central topics addressed by European Jewish intellectuals from the eighteenth century onward. Yet these same readers—including, alas, Middle East specialists—usually know little or nothing about Jewish intellectuals hailing from within the modern Arab Middle East.

In undertaking this project, we have been emboldened by the fact that in recent years some scholars have spoken about the need for such a volume. Ammiel Alcalay concludes his unique overview of Middle Eastern Jewish intellectual life with a call "to begin filling in the contours and details of this rich and varied intellectual history," stressing that this task "will take the collective efforts of many."[15] Indeed, it must be a collective effort—and the rationale behind starting with an anthology, rather than a monograph, is that an anthology can begin to "fill in the contours." The writers and thinkers featured here by no means represent the full array of Middle Eastern Jewish intellectual life; our anthology is merely one step toward a more comprehensive and fuller intellectual history of Middle Eastern Jewry. First and foremost, this step involves beginning to turn these "voices" into a history.

Contours of Place and Time

The anthology's context and chronology require a bit more by way of introduction. The body of knowledge presented here is almost completely unknown in that sense. Thus it seems best to introduce it cautiously—in a way that opens it up for consideration rather than one that asserts definitive conclusions. This collection of writings is above all an invitation to study its implications for Middle Eastern and Jewish history. It offers a collection of sources that were written in Arabic, Hebrew, English, and French in the major urban centers of the Mashriq (the Arab East)—Cairo, Beirut, Jerusalem, and Baghdad—by writers who can collectively be termed here Middle Eastern Jewish intellectuals. With only a few exceptions, the anthology proceeds in chronological order, from 1893 to 1958. The earliest text is a lecture on Islam by an Egyptian Jew delivered in Chicago, at the World's Parliament of Religions and Religious Congresses; the last text is a report on the social conditions of Middle Eastern Jews living in Israel by a Syrian-born Israeli parliamentarian representing the Ahdut Ha-'avoda Party—during the 1950s, a major part of the ruling coalition and historically an important element within Israel's ruling Labor Party.

The endpoint of 1959 is deliberate. The essay ending the anthology meticulously discusses Mizrahim a decade after the creation of the State of Israel.

During this decade, the Middle Eastern Jewish diaspora effectively came to an end. The overwhelming majority of the Jews in many major Middle Eastern communities left their homes and emigrated, mostly to Israel, which has the largest concentration of Jews of Middle Eastern origin. At this point the Jews of the Middle East cease to be the Middle Eastern version of the so-called Jewish Question and become—as they remain today—an Israeli social, political, and cultural problem.[16]

Although the selection of writings in this anthology suggests a certain historical trajectory of modern Middle Eastern thought from the 1890s to the late 1950s, we emphasize that this trajectory is, at best, skeletal. This collection traces only the central questions that concerned Mizrahi intellectuals during those decades: the place and role of Jews in a modern Middle East; how to define Judaism and how to identify as Jews in a region increasingly dominated by European power and culture; the relationships between Jews and Muslims, Jews and Arabs, as well as Jewish and Arab culture; how to relate to Zionism and the proper form for a modern Jewish state in Palestine; and, finally, how to integrate with the new Israeli society—a society created and dominated by Ashkenazi Jews whose identity, writ large, was based exclusively on European and European Jewish experiences, ideologies, identities, and orientations. Albeit in different forms and for different purposes, these questions are being asked today, too, despite—or perhaps precisely because of—the transformations stemming from the creation of the State of Israel in 1948.

The answers provided by the authors in this collection to the questions above are not comprehensive. In making our selections we strove to give the reader a sense of how very wide was the range of possibilities that different writers envisioned at different points in history. This is crucial, for it enables us to recover, and sometimes present for the first time in English, ideas that were once considered viable but that were forgotten as the history of the Middle East shifted and turned. For instance, the call for full Jewish integration with the emerging Arabic-based culture might sound eccentric to contemporary ears, but at a time when some of the early intellectuals featured here, and numerous other authors, were writing in Arabic, such integration seemed a real possibility. The same can be said concerning Jewish relationships with Arab nationalism, both in Palestine and the wider Middle East. Strange as it sounds today, playing a role, even a significant one, within Arab national movements and parties was a more viable option for many Jewish intellectuals of earlier times than keeping themselves separate or emigrating. Perhaps the clearest indication of this is the very late and lukewarm (to say the least) response to Zionism among Middle Eastern Jews, which at times is described as a failure on their part and is often cited as the cause of their problematic integration into the Israeli state and society.[17]

A final example would be the various suggestions and programs discussed in the selections here for a more equal participation of Jews and Arabs in the building of a modern state in Palestine. These proposals may seem fantastic today, but to reject them as unrepresentative or illusory is to deny their historicity. In the context of their time, they seemed plausible and logical, one of the many possible trajectories the Jewish national movement in Palestine could take. We revisit some of these issues below.

Mizrahi Intellectuals

It is hard to define the term "modern Jewish intellectuals." Such a conscious attempt to identify Middle Eastern Jewish intellectuals has never been made before, and the word "Mizrahim" has never been neutral and sometimes seems fraught with contradictions, geographical inconsistencies, anomalies, and incoherencies.[18] Following Paul Mendes-Flohr, we also are interested in "the emotive and normative character of the term *intellectual* rather than its strict sociological definition." We therefore adopt one of the less rigid definitions that Mendes-Flohr, following Michael Confino, offers: not "simply men of letters or scholastic achievement, but . . . individuals who exhibit a particular focus to their thinking."[19] We thus identify Middle Eastern Jewish intellectuals as Jewish men and women whose thinking was informed and shaped by their expressed affinities with, and sense of belonging to, the Middle East, or Orient, and its peoples and cultures.

Like Jewish intellectuals in Europe, their Middle Eastern counterparts wrestled with modernity. At the same time, Jewish intellectuals and others in the Middle East grappled with the idea of Europe. Inasmuch as modernity sprang from local Middle Eastern historical currents, and inasmuch as it was subject to the European presence, dominance, and colonization, modern Jewish thought in the Middle East was closely linked to both.[20] These intertwined trajectories gave rise to weighty challenges and questions, such as how one negotiates individual and collective Jewish existence in a modern Middle East. The rise of literacy in the Middle East—the product of the modernization of education in most major urban centers of the region—produced large numbers of writers who expressed their views in new modes of expression and genres. Furthermore, Jews began, slowly but with increasing intensity, to write in the European languages that were introduced into the Middle East, primarily French and English. At the same time, Jews also wrote in Arabic and Hebrew.

Jewish fiction and nonfiction written in a variety of languages appeared with the rise of modern journalism and print culture in the region. These processes accelerated after the disintegration of the Ottoman Empire in 1914.[21] The strong Western impact on modern Middle Eastern education and the rapidly emerging print culture shaped the local Jews' intellectual work. Although many Jews began attending modern state schools, still more attended modern Jewish schools whose origins were external. For instance, many of the intellectuals were graduates of the Francophone Alliance Israélite Universelle, whose network of schools spread in many Ottoman and Middle Eastern regions beginning in 1862. By the 1900s there were 26,000 students in more than one hundred Alliance schools alone.[22] Many others continued their education in Europe or attended branches of European schools in their home countries where Jews and Christians were disproportionately represented. It was reported, for instance, that 90 percent of the Iraqi candidates for the matriculation exam in London were Jews. In the English department in Baghdad's Normal School, four students—half of the class—were Jews.[23] This was at a time when Jews made up less than 4 percent of the Iraqi population (but 20 percent of the population of Baghdad).

Intellectual Engagement and Debates

Sometimes taking leading positions, Jews participated actively in almost all of the significant political, social, and cultural movements that shaped the modern Middle East from the middle of the nineteenth century onward, and particularly from the beginning of the twentieth century.[24] And Western and Middle Eastern currents were clearly visible within Jewish intellectual thought and activity. As Lital Levy explains, "at the twilight of the Ottoman Empire, in urban centers such as Baghdad, Beirut, Cairo, and Jaffa, Jewish intellectuals participated in the modem Hebrew and Arabic enlightenment movements (the *haskala* and the *nahda*-awakening). They immersed themselves in the ideological and political currents of their time, responding to the competing pulls of Ottomanism, Zionism, and territorial nationalism."[25] To the above list of isms and ideologies, we might add Marxism, communism, and theosophy.[26] In this anthology we meet, for instance, writers such as Ya'qub Sannu' and Esther Moyal, active leaders in the *nahda* movement in Egypt during the late nineteenth century. Avraham Elmaleh's *haskala*-like call for collecting and researching the reaches of Mizrahi culture was published in Jerusalem nearly a century ago. This call remains apt today, and we open this volume with it even though it is not the earliest item in our selection. Another powerful essay on Mizrahi culture in the context of the encounter between European and Middle Eastern Jews in early-twentieth-century Palestine is by Hayyim Ben-Kiki, who insisted in 1921 on returning to "our Oriental culture" (*tarbutenu ha-mizrahit*). Also included here are an essay on religions in the Middle East by the prolific Egyptian poet and essayist Murād Farag, and an essay on solidarity and diversity by Joseph Cattaui, one of Egypt's first modern historians.

These themes resonate in the discussions and elaborations of other authors represented here. For example, behind the discussion about Arabs and Arabic culture there is another important question about the Jewish attitude toward Islam and Islamic history and culture. Several authors address this question and also questions of religion in general. As Levy puts it eloquently, Middle Eastern Jewish intellectuals "explored what it meant to be Arab, Jewish, and modern, re-imagining themselves and their communities through the regional vocabulary of modernity and enlightenment."[27]

It is important to realize that intellectual endeavors such as exploring "what it meant to be Arab, Jewish, and modern" in the Middle East, and negotiating a "regional vocabulary of modernity" were not carried out in a political or cultural vacuum. One can certainly see some of these issues intersecting in early essays touching on questions of what should be the cultural orientation of the Jewish Yishuv in Palestine. The reader might find that the early discussions are precursors to some recent Mizrahi ideas about Israel's own cultural orientation.[28] We should reiterate that some of the ideas that have been associated with Mizrahi intellectuals and activists since the 1970s had been articulated impressively at least sixty years earlier by individuals who identified themselves in similar terms yet who remain largely obscure today.

The building of a Jewish nation particularly affected the Jewish communities nearest to it—namely, those living in the Mashriq.[29] In the context of the encounter with modern European Jewish nationalism and thought, Jerusalem was the site that made the imagining of a Middle Eastern Jewish collective possible. Indeed, this collective was one that was to be imagined in as much detail by Middle Eastern Jews as by European Jews. This vision turned into reality when—in the wake of decolonization and the creation of the State of Israel—the majority of Middle Eastern Jewry found itself in Israel. These Jews and their children did indeed indisputably end up imagining themselves as one Mizrahi collective, and they are imagined as such by others, as well.[30]

What the intellectual history of this collective is, and where to locate the collective, should remain an open question. But the general outline we sketch here explains our perhaps not-so-obvious choice to end this anthology in Israel in the 1950s, before the outbreak of the Mizrahi Wadi Salib rebellion—a series of violent clashes between Mizrahi immigrants and the Israeli authorities over housing issues that broke out in 1959. It is this period that can be seen as concluding the early phase of Middle Eastern Jewish intellectual history. Until that moment, most Middle Eastern intellectuals hailed from their original communities in the Arab East. The 1950s marked a geographical and demographic transformation that unleashed radical intellectual, sociopolitical, and cultural change. Engaging modernity in their original communities was now replaced by discussing the hardships of the modernization and Israelization projects demanded by the Israeli government. The big questions with which Mizrahi intellectuals contended before the creation of the State of Israel—the shape of the national Jewish home and the Jewish attitude toward Arabs and Arabic culture—were completely transformed, but not entirely forgotten. Finally, the process of concentrating Middle Eastern Jewry in Israel meant a transformation in linguistic terms as well. Earlier intellectuals wrote in Arabic, French, English, and classical Hebrew, but their successors gradually transitioned to writing in the new "demotic"—or vernacular—Hebrew that was emerging in Israel. Many authors, alas, simply ceased to write altogether. We present here one essay by the Iraqi author Sami Michael, written and published in Arabic in Israel in 1954 in the leading Palestinian journal a few years after his immigration. Michael, now known as one of Israel's leading literary figures, began his career as a writer in Iraq yet made a conscious choice to emigrate and write in Hebrew. Michael and a few others like Shimon Ballas and David Semach are unique in this regard. Other writers in Arabic either disappeared or became mute.[31]

Since the 1950s, the main group of what we would now call "Mizrahi intellectuals" has been increasingly educated in the Israeli education system, most often only in Hebrew. The essays from the 1950s that are included in this anthology are designed to capture these early moments of dislocation and transition from engaging modernity to grappling with Israeli-style modernization.[32] For better or worse, Middle Eastern Jews—for the first time in their long history—became part of a majority (Jewish) community, albeit as second-class citizens. Two of the last three essays in this collection, by Jacqueline Shohet Kahanoff and Avraham Abbas, describe this moment in the history of Middle Eastern Jews. These essays are particularly important because they strike a tone that seems to anticipate the two dominant features of Mizrahi discourses today. Abbas's empirical approach and meticulous emphasis on the social conditions of Mizrahi life in Israel anticipates the rise of a Mizrahi discourse in the 1970s that stressed the need for equality in housing, work, and education. Conversely, Kahanoff's forays into the psychological conditions of her fellow Mizrahi Israelis, whom she encounters in the transit camps, effectively foretell the postcolonial turn in the Mizrahi discourse of the past two decades.[33]

Contemporary Mizrahi Intellectuals

The need to write a critical history of Middle Eastern Jewish thought has become clear in recent years. The inclusion of a chapter on "intellectual life" in a comprehensive new book on Middle Eastern Jewry testifies most elegantly to this development.[34] Yet why, to begin with, is there such need? The recent rise of individuals identifying themselves as Mizrahi intellectuals or activists marks a turn in the short history of the collectivity known as Mizrahim. In previous decades, the most prominent form of Mizrahi self-expression was protest movements and political parties—most notably the Black Panthers movement of 1970s Israel.[35] These movements largely failed or disappeared, giving way to the post-1980 rise of the ultra-Orthodox Shas Party, whose political agenda is ultimately exclusively Haredi.[36] Absent party politics, Mizrahi writing and scholarship have become the principal vehicle of the group's self-expression. Mostly living in Israel, although also in the English- and French-speaking worlds, Mizrahi intellectuals represent a rainbow of views and opinions but are roughly grouped together. The appearance of such a group has certainly been noted as one of the new developments within contemporary Jewish culture and thought worldwide, particularly in Israel. At the same time, this development is affecting the fields of Jewish studies and Israel or Palestine studies, in Israel, Palestine, and elsewhere.[37] Indeed, Mizrahi studies now probably constitutes a scholarly field by itself. This is certainly the main contribution of contemporary Mizrahi intellectuals—even if it was not their specified aim.[38]

Numerous social, political, and cultural reasons underlie the contemporary rise of these Mizrahi intellectuals and set them apart from their predecessors whose work appears here. Contemporary Mizrahi intellectuals consider their Middle Eastern identity and their affinities to the Middle East as crucial elements that shape and inform their thinking.[39] At the same time, these intellectuals consider themselves to be in dialogue with Europe, European Jewish historical experience, and Arabs generally and the Palestinians in particular.

The exact space these intellectuals occupy within contemporary Jewish thought has not yet been rigorously delineated. The nature of their affinities to the Middle East and its history and peoples is still contested. Yet the mere fact that it is easy to see today an ever-growing group of intellectuals and writers who identify themselves as Mizrahi intellectuals raises questions about their intellectual tradition. Affinities between the two groups—the current Mizrahi intellectuals and their predecessors—clearly exist. Our survey of numerous texts has taught us that by the 1920s, the consciousness of belonging to the Orient (Mizrah) and of being Oriental led many Middle Eastern Jews to identify themselves as Mizrahi. This term was closely associated with being Sephardi as opposed to being Ashkenazi—just as it is today. Then and now, the terms "Mizrahi" and "Sephardi" are virtually interchangeable (except, perhaps, to "true" Sephardim—that is, Jews with a strong Portuguese or Spanish identity).[40]

But names are merely one dimension of the situation. With increasing intensity, contemporary Mizrahi intellectuals turn their attention today to writers they see as their precursors. Accordingly, Eliachar's *Ha-Mizrah* (founded 1942) is now viewed as a Mizrahi publication; the Youngsters of Mesopotamia (Tse'ire Aram Nahrayyim), a group of Iraqi Jewish intellectuals active in Palestine and Israel between 1946 and 1951, are now studied as Mizrahi intellectuals, and their journal, *Nahrayyim* (Mesopotamia), is, quite justly, presented as "the forerunner of [contemporary] Mizrahi discourse."[41] The Egyptian-born writer Jacqueline Kahanoff is seen today as anticipating Mizrahi and Mizrahi-feminist thought;[42] Michael Selzer (b. 1940), who wrote extensively in pioneering Sephardi and Mizrahi journals during the late 1950s and early 1960s, has received similar, albeit insufficient, treatment as a Mizrahi intellectual anticipating Mizrahi thought.[43] A revival of interest in the persona and writing of Elie (Eliyahu) Eliachar is evident as well.[44] Iraqi Jewish writing in Arabic—part of the monumental literary Arabization project of the Iraqi Jewish intelligentsia from the 1860s on—is studied meticulously as the direct precursor of Iraqi writing in Hebrew and Arabic in Israel.[45]

Different Mizrahi authors predictably use earlier intellectuals in different ways, often as the precursors of projects they are advocating today. For instance, a mainstream intellectual historian of Moroccan descent, an advocate of the "Mediterranean" or "Levantine" categorization, writes: "The writer and essayist Jacqueline Kahanoff (1917–79) was the forerunner of the Mediterranean option in Israel. Her early polyphonic voice represented a radical challenge to the crystallizing Israeli hegemonic ideology and culture. She should therefore be considered a unique example of a woman providing an avant-garde voice in the public sphere, and fostering debates regarding both Mediterranean and gender issues."[46] Advocates of the Mediterranean-Levantine option have been accused of proposing for Israeli society nothing less than an expression of nostalgia for coffee shops in Alexandria—that is, a nostalgia for a supposedly multicultural past that, critics argue, never truly existed.[47] Less than the debate itself, what is relevant here is that such thinkers as Kahanoff are now regarded as "forerunners" in the "avant-garde" of some subsequent tradition.

A similar phenomenon that has generated even more heated debate is the contemporary trend to (alternately) return to or rethink the links between current Mizrahi intellectuals and their real (or imagined) cultural roots. It is clearer now that there is a certain Arab-Jewish revival in Israel (and to a certain extent in the West) that has generated passionate debate, both inside and outside Mizrahi circles. In a way, this intellectual effort parallels the attempts of Middle Eastern Jewish intellectuals of past generations to grapple with their relationship qua Jews to Arabs and Arabic culture. Today, musical experiments with Arabic music are widely accepted, even celebrated, in Israel, just as Jewish participation in the musical life of the Arab world was until the 1950s. The same is true of recent Mizrahi literary experiments.[48] In the intellectual realm the issues are far more complex, with the existence of past Middle Eastern Jewish intellectuals invoked either as evidence for a close link between Arabs and Jews or as proof that such a link never existed.

With this collection of little-known essays, we hope to foster more direct engagements with questions that Middle Eastern Jewish intellectuals faced then—and that we all face today. We believe that this anthology could help our contemporaries to rethink and reinvigorate the histories of both modern Middle Eastern and Jewish thought.

Notes

1. The scope of this introduction is far too limited to cover all of this material. We refer the reader to the endnotes throughout and to our suggestions for further reading of secondary studies that follow each selection in the anthology. In this introduction we focus mostly on English publications, the volume of which should be taken as an indication of the much greater volume of material in Hebrew.

2. See, for instance, the partly academic and partly political collection of four essays titled "Mizrahim and Zionism: History, Political Discourse, Struggle," a special supplement edited and introduced by Tikva Honig-Parnass (*News from Within* 13, no. 1 [1997]: 28–75). These English essays were later published in Hebrew and Arabic as well.

3. This pair of terms has been in use since the creation of the International Congress on the Sephardi and Oriental Jewry in 1978, not coincidentally following the rise of the Likud Party to power in Israel. See for example, the publication of the second congress dedicated to the memory of Elie (Eliyahu) Eliachar (Issachar Ben-Ami, ed., *The Sephardi and Oriental Jewish Heritage: Studies* [Jerusalem: Magnes, 1982]). The choice of the word "heritage" (rather than "history," for example) is symptomatic of those years.

4. Thus, for instance, we see a Series in Sephardi and Mizrahi Studies published by Indiana University Press; the *Journal for the Study of Sephardic and Mizrahi Jewry*, based at the University of Florida; and a Sephardi Mizrahi Studies Caucus, based at Princeton University. In Israel the field of Mizrahi studies is even more advanced, as the copious examples in the following notes demonstrate. The relationship between the terms "Mizrahim" and "Sephardim" is addressed below. But it is quite clear that the former term is now superseding all other labels and terms, both when earlier geographical terms continue to be applicable and when they have become anachronistic. For instance, both the French philosopher Bernard Henri-Lévy (b. 1948, French Algeria), and Les Gara, a member of the Alaska House of Representatives who was born to Iraqi parents, are listed among the "Notable Mizrahim" in the Wikipedia article on Mizrahim (http://en.wikipedia.org/wiki/Mizrahi_Jews, accessed June 4, 2012).

5. Yitzhak Dahan, "Separationists and Assimilationists: Mizrahi Intellectuals in Israel" [in Hebrew], *Iyunim Bitkumat Israel* 17 (2007): 239–65.

6. Peter Medding, *Sephardic Jewry and Mizrahi Jews* (Oxford: Oxford University Press, 2007), xi.

7. For instance, the well established Hebrew journal *Pe'amim* recently dedicated a 502-page special issue on the "Arab-Jews controversy" that touches issues intimately linked to Middle Eastern, and Middle Eastern Jewish, history. See Avriel Bar Levav, Miryan Frenkel, and Yair Adiel, eds., "Arab-Jews? A Controversy on Identity," special triple issue, *Pe'amim*, nos. 125–27 (Autumn 2010–Spring 2011). This special issue could also be seen as another example of how the contemporary Mizrahi conversation affects the more traditional historiography of Middle Eastern Jewry.

8. See, for instance, Yaron Tsur, "Israeli Historiography and the Ethnic Problem," in *Making Israel*, ed. Benny Morris (Ann Arbor: University of Michigan Press, 2007), 231–78.

9. Quoted in Abigail Jacobson, "From Empire to Empire: Jerusalem in the Transition between Ottoman and British Rule, 1912–1920" (PhD diss., University of Chicago, 2006), 129.

10. Specifically we are referring to the literary scholars Ammiel Alcalay and Reuven Snir. This interesting fact is probably related to both the scholarly blind eye in other fields toward these intellectuals and the reluctance to see them as political thinkers. Literary scholars, therefore, have forged ahead of everyone else.

11. One of the few modern scholars who takes a systematic and comprehensive approach is Ammiel Alcalay. See in particular his "Intellectual Life," in *The Jews of the Middle East and North Africa in Modern Times*, ed. Reeva Simon, Michael M. Laskier, and Sara Reguer (New York: Columbia University Press, 2003), 85–112. Alcalay was also one of the first scholars in the United States to treat the modern literary tradition of Middle Eastern Jewry as a whole. See his *After Jews and Arabs: Remaking Levantine Culture* (Minneapolis: University of Minnesota Press, 1993), and *Keys to the Garden: New Israeli Writing* (San Francisco: City Lights, 1996).

Alcalay's comprehensive overview of Middle Eastern Jewish intellectual history covers rabbinic and literary works and authors of fiction and poetry. In this anthology, we limit ourselves chiefly to political and social commentary.

12. Again, the literature on this subject is vast. For a comprehensive treatment of the subject of Jewish intellectuals, see Paul R. Mendes-Flohr, *Divided Passions: Jewish Intellectuals and the Experience of Modernity* (Detroit: Wayne State University Press, 1991), 23–53; and Mendes-Flohr, *Kidmah ye-naftuleha: ma'avakam shel intelektu'alim Yehudim 'im ha-modernah* (Tel Aviv: Am Oved, 2010), 13–30. In his comprehensive introduction to *Divided Passions*, Mendes-Flohr discusses several theories and approaches to the question of the Jewish intellectual. None of them addresses or encompasses Middle Eastern intellectuals.

13. See, for instance, Gai Abutbul, Lev Luis Grinberg, and Pnina Motzafi-Haller, *Kolot Mizrahiyim: likrat siah Mizrahi hadash 'al ha-hevrah veha-tarbut ha-Yisre'elit* (Tel-Aviv: Masadah, 2005).

14. I. Gershoni and Amy Singer, "Introduction: Intellectual History in Middle Eastern Studies," *Comparative Studies of South Asia, Africa and the Middle East* 28, no. 3 (2008): 383–89.

15. Alcalay, "Intellectual Life," 112.

16. The existence of Israel's "Mizrahi problem" was denied in the past but is not denied by anyone, it seems, in the twenty-first century. Again, the literature on the Mizrahim as an Israeli problem is quite vast, covering the social, political, and cultural dimensions referred to in the text and more. Some of the main studies are cited below.

17. In Iraq, for instance, a Zionist movement was established only in 1941, after emissaries from the Yishuv organized it. At the height of its popularity, only a little over 1 percent of the Jewish population in Iraq belonged to the movement. For a comprehensive study in English, see Moshe Gat, *The Jewish Exodus from Iraq, 1948–1951* (London: Frank Cass, 1997). For a general treatment of the problem of Middle Eastern Jews and nationalism, see Moshe Behar, *Nationalism at Its Edges: Arabized-Jews and the Unintended Consequences of Arab and Jewish Nationalism, 1917–1967* (PhD diss., Columbia University, 2001).

18. See Ella Shohat, "The Invention of the Mizrahim," *Journal of Palestine Studies* 29, no. 1 (1999): 5–20; Moshe Behar, "Mizrahim, Abstracted: Action, Reflection, and the Academization of the Mizrahi Cause," *Journal of Palestine Studies* 37, no. 2 (2008): 89–100; Moshe Behar, "What's in a Name? Socio-Terminological Formations and the Case for 'Arabized-Jews,'" *Social Identities* 15, no. 6 (2009): 747–71.

19. Mendes-Flohr, *Divided Passions*, 29. Mendes-Flohr offers a careful and comprehensive discussion of the term (23–53); for a newer version of this book, see Mendes-Flohr, *Kidmah ye-naftuleha*, where the relevant pages are 13–30.

20. Reuven Snir, "'Religion Is for God, the Fatherland Is for Everyone': Arab-Jewish Writers in Modern Iraq and the Clash of Narratives after Their Immigration to Israel," *Journal of American Oriental Society* 126, no. 3 (2006): 379–400.

21. See, for example, Reuven Snir, "Arabic Journalism as a Vehicle for Enlightenment," *Journal of Modern Jewish Studies* 6, no. 3 (2007): 219–37.

22. Norman A. Stillman, *The Jews of Arab Lands in Modern Times*, paperback ed. (Philadelphia: Jewish Publication Society, 1991, 2003), 23–25. See also Onur Sar, *Alliance Israelite Universelle Schools within the Existing School Networks in the Ottoman Empire* (Istanbul: Boğaziçi University, 2010); Aron Rodrigue, *French Jews, Turkish Jews: The Alliance Israélite Universelle and the Politics*

of Jewish Schooling in Turkey, 1860–1925 (Bloomington: Indiana University Press, 1990); Aron Rodrigue, *Images of Sephardi and Eastern Jewries in Transition: The Teachers of the Alliance Israélite Universelle, 1860–1939* (Seattle: University of Washington Press, 1993); Michael Menachem Laskier, *The Jewish Communities of Morocco and the Alliance Israélite Universelle, 1860–1956* (Ann Arbor, MI: University Microfilms International, 1980).

23. Reuven Snir, *Arabness, Jewishness, Zionism: A Clash of Identities in the Literature of Iraqi Jews* [in Hebrew] (Jerusalem: Yad Ben-Zvi, 2005), 48.

24. Joel Beinin, *The Dispersion of Egyptian Jewry: Culture, Politics, and the Formation of a Modern Diaspora* (Berkeley: University of California Press, 1998), 1–89; Abbas Shiblak, *The Lure of Zion: The Case of the Iraqi Jews* (London: Al Saqi, 2005), 33–54; Orit Bashkin, *The Other Iraq: Pluralism and Culture in Hashemite Iraq* (Stanford: Stanford University Press, 2009), 19–51.

25. Lital Levy, "Jewish Writers in the Arab East: Literature, History, and the Politics of Enlightenment, 1863–1914" (PhD diss., University of California, Berkeley, 2007), 1–2.

26. The Jewish community of Basra, Iraq, had a strong theosophical movement that disappeared when the community immigrated to Israel. Many of those active in the movement were graduates of the local Alliance school. See David Sagiv, *Yahadut be-mifgash ha-naharayim: kehilat Yehude Batsrah 1914–1952* (Jerusalem: Karmel, 2004).

27. Levy, "Jewish Writers in the Arab East," 2.

28. Perhaps the best articulation of this position is by the Tunisian-French Jewish intellectual Albert Memmi (b. 1920), in his *Juifs et Arabes* (Paris: Gallimard, 1974) translated by Eleanor Levieux as *Jews and Arabs* (Chicago: J. P. O'Hara, 1975). See also Elie Kedourie, *Arabic Political Memoirs and Other Studies* (London: Frank Cass, 1974).

29. See Moshe Behar, "Palestine, Arabized Jews and the Elusive Consequences of Jewish and Arab National Formations," *Nationalism and Ethnic Politics* 13, no. 7 (2007): 581–611; Moshe Behar, "One-State, Two-States, Bi-National State: Mandated Imaginations in a Regional Void," *Middle East Studies Online Journal* 5, no. 2 (2011): 97–136.

30. The literature supporting this statement today is vast. For two examples, see Henriette Dahan-Kalev, "The 'Other' in Zionism: The Case of the Mizrahim," *Peace Research Abstracts* 39, no. 3 (2002): 311–456; E. Tzfadia and O. Yiftachel, "Between Urban and National: Political Mobilization among Mizrahim in Israel's Development Towns," *Cities* 21, no. 1 (2004): 41–55. Perhaps the most telling testimonies are studies that explore the distinct history of Mizrahi attitudes toward the Holocaust. See Hanna Yablonka, "Oriental Jewry and the Holocaust: A Tri-Generational Perspective," *Israel Studies* 14, no. 1 (2009): 94–122; Hanna Yablonka, *Harhek meha-mesilah: ha-Mizrahim yeha-sho'ah* (Tel Aviv: Yedi'ot aharonot, 2008).

31. Nancy E. Berg, *Exile from Exile: Israeli Writers from Iraq* (Albany: State University of New York Press, 1996); Zvi Ben Dor, "Invisible Exile: Iraqi Jews in Israel," *Journal of the Interdisciplinary Crossroads* 3, no. 1 (2006): 135–62.

32. See Deborah Bernstein and Shlomo Swirski, "The Rapid Economic Development of Israel and the Emergence of the Ethnic Division of Labour," *British Journal of Sociology* 33, no. 1 (1982): 64–85.

33. For a characterization of this trend, see Ella Shohat, "The Postcolonial in Translation: Reading Said in Hebrew," *Journal of Palestine Studies* 33, no. 3 (2004): 55–75.

34. Alcalay, "Intellectual Life."

35. The first introduction of the movement to the English-speaking world may have been a pamphlet by the Israeli Revolutionary Action Committee Abroad, *Black Panthers in Israel* (London, 1971). See also Albert Axelrad, *The Black Panthers, Jews and Israel* (New York: Jewish Currents, 1971). For scholarly works see, Sammy Smooha, "Black Panthers: The Ethnic Dilemma; Israel and Its Third World Jews," *Society* 9, no. 7 (1972): 30–36; Deborah Bernstein, "The Black Panthers of Israel, 1971–1972: Contradictions and Protest in the Process of Nation-Building," PhD diss., University of Sussex, 1976.

36. For a study of Mizrahi political parties and protest movements, see Sami Chetrit, *Intra-Jewish Conflict in Israel: White Jews, Black Jews* (London: Routledge, 2010).

37. Thus, for instance, the "central aim" of the Sephardi/Mizrahi Studies Caucus that was founded in Princeton in 1999 is "to promote the integration of Sephardi and Mizrahi Studies into general Jewish Studies, both in teaching and in scholarship" (http://www.princeton .edu/). A new journal was established as well, the *Journal for the Study of Sephardic and Mizrahi Jewry*. See Zion Zohar, *Sephardic and Mizrahi Jewry: From the Golden Age of Spain to Modern Times* (New York: New York University Press, 2005).

38. Behar, "Mizrahim, Abstracted."

39. A round-table discussion by the Social and Cultural Studies Forum at Jerusalem's Van Leer Institute of the "mechanisms of Mizrahi production of knowledge" was edited into a single essay and included in a book on Mizrahim (Social and Cultural Studies Forum, "Mechanisms of Construction and Production of Canonical Knowledge on Mizrahim in Israel," in *Mizrahim in Israel: A Critical Observation into Israel's Ethnicity*, ed. Hannan Hever, Yehouda Shenhav, and Pnina Motzafi-Haller [Jerusalem: Van Leer, 2002], 288–305).

40. On the interchangeability of and affinities between the terms "Mizrahi" and "Sephardi," see Harvey E. Goldberg, "From Sephardi to Mizrahi and Back Again: Changing Meanings of 'Sephardi' in Its Social Environments," *Jewish Social Studies*, n.s. 15, no. 1 (2008): 165–88. For a more social approach to the connection between Sephardi Jewry and Mizrahim, see Peter Medding, *Sephardic Jewry and Mizrahi Jews* (Oxford: Oxford University Press, 2007).

41. Pnina Motzafi-Haller, "Intellectualim Mizrahim 1946–1951: Ha-Zehut Ha-Etnit u-gevuloteha," in *Mizrahim in Israel*, ed. Hever, Shenhav, and Motzafi-Haller, 152–90.

42. See Ronit Matalon, "Jackeline Kahanov ve Felix Matalon, kolot Matrimim," in *Mizrahim in Israel*, ed. Hever, Shenhav, and Motzafi-Haller, 28–35; Doli Benhabib, "Women's Skirts Are Shorter Now: Levantine, Female Identity as Elitist Disguise in Jacqueline Kahanoff's Writings," *Women's Studies International Forum* 20, nos. 5–6 (1997): 689–96. (This article appeared two years earlier in Hebrew.)

43. Zvi Ben-Dor Benite, "The Jewish State as an Aryan State: Michael Selzer, the Oriental Jews, and the 'Third Exile'" [in Hebrew], *Theory and Criticism*, no. 26 (2005): 255–60.

44. See Chetrit, *Intra-Jewish Conflict in Israel*, 69–139.

45. Snir, "Arabic Journalism as a Vehicle for Enlightenment"; Reuven Snir, "Arabic Literature by Iraqi Jews in the Twentieth Century: The Case of Ishaq Bar-Moshe (1927–2003)," *Middle Eastern Studies* 41, no. 1 (2005): 7–30; Reuven Snir, "'Mosaic Arabs' between Total and Conditioned Arabization: The Participation of Jews in Arabic Press and Journalism in Muslim Societies during the Nineteenth and Twentieth Centuries," *Journal of Muslim Minority Affairs* 27, no. 2 (2007): 261–95.

46. David Ohana, "The Mediterranean Option in Israel: An Introduction to the Thought of Jacqueline Kahanoff," *Mediterranean Historical Review* 21, no. 2 (2006): 239–63.

47. On the "Levantine option," see, for example, Alexandra Nocke, "Israel and the Emergence of Mediterranean Identity: Expressions of Locality in Music and Literature," *Israel Studies* 11, no. 1 (2006): 143–73.

48. See Galit Saada-Ophir, "Borderland Pop: Arab Jewish Musicians and the Politics of Performance," *Cultural Anthropology* 21, no. 2 (2006): 205–33.

Modern Middle Eastern
Jewish Thought

Avraham Elmaleh

Avraham Elmaleh (1876–1967) was a prolific scholar, essayist, linguist, translator, editor, ethnographer, historian, and journalist. He was also a Sephardic leader and politician in Jerusalem. Elmaleh received an extensive rabbinic education, first at the Mugrabi Talmud Torah of Rabbi Yehouda Kastil in the Old City of Jerusalem, and later at Yeshiva Doresh Tsiyyon and Yeshiva Tiferet Yisrael. He also attended the Jerusalemite Alliance school and later the Jerusalem-based Ecole Biblique et Archéologique Français. Between 1902 and 1912 Elmaleh taught French at the Alliance school. A committed advocate of the use of Hebrew, Elmaleh was one of the founders of the Society of the Youth of Jerusalem, which promoted national consciousness and using Hebrew among Sephardic youth. In 1911 he was appointed secretary of the Jewish community in Damascus and principal of its community school. He returned to Palestine in 1913, briefly serving as a bank manager in Gaza and a schoolteacher in Jaffa. In 1916 Elmaleh was exiled to Damascus. During the British Mandate years, he held several official positions on the Sephardic Community Council in Jerusalem. After the founding of the State of Israel, Elmaleh was elected to the first Knesset, as a representative of the Sephardi-Edot Ha-Mizrah Party. He served on the Parliamentary Committee for Education and Culture and was awarded several honors by the French government, including *officier de l'Académie Française* in 1934 and *officier de la Légion d'honneur* in 1960.

Elmaleh had a rich journalistic career for many decades. His first essay was published in 1903 in the Jerusalem newspaper *Hashkafa* (The outlook). In 1909 he founded the Hebrew publication *Ha-Herut*, and he was editor of *Do'ar Hayom* from 1921 to 1932. He also briefly edited *Do'ar Hayom*'s Arabic version, *Barid alyawm*. Even more impressive was Elmaleh's scholarly career. He published over 700 scholarly works in various languages, including Hebrew, Arabic, French, and Turkish. In 1923 Elmaleh was sent by the Jewish National Fund to North Africa, and as a result he produced a series of essays on the history and ethnography of the Jewish communities of the Maghreb. After 1948 Elmaleh contributed to leading Sephardic or Mizrahi publications such as *Hed Ha-Mizrah* (Eastern echo), *Shevet ve-'Am* (A tribe and a people), and *Ba-Ma'aracha* (In the battle). In 1920 Elmaleh founded the scholarly journal *Mizrah u-Ma'arav* (East and West), whose opening essay is included here.

1 | East and West

Excerpt from Avraham Elmaleh, "Te'udatenu" (Our mission), *Mizrah u-Ma'arav*, Sivan 1928, 1–7.

This Hebrew essay was first published in Jaffa in 1919 and a year later became the inaugural essay of the new journal *Mizrah u-Ma'arav* (East and West), cofounded by Elmaleh. The journal was published regularly for a few years but then was discontinued for lack of funds. The same essay was republished when the journal reappeared in 1928. In this essay Elmaleh laid out the new journal's mission and vision. Our translating efforts notwithstanding, we are regretfully unable to transmit fully into English the essay's sublime Hebrew.

OUR MISSION

We had a noble dream!

To gather, investigate, and publish everything pertaining to Sephardic, Eastern,[1] and North African Jewish life from the most ancient times to the present.[2] This was our ambition ever since we were able to use the scribe's pen. This idea—to commit to paper the history of Eastern Jewry with all of its branches, customs, virtues, beliefs, literature, activities, etc.—has been burning in our minds for several years, and finally the day has come when we can realize this aspiration.

A comprehensive Jewish history is made up of the history of each group and

1. [It is important to note that the word "West" in the selection title does not refer to the Euro-American West. It is a translation of the word *maghrib* (Arabic for "west") and refers to North Africa (Tunisia, Algeria, Morocco). In this context, therefore, Elmaleh is referring to the entirety of Middle Eastern Jewry in the Arab world, both in the *Mashriq* (Arabic for East), and in the *Maghrib*. Furthermore, Elmaleh specifically uses the Hebrew word "Mizrahit," which we translate here as "Eastern." It is very clear that he views the three Jewish collectives—Sephardic, Eastern, and North African—as tightly connected to one another.]

2. [For Elmaleh, based in Palestine in 1918–19, Jews in the West for the most part denote Jews in the Arab world's western part—the Maghreb—rather than meaning Western or European Jews, as the term is commonly employed today. Elmaleh certainly understands and appreciates the historical diversity within Asian and African Jewries.]

collective scattered around the globe. In Africa and the East there are treasure troves and burrows that lovers of history, archaeology, and folklore can explore to their hearts' content. The edifices and tombstones, the archives found in each community, the genealogies of ancient families—they are all precious sources for researching Eastern Jewry.

Knowledge of the history of every people—and the stories of their eminent figures and sages—is imperative and honorable for the purpose of telling the present generation the chronicles of their forebears who excelled in wisdom, might, and deed. The aim of such historical knowledge is not just to demonstrate the struggles of those who preceded us so that we may observe all the details, victories and defeats, crimes and acquittals, sagacity and folly, sacrifices and selfishness, falsehoods and truths, virtues and disgraces, cowardice and courage; the aim of such historical knowledge is also to bring us into contact with our ancestors when they were frightened and confident, doubtful and brave, great and petty, admirable and repugnant, hoping to find light when angrily throwing themselves into the mist, despairing at a time when they should have been hopeful. Briefly put, then, history is the mute language of our life unfurling before our eyes the remains of our distant past and presenting us with the faces of our ancestors as they truly were. However, whether history is paradise or perdition, one must immerse oneself in history—and in history alone!—in order to locate guides and good examples, a support and moral hope.

And as each nation cherishes its knowledge of the history of its eminent ones and sages, so the history of our own nation and sages should be treasured. For knowledge of our history will not be attained until all past times are revealed in front of us as an open book where all the names of the sages and men of valor— who were precious to Israel, its pride and glory for all the nations to see—can be read by themselves. Jewry still has not shed a bright light on its eminent people, particularly those who, by virtue of their skills and qualities, bequeathed honor to it, served it with their wisdom and their knowledge, and elevated it with their creations and lives.

There are now many scribes [scholars, chroniclers] from our nation tracing, searching, and investigating the origins of the cities and ancient Jewish communities, their beginnings and ends. This is in order to know their history, to count all the rabbis and the great thinkers who were shepherds and guides, to shed light on the shining noble face of a certain genius or creator, to search for their origins and roots and their places of death, and to laboriously write the history of these communities and to erect for them in Jewish history a stable, lasting memorial.

Alas, so much depends on chance!

There is sometimes a small community placed at the earth's edge, yet everyone still knows what is going on there around it: who rises and who falls, who lives and who dies, its qualities and news, its transformations and shifts, what quarrels it experiences and how they are settled. There are, conversely, large and important communities from which one hears no voices because none of the researching authors has emerged to redeem their history and shed explanatory light on them.

There are, moreover, whole nations that perished from the face of the earth many years ago and piles of ashes have accumulated on their tombs over the generations. Yet their name is still ringing among the living and among students of history and antiquity who ceaselessly scour the tombs' ashes in order to discover these nations' mysteries, customs, modes of life; how developed and civilized they were culturally and materially; and how many books and scrolls they left behind. There are, conversely, nations existing today whose characteristics and customs, ambitions and deeds, beliefs and delusions, past and present—briefly, whose entire civilizations—merit special attention so that their histories will be at least as deserving and valued as the histories of those long-gone nations. Yet our scholars still do not pay sufficient attention to these living nations—as if their scholarly attitude vis-à-vis them resembles a magnet pulling their scholarly attention only to the ancient history of these still-existing nations.

This, I submit, is what happened to the Sephardic communities in North Africa and the East.

There are many such communities—and the number of our brethren in them is great—whose histories emerged many long centuries ago. Over the years these communities produced rabbis and excellent authors who greatly enriched our rabbinic literature, the liturgy, and the Midrashic lore. These communities built many presses and printing houses where books by the thousands were printed about Israel's wisdom and literature. Furthermore, many historical transformations occurred within these communities and in relation to them. There was still no one among us who considered it their duty to investigate these communities thoroughly, study them comprehensively, collect everything related to their customs, and search for evidence about their history, chronicles, and creative works. No one thought that such an endeavor was worth the time it would consume.

The absence of a collection containing a full, accurate picture of all that is going on with our brethren in the East and the *Maghrib* [Western North Africa]

—from the time of their exile until this very day—is acutely felt in our recent literature. Historical writing was deserted completely by our Hebrew writers and—with the exception of a few short, fragmentary articles that appeared here and there in some journals, collections, or special books that do not shed even minimal light on this topic—there is no decent book or article on the subject. (The important books by the Sephardic Rabbi Salamon Rosanes and the scholar Rabbi Abraham Danon are obviously the exceptions to the rule.)

It is wonderful that our authors and scholars working on foreign literature employ their talents intensively in the discipline of history. In their historical investigations they have succeeded in gathering precious and invaluable material relating to the history of the people of Israel in the Diaspora's four corners. But at the same time it is incredible that the histories of our brethren in North Africa, Syria, Turkey, the Balkans, the cities of Persia, India, Yemen—the countries where the number of our brethren is large and whose communities shone with a great bright Jewish light—these histories remain completely covered with mist and have yet to be written.

It is true that some attempts in this profession were undertaken: Mr. Franco, head of the Alliance School, wrote the *Histoire des Israélites de l'Empire Ottoman*; Mr. David Cazès, head of the Alliance School in Tunis, wrote the *Histoire des Israélites de Tunisie*; Rabbi Abraham Danon founded the journal *Yosef Da'at [o El Progreso]*; and the scholar S. Rosanes authored his *Divere Yeme Yisarel be-Togarma* (History of the Jews in Turkey).[3] Still, the first and second authors—notwithstanding their being knowledgeable about foreign literature—wrote their essays in French. They did not possess sufficient knowledge of the languages of the Talmudic and *responsa* literature vital for this subject. They were therefore unable to write much out of thin air, to unearth all the material necessary for the project since it is

3. [Rabbi Moise Franco was the rabbi and Alliance schoolmaster of the Jewish community in Akhisar (Thyatira), Turkey. The book to which Elmalah refers is Moïse Franco, *Essai sur l'histoire des Israeïlites de l'Empire ottoman depuis les origines jusqu'aì nos jours* (Paris: A. Durlacher, 1897). David Cazès (b. 1851) was a Moroccan Jewish educator and writer active in the Maghreb, Paris, and the Argentine. His book's title is *Essai sur l'histoire des Israélites de Tunisie, depuis les temps les plus reculés jusqu'à l'établissement du protectorat de la France en Tunisie* (Paris: A. Durlacher, 1887). Abraham Danon (1857–1925), a rabbi from Edirne, was a journalist and historian. *Yosef Da'at o El Progreso* was a Hebrew and Ladino journal published in Turkey. Salomon Rosanes (1862–1938) was a prolific Sephardic historian of Ottoman Jewry and the author of the classic that Elmalah mentions, *Divre yeme Yisrael be-Togarmah: 'al pi mekorim yesharim* (History of the Jews in Turkey: according to reliable sources) (Husiatin, Turkey, 1907).]

scattered all over. All that these authors could do is provide the material for the history of the Jews in Tunis and Turkey. The journal *Yosef Da'at*—which was published about thirty years ago in Hebrew and Ladino [Judeo-Spanish]—ceased publication after only a few issues. Rosanes's volume covers only the history of the Jews in Turkey and not the history of the Sephardic communities in their entirety.

Moreover, anyone attempting to carry out this kind of research immediately ran into trouble and distress, stemming from a lack of knowledge and sources. The stressful conditions and political situation of the Jewish community in all these aforementioned places—coupled with the lack of printing houses especially in North Africa and for other, similar, reasons—resulted in a severe lack of communication for many generations between the Jews living there and the Jews living in the rest of the Diaspora. That is why all of their memories, histories, and chronicles are shrouded in darkness.

It is time, then, to turn our attention to the great works in the field of our Eastern histories as well as to gather bricks and mortar for this distinguished edifice.

Precious treasures are hidden in the vineyard of our Eastern histories; we are neither very familiar either with the internal life of the communities and their attitude toward their governments, nor with their governments' attitude toward them. Once we acquire that knowledge we will resolve many questions hitherto disregarded. We likewise have no knowledge of the manuscripts, books, notes, poems (etc.) hidden deep inside individual collections—or sealed in a community chest—that are certain to shed some light on many unresolved issues.

These and similar thoughts are what encouraged us to try and undertake the project associated with this new journal *East and West*. We thought that the time had come to establish in the land of the past and future a modest fortress to hold the spiritual treasures of Eastern and Sephardic Jewry.

Our brothers in exile, scattered all over the land, were never closer in spirit—and as united in thinking about general issues—as they are now. The horizon of public Hebrew work has expanded to the degree that its particular, localized form has given way to one Jewish organization encompassing all of our nation's life. An organization whose different institutions are just one link in the larger organized chain: the people of Israel. This transformation is felt especially through the increasing closeness—in both spirit and location—between Sephardic and Ashkenazic Jewries. *East and West* is not founded in order to separate these two entities but, rather, to bring hearts closer and reconcile all that is presently happening in our region and the world. The diversity of shades and different forces—each operating according to its own logic within a certain society—create a holistic and harmonious society where each distinctive voice can be expressed to its fullest. The value of such shared work lies in different forces working conjointly and mutually affecting each other—giving and receiving each other's creative achievements, each according to its own distinctively autonomous character, without losing its unique identity and shape.

The Eastern and Sephardic Jewry is established on strong foundations in a variety of domains. The waves of the surrounding cultures that have fractured Judaism's strong wall could not shatter the essentials, which are resting on strong foundations that do not collapse easily. The Eastern and Sephardic Jewry has a loyal base—its human material—that is holistic and healthy in its essence and sources and that could provide the substance for both a great national creative project and popular projects. It is true that Sephardic Jewry appears somewhat unskilled, while its public institutions lack a measure of law and order. But these institutions are nevertheless rich in content; they draw on Judaism's original spirit that is a resource in and of itself.

East and West will therefore try to blow new breath and fresh currents of life into Sephardic Jewry, whose spring of national life gurgles slowly. *East and West* will enrich this life and draw the community close to its original reliable sources. It is time for our Sephardic brethren to get closer to the original Jewish sources, the original Hebrew language and literature, and to the Torah. Here is a summary of what we aim to provide in *East and West*.

Lore [. . .].

Opinion [. . .].

Criticism [. . .].

Literature [. . .].

Events [. . .].

News about what is ongoing among our neighbors. There are in our vicinity different nations and peoples: Arabs, Druze, the Mutawalli's [Shi'is], [Christian] Maronites, etc. We have no knowledge about their histories, religions, customs, codes of propriety, and ways of life. *East and West* will devote a section to surveying these nations, exploring their relationships with us and our relationship with them, and will clarify the issues standing between us.

Biographies [. . .].

Bibliography and books [. . .].

In short, *East and West* will plow through the hidden channels of time to unearth from the abyss of loss and oblivion all the remains of every story and issue that can be recovered. There are many precious jewels and treasures in this abyss, and they are needed because they form the foundation on which we will build our nation. [. . .] Who knows whether in a few years' time—as progress and modernization develop deeper roots—we will run the risk of losing completely the memory of popular beliefs—very often so original, idiosyncratic, poetic.

East and West will call for a national revival among the Jews of the East and will serve those who read and studied the ancient rabbinic literature as a bridge to our modern literature. It will also stimulate among Eastern Jews a love for our language and national treasures. It will particularly aspire to develop among Eastern and North African Jews the ambition to be creative in original Hebrew writings; to become influential within the process of spiritual development and the renewal of education in Jewish communities in the East and the West.

For the outside world, *East and West* will serve as a mirror in which Jewish life is reflected with all its colors and varieties, light and shadows. *East and West* will be an Eastern Hebrew journal dedicated to the dissemination of Hebrew knowledge and literature and will be a source of information about the fervent life and the activities in Jewish communities everywhere. It will proudly defend the spiritual treasures in the form of the [Hebrew] language, literature, and national culture.

There always has been, and there remains, a strong national awareness among the Sephardic Jewish masses. It is on the basis of this natural and healthy national awareness that we aspire to build a tower to the glory of Sephardic Jewry. Hebrew has been neglected by our Sephardic brethren for various reasons. Hebrew is the national language that stitches together the rifts within our nation; it gathers our scattered people from the earth's four quarters. Hebrew is the tongue in which all our treasures are hidden, the rich land of our fathers, the only relic from our great past. Yet the grandsons and great-grandsons of Maimonides, Rabbi Yehuda Halevi, and Ibn Ezra have grown distant from our source of life—our language and national literature—to the extent that many regard Hebrew only as a language for prayer. Thus, the national creation among our Sephardic brethren has halted. But it is only unconsciously that these brothers of ours have forgotten our national language. Hebrew is the language with which our ancestors created such a sublime national literature, one that remains a treasure in world literature and culture. Only unintentionally did Sephardic Jewry forget the language inherited from Isaiah, Jeremiah, and Ezekiel.

Sephardic Jewish life has not yet acquired a steady and defined form. Sephardic Jews are indeed gradually becoming homogeneous, slowly changing their distinct shapes and faces and becoming one body with one image. But until these separate entities become closer and until the Eastern and Sephardic Jewries become one Hebrew public sharing similar education and characteristics—exceptional occurrences and unique events are in any event taking place within Eastern Jewry and within different communities that otherwise live differently and separately. Sephardim have their special historical trajectory, the Ashkenazim their historical path, and so on and so forth. It is therefore of great necessity to record the respective developments in matter and spirit of each of those parties and the ways of those different people from different countries who are of one race and origin.

Will we succeed in this goal we have set for ourselves?

This goal is not up to me alone. For myself, I can say—while employing no false modesty—that I am carrying out this task in good faith. As a Sephardic Jewish writer living among his brothers and observing the development of Hebrew life—in all its varieties and ways, from all its sides and facets, in shadow and light in all Eastern countries—I shall try, as far as I am capable, to shed light on every corner of the history of Sephardic and Mizrahi Judaism and unveil that which cloaks any group, man, or book. And if I can manage to add to this the contribution of the best authors and scientists in the Holy Land and abroad who will commit themselves to help, then this general plan as we conceive it may indeed be realized in its entirety.

Further Readings

Elmaleh, Abraham. *Hommage à Abraham: recueil littéraire en l'honneur de Abraham Elmaleh, citoyen de Jérusalem, écrivain et homme de lettres: à l'occasion de son 70ème anniversaire 1885–1955.* 1959.

———. *Zakhor le-Abraham: Mélanges Abraham Elmaleh, à l'occasion du 5ème anniversaire de sa mort . . .* Edited by H. Z. Hirschberg. Jerusalem: Comité de la communauté marocaine, 5732 [1972].

Saposnik, Arieh Bruce. *Becoming Hebrew: The Creation of a Jewish National Culture in Ottoman Palestine,* New York: Oxford University Press, 2008.

Ya'qub Sannu'

Also called James Sanua—and widely known by his nom de plume, Abou Naddara Zarqa[1] ("the man with the blue spectacles")—Ya'qub Sannu'[2] (1839–1912) was an Egyptian nationalist, playwright, colorful satirist, dramatist, journalist, publisher, cartoonist, teacher, lecturer, anticolonialist, protofeminist, and self-proclaimed deist. Born in Cairo to Egyptian Jews, Sannu' was raised and schooled in an environment where Arabic, French, Hebrew, and English were all common. When he turned thirteen, his parents managed to secure a scholarship to send him to Italy for three years to study political economy, law, science, and fine arts. When Sannu' was twenty-four, Cairo's Polytechnic School offered him a teaching position. The many students he taught included young bureaucrats and soldiers who, by 1881–82, would constitute the societal cadre sustaining the [Ahmad] 'Urabi revolt.

In the late 1860s Sannu' befriended philosophers of reformist-modernist Islam, especially Jamal al-Din al-Afghānī (1837–97) and Mohammad 'Abduh (1849–1905). Sannu' began to write plays and established Egypt's first theater company. The plays were revolutionary: most were performed in colloquial Egyptian Arabic, included female actors, and addressed social and political issues and themes. The plays chiefly highlighted the regime's authoritarianism while advocating a just and free society based on egalitarian principles. As his theatrical activities grew more nationalist and critical of the reign of Khedive Isma'il Pasha, they were banned. No longer permitted to stage his plays publicly, Sannu' had the idea of printing anonymous broadsides criticizing the khedive's government. By 1877 these broadsides turned into his legendary satirical weekly, *Abou Naddara Zarqa* (the title of the publication as well as his nom de plume). Each issue contained a sketch whose characters exchanged commentary—written in colloquial Egyptian—on the deeds of the khedive or the government. Egyptian authorities were infuriated and—following two failed attempts to assassinate Sannu'—exiled him to France at the age of

1. [The transliteration of the nickname "Abou Naddara" here follows the spelling that Sannu' uses when he writes in Latin script and when that script appears in his Arabic publications.]

2. [Scholars have transliterated the author's Arabic name in many ways. We opted for the one that seems most common in the secondary literature.]

thirty-nine. A resident of Paris until his death, Sannu' continued publishing *Abou Naddara Zarqa*—smuggling the publication into Egypt hidden in respectable documents while also evading censors by frequently changing its name. Around the time of the British invasion of Egypt, Sannu' added sections in French to the publication, which was divided equally between the two languages in 1885. In Paris, Sannu' was reunited with other Egyptian exiles who supported his work, and he also helped al-Afghānī and 'Abduh improve their French.

Sannu' remained a deist Jew. He lectured European and North African audiences almost weekly on topics pertaining to Egypt and Islam—some 1,100 talks, by his own count in 1910. His writings and talks praised French culture while also aiming to harness Anglophobic feelings on behalf of Egyptian causes (in part, a reverse "divide and conquer" strategy). In 1907 Sannu' founded *L'Univers Musulman*—a journal exclusively in French intended to counter stereotypical European views of Islam and Muslim societies. Because of his severely diminished sight, in December 1910 Sannu' stopped writing and publishing on the orders of his Parisian optometrists. The flamboyant Abou Naddara Zarqa died less than two years later.

2 | Some Teachings of the Koran

Ya'qub Sannu', "Some Teachings of the Koran," in *Neely's History of the Parliament of Religions and Religious Congresses at the World's Columbian Exposition: Compiled from Orig. Manuscripts and Stenographic Reports*, ed. Walter Raleigh Houghton, (Chicago: Neely, 1894), 654–56.

In 1893 the organizers of the World's Parliament of Religions and Religious Congresses asked Ya'qub Sannu' to present a short paper outlining his opinions about the Qur'an. Sannu' agreed and sent a short letter to the conference, where it was read in part.

SOME TEACHINGS OF THE KORAN

An interesting paper prepared by J. Sanna Abou Naddara of Paris was read by Professor Snell, on the Koran and other sacred scriptures. The paper said in part:

You desire me to speak freely about my opinion about the Koran.

The Koran has been translated into all languages. I shall not speak of its holiness, lest I profane it, and, besides, I am not a Mohammedan priest—I am a deist—a very faithful believer in God and a sincere admirer of all those who make Him known to men, and celebrate His sublime work. The Koran is tolerant, humane, and moral. The Koran has mercy upon slaves. I may even say Mohammed was the slave's friend. Allow me to show you that Mohammed and his followers are not, as some suppose them to be, adversaries to instruction: nay, they are great friends of knowledge. The Koran says, "Learned men are the heirs of prophets," and that learning is a divine precept that every Mussulman must fulfill. These words show us how greatly the Prophet of Islam appreciated instruction, as he bids his followers to go and acquire knowledge, even if it were to China, a very long voyage at that time, when steamboats and railways were unknown. Mohammed also said: "Expect no good from a man who is neither learned nor a student." Moslem doctors, philosophers, and poets have written and said much upon this subject. In Turkey, in Syria, and in Egypt, not only numerous schools for boys were founded but for girls also, as women are highly regarded by the Prophet Mohammed and his followers.

Islam had and has still many female writers and poets. Mohammed said of women: "Happy and fortunate is the man who has only one wife, pious and virtuous." This is favorable to monogamy, otherwise he would have said: "Happy is he who possesses a good number of wives." He said also to his friends: "I love three things in your world—namely, women, perfume, and prayer." This denotes that the Prophet of Islam appreciates woman, since he places her first in what he cherished in this world. The Koran is so favorable to the fair sex that its fourth chapter, which is long enough, is consecrated to woman, whose cause it gallantly pleads, and in speaking of divorce, the apostle of Allah says that, even if a man had given his wife a talent [a measure of money], if he divorces her he has no right to take anything back from her.

I terminate my humble words by calling divine blessings on the enlightened members of the Parliament of Religions and by praying to the Lord to crown their undertakings with happy success.

Transvaal's Exemplary Rebels

Ya'qub Sannu', untitled essay in Arabic, *Le Journal D'Abou Naddara*, 18 Shawwal, 1318 Hijri [February 8, 1901], 1–2.

Sannu' refers here to the Second Boer War between the British and the Boers— Dutch-speaking settlers in South Africa—that began in 1899 and ended in 1902. This text was left untitled by Sannu'. The original Arabic text is composed in rhyme and contains a great deal of sarcasm (typical of the author's writings); both are difficult to reproduce in English without compromising the text's clarity.

Happy 'Id al-Fitr! Happy Afranji [here, meaning European] New Year! Like dewdrops and like the stars sparkling during these days of 'Id al-Fitr, I extend my regards and warmest wishes to my Muslim brothers. I ask the Almighty to let joy and bliss prevail for his great caliph, our sultan, and for all the kings, princes, and leaders of the believers whom I am joyous to see happy and prosperous. God alone knows my full love and fondness toward the Muslim community. I thus ask of Him victory for Abd al-Hamid Khan our sultan; victories for my dear friend Muzzafar al-Din, shah of Iran, and to my friend Ali II, king of Zanzibar, and to my companion al-Sayyid Muhammad, the darling of the princes of An-jawan; victory to the leader of the kingdom of Tunisia as well, the dearest of my friends. May God hear my prayers and help me achieve my aims and goals.

I similarly wish to congratulate the followers of the Prophet Jesus and of the Prophet Moses. Happy Afranji New Year! A year full of blessings and happiness in which I will see the East [free and independent] as my heart wishes; a promising year for Transvaal [South Africa]—that hopefully will culminate with freedom and independence; a promising year for India, Sudan, and Egypt—ushering in triumph and victory. Never stop seeking God's forgiveness, my dear reader. The Almighty is capable of saving the Nile Valley from the British: His power is astonishing, His deliverance imminent. I now wish to offer you evidence and proof of the Almighty's kindness and mercy.

After the British won and the Boers were defeated and crushed, God crushed the victorious and made the defeated glorious. This made Mr. Bull[3] scream and

3. [John Bull—following his literary creation by John Arbuthnot in 1712—became the

exclaim and say: "Perish the Boer nation, on its gold mines I shall lay my strong hands." That is useless nonsense; the guns and cannons exposed these lies. The weaponry and splendid cannons of the British were taken by the Transvaal's brave rebels. General Kitchener[4] and his soldiers were beaten to within an inch of their lives and ran for their lives in front of the Boer heroes. Lord Roberts, commander of the British troops, escaped to the British capital. There he met Queen Victoria and told her the truth. As her heart shattered, the poor dear fainted and, later, died. The people were saddened.

In my *Journal* I paid tribute to the queen since I respect the dead even when they are my mortal enemies. Whoever said to speak no ill of the dead was right; as the noble *Hadith* stipulates, "speak well of the dead." So if you, *mon cher*[5] reader, tell me that the queen is not one of our dead, I will answer you: we are Arabs, and mercy and forgiveness are part of our character and traditions. Furthermore, it is not the queen who offends us, but her moronic government. It happened that my London office informed me that both this Christmas and New Year were ghastly for the Englishman (may you yourself be spared from such fate): why would it be otherwise? The British lost 60,000 men in the Transvaal war even as they spent 160 million of their strong pounds. Poor Englishmen—that is the Almighty's punishment.

Wrap up your article, Abou Naddara, with prayers to your Muslim, Jewish, and Christian brothers. May God grant them all a long life and everything they wish for [the rise of the Eastern nations over Britain]. For your good taste, dear reader, I reward you with a great picture in this issue.[6] Observe it, ponder, and you will need no additional explanation to understand it. The four individuals you see standing on the mountain are of the best born believers: the Egyptian, the Sudanese, the Indian, and the Afghan. They all watch the pasha of the scoundrels,

---

national symbol of Great Britain around the world, including in such graphic works as political cartoons.]

4. [Opposed by Asian and African anticolonialists, Sir Herbert Kitchener (1850–1916) was a leading British field marshal. He secured British control over the Sudan (1898), was chief of staff during the Second Boer War, and then served in India (1902–07) and Egypt (1908–15). At the outbreak of World War I, he was appointed secretary of state for war.]

5. [The French *mon cher* (my dear) is transliterated in the Arabic original.]

6. [Each issue included a cartoon, at the time a pathbreaking idea. The cartoon was meant to improve communication with Egypt's illiterate public. Likewise, the publication's "innovative use of the Egyptian colloquial set a precedent for Arabic journalism and made the journal accessible to the (predominantly illiterate) masses who heard it read aloud" (Levy 2007, 150–51).]

General Kitchener. He and his soldiers are frightened and escape from the heroic Boers. Look at the British soldiers stepping on each other while running for their lives. Poor they indeed are, yet the blame falls squarely on their government's shoulders. While the discussion between our dear four brothers is ongoing, it regrettably cannot be transmitted in its entirety in this small journal. Permit me then to explain the content of this brotherly discussion with a brief summary. [...] I am going to talk to you, my readers, in the [Arabic] colloquial tongue—at times in the traditional way, at other times in the manner of peasants.

Listen up, my fellows, to the ideas of the East's sons. Know beforehand that al-Sayyid Abd al-Rahman—emir of the Afghans—is today ready to fight against 200,000 British. His soldiers are lions who would prefer to die rather than run for their lives. He has great weapons and magnificent guns and cannons. What will happen is that when a British knight [cavalryman] sees an Afghan soldier from afar, he will lay down his sword and rifle and say: "O, my legs, run as fast as you can." That is why whenever Emir Abd al-Rahman calls on India's British rulers, they hurry to obey his orders. That is now especially so because wars and epidemics are eating up British money and soldiers.

On the other hand, al-Sayyid Ali Dinar—emir of Kurdufan—is stationed and ready on Sudan's borders with a large army, awaiting the British who wish to occupy and steal the land. And after the Afghans, both the Indians and the Sudanese appreciated the efforts of the Egyptians—who magically brought them from their countries to the Transvaal—and after that, when they happily witnessed their enemies retreating and suffering bad morale, the Indian told his Afghan brother: it is time for Emir Abd al-Rahman to drive out the British from all Indian lands. If he does not take this opportunity now, it may never come again. As the Egyptian brother told the Sudanese—an accidental encounter is better than a thousand planned ones. There are few British soldiers in the Nile Valley, and the emir of Kurdufan is capable of driving them out of the lands to rescue both Sudan and Egypt from their cruelty. So the Afghan and the Sudanese brothers told the Indian and the Egyptian that it was in their best interest that Emir Abd al-Rahman and al-Sayyid Ali Dinar should save India and the Nile Valley from the claws of the invaders, and that they await the peoples of India, Sudan, and Egypt to overtake the redcoats wanting to occupy them.

The East's sons are now uniting to fight against the British nation. I believe that they have the right to do so, that the oppressed should resist their oppressors, and that the oppressed will eventually be assisted and rescued by their friends. My heart tells me that this will happen because all the nations of the contemporary world have become civilized: they know what to do and what not to do. Allow no one to enslave you. Enjoy—instead—freedom: God created man free; he did not create him a slave. The awakening of Eastern nations is evident and resisting the British nation is possible. O reader, may you live to see the Eastern nations as happy as Western nations are.

4 | The Koran

Ya'qub Sannu', "Le Koran," *L'Univers Musulman* (The Muslim world),
March 15, 1907, 3–4.

Following is a speech in French on the Qur'an that Sannu' delivered in Paris and
that was published in *L'Univers Musulman*.

Islam's holy book, called by its faithful believers *Kitabuhu al-'Aziz* [His dear
book], is nowadays studied more than ever by scholars and intellectuals and
read by the public. All wish to familiarize themselves with the religion, laws,
literature, and morals of the 300 million Muslims residing in every country and
confidently marching forth on the path of progress and civilization.

Ever desirous to please the thirty million Muslims living in its colonies and
countries under its protectorate, the French government has decreed that its
Grand Imprimerie Nationale shall print the Koran in Arabic—while using
brand-new type font, special ink, and magnificent paper. This edition—made
with care and attention—will soon be appearing, printed in thousands of
copies; this is to serve the faithful believers in God and Muhammad, his holy
prophet. [. . .]

Ah! If only Europeans knew the Koran as Muslims know the Bible and the
New Testament, they would no longer say that this book inspires—in *Allah's*
faithful believers—aversion toward those who do not follow their religion. European readers of the Koran would instead find it just as tolerant, philanthropic,
and humane as the Holy Scriptures of Moses and Jesus are. The Koran sings the
praises of every biblical prophet and considers them all as sent by the Almighty
to guide mankind in the ways of righteousness, make man's life happy and ensure him a reward in the company of the chosen.

If the Bible tells us that Moses talked to the Lord *face to face, like a man would talk
to his companion,* and the New Testament assures us that Jesus Christ *is the son of
God*—the Koran simply informs us that this sacred book was communicated
through the Angel Gabriel verse by verse to Muhammad—who was a self-
confessed illiterate. But the Koran is written in a sublime language; it is the *chef
d'oeuvre* of Arabic literature, and any one of us would be proud to have written
one of its numerous chapters. I myself have given the Holy Scriptures in Hebrew

careful and serious study, and they charmed my heart and enchanted my soul with the beauty, sweetness, and solemnity of their language. I have also studied the Koran in Arabic—a rich, august, and sonorous language. I would dare say that I do not find the book of Muhammad any less sublime than those of Moses and Jesus: I read all three of them with equal joy and pleasure, and I find them all appropriate to guide their adepts in the way of virtue and honor.

And now, so as not to abuse the kindly attention of my listeners by prolonging my digression on the Koran, I will restrict myself to quoting several verses of this book of Islam to them, in order to prove its spirit of tolerance, morality, and philanthropy:

Lo! Those who believe, Muslims, Jews, Christians and Sabaeans, in a word whoever believes in God and the Last Day, and who does right; all of them will receive their reward from their Lord, etc. (Koran, chapter II, verse 62).

In which other religion can you find a tolerance so plain and so comprehensive! While the other religions only promise to their faithful rewards in the afterlife, Islam considers that *any* man who has done good works will be rewarded after his death:

Good and evil shall not walk together. Repay evil with good and you will see your enemy transformed into a friend and a protector! (Koran, chapter XLI, verse 34).

Could one preach any better than that love for one's neighbor and the pardoning of offenses? Furthermore, the Koran is the enemy of vengeance: it shows us that the Creator has not made us to hate one another and to dispute with one another but to love one another and to understand one another. It proves this in the following verses:

An honest word and the forgiveness of offenses are worth more than the giving of alms to repay an injury or offense caused to him that receives them. God is rich and clement. (Koran, chapter II, verse 263.)

Here is how the Koran preaches charity:

They will ask you how to give alms. Say to them: you must help your parents, relatives and close friends, orphans, the poor, and travelers. The good that you do will be known by God. (Koran, chapter II, verse 215).

Should some idolater ask you for asylum, grant it to him, so that he may hear the word of God; then send him on his way to safety. (Koran, chapter IX, verse 6).

As for slaves, the Koran demands they should be treated as follows:

If one of your slaves asks you for his freedom, grant it to him, if you judge him worthy. Give them of what little goods God has accorded you, etc. (Koran, chapter XXIV, verse 33).

Slavery in the Islamic countries has now been almost entirely wiped out.

American Hebrew Academy Library

I could quote hundreds of analogous verses to support my contention, but those quoted should suffice to convey that the Koran is not a book of fanaticism, superstition, and barbarity. Prophet Muhammad's followers ask nothing better than to live in peace with their neighboring countries. May those neighboring countries treat them as brothers!

5 | Ottoman Imperial Schools

Ya'qub Sannu', "Les Écoles Impériale Ottomanes," *L'Univers Musulman*
(The Muslim world), March 15, 1907, 4.

This is an excerpt from an address in French given by Sannu' at the Fête des Elèves
at the Graillot Institute in Paris, on March 11, 1906. It was published the following year.

The Ottoman emperor has learned the value of knowledge and knows that
education is the source of happiness and prosperity among peoples. Was it not
the worthy successor of the great Prophet of Islam who said: "Cultivate science,
for the study of the sciences, to the glory of God, is an act of good, research into
them is an act of merit, and the cultivation thereof adds depth to a holy struggle,
the pursuit thereof is an act of piety, the teaching thereof an act of charity, and
for those who are worthy, the act of taking part in scientific endeavors is an
act that brings them closer to God." He further expounded: "Science is a river
and wisdom is a sea; those persons of knowledge walk around this river, the
angels dive to the bottom of this sea, and those persons who are instructed in the
knowledge of God sail in vessels of salvation."

O my dear friends, if I were to repeat to you all the good things that the blessed
Prophet of Islam and his august successors have said in praise of knowledge, I
would have to stay here until tomorrow! Suffice it to quote a few of their sublime
thoughts to give an idea of their love for science.

Science is the heart's life and the soul's fire.
Knowledge is the immortal son of man.
The wise are to the earth as the stars are to the sky.

You must not believe, ladies and gentlemen, those who tell you that Islam is
the enemy of education. If this were true, then the august caliph would not have
founded schools for boys and for girls throughout his vast empire. I visited the
civil and military schools of Constantinople [founded] by imperial decree, and I
can assure you that they are the rival of those in the most civilized countries in
the world. That visit took me eight days, and I had the pleasure and satisfaction

of chatting in Arabic, French, English, German, and other languages to the students, who surprised me with their knowledge and eloquence.

Regarding women's education, it is developing well as a consequence of the encouragement of H.I.M. [his imperial majesty] the sultan. In one of the imperial schools for young women I was received by the strains of the Hamidiye[7] march, a piano duet for four hands, exceptionally well played. They [the students] recited verses in Turkish, Arabic, Persian, and French. I shall never forget the memories of this visit, and I shall care religiously for the embroidered fabrics that they gave me, made by those gracious girls themselves. On that day, I would have liked to have with me those French ladies who are here now; they would have been enchanted by their Ottoman comrades.

7. [A popular Turkish tune, still heard today.]

My Last Dream

Ya'qub Sannu', "Mon Dernier Rêve," *L'Univers Musulman* and *Abou Naddara*,
fourth joint French-Arabic issue, December 1910, 1–2.

The lead headline of the issue in which this item appeared reads as follows: "Sheikh Abou Naddara ends his career of eleven *lustra* [fifty-five years] as a publicist and lecturer." It later explains: "Abou Naddara began to write for Egyptian and European papers, and take up public speaking, fifty-five years ago (in 1855). [. . .] He consequently well deserves the break which he plans to take at the beginning of 1911. As he is—thanks be to God—in good health, he would have liked to continue in his career, but alas! Abou Naddara's eyesight no longer permits him to work, as the greatest opticians of Paris have forbidden him to do further reading and writing."[8]

May the Merciful and Compassionate God—who for half a century has deigned to realize almost all of my dreams—bring this last dream, which has charmed my night and made my morning joyful, to reality! As an Eastern poet once said—the lover dreams only of his beloved and of her beauty, which charms his heart and enchants his soul. The humble exile from the land of the Nile only dreams of his darling Egypt and his oppressed compatriots.

In my dream I received a visit from the famous Blériot, the celebrated French aeronaut, whose praises are justly sung by the Old and New Worlds.[9] I welcomed

8. [In this context Ziad Fahmi remarks: "It is important to note that Sannu' continued to print his newspapers until December 1910 and did not retire in 1907 as cited in the literature. In the conclusion of *The Practical Visions of Ya'qub Sanu'*, which is the only non-Arabic book-length biography of Sannu', Gendzier [*The Practical Visions of Ya'qub Sanu'*, 1966] mistakenly claims that Sannu' retired in November 1907, 'without formally taking leave of his readers.' In fact, Sannu' continued to publish both newspapers until December 1910. [. . .] Scholars relying on Gendzier for Sannu''s biographical information are continuing to date 1907 as the year of Sannu''s retirement from journalism" ("Francophone Egyptian Nationalists, Anti-British Discourse, and European Public Opinion, 1885–1910," 170).]

9. [Louis Blériot (1872–1936) was a French aviator, engineer, and inventor. A year before Sannu' wrote this text, Blériot became the first person to fly across the English Channel. Albeit in a different context, Esther Moyal also refers to aviation issues of the time (see selection 12).]

him graciously and cordially, offering him a delicious cup of mocha-flavored coffee and an appetizing cigarette, made of Turkish tobacco and perfumed with rose and jasmine. I then put myself at his disposition. Blériot drank my coffee, smoked the cigarette, thanked me heartily for my warm and accommodating welcome, and said: "But it is I, my good sheikh, who wish to put myself at your disposition, to carry you by biplane to Cairo where they are currently celebrating the festival of the Egyptian Constitution. You will see the Great Pyramid at Giza covered with people, both Egyptian patriots and foreigners, friends of the Nile Valley, all singing the national anthem, acclaiming the khedive and the Constitution, and celebrating liberty, equality, and fraternity of which the country had been deprived by invaders."

Invoking the help of the Most High, I accepted Blériot's gracious invitation and climbed into his celestial chariot. Under the encouragement of its daring cavalier, the chariot bravely flung itself into the air and—quick as a flash—hurtled across the immense space separating Egypt, land of my birth, from France, my country of exile.

I am afraid that I am unable to provide an account of my air travel as I have forgotten all its details. I remember only that the scene changed and that I found myself at the foot of the Great Pyramid, the top of which has been dreamed about by the glorious ancestors of our friends the French for some forty centuries. My two honorable friends, Faridassrou and Aliyouchan—those illustrious and universally recognized patriots—came to meet me. Each one taking my hand, they climbed up with me to the top of the gigantic pyramid, in the midst of enthusiastic acclamations and joyous shouts of "Long live young Egypt! Long live Abou Naddara, father of liberty!" Faridassrou, that eloquent Nilotic statesman, presented me with charm and eloquence to the multitudes, according to my merit.

The love of my motherland and my nation inspired me to speak in sweet and tender tones that seem to have moved my audience to tears. Applause was therefore forthcoming. What a shame that Blériot—in place of the biplane that he had quickly built for my journey to Cairo—had not made a triplane; I would have taken my stenographer with me and you, dear reader, would have had the text of my speech *in extenso*, which was imbued with the spirit of those forty centuries. All I know is that I spoke of our dear Egypt, whence tyrants expelled me for having defended the rights of my dear Egyptian brothers against that which the children of the Nile Valley have suffered from the time of the ill-fated [British] invasion up to the happy proclamation of the blessed Constitution. I also spoke of my thirty-two years of exile in Paris, where I was always treated as a brother, for France is a great friend to the Eastern nations.

Once my speech was over, the brave Blériot took flight to find me at the top of the pyramid. Enthusiastic cries of "Long live Blériot! Long live France!" filled the vast Sahara Desert and echoed from one side of the Nile Valley to the other. Moved, enraptured, enchanted, Blériot and I broke into tears of joy. I asked myself: was this a dream or was this reality? Alas, it was nought but a dream. But my heart tells me that God will bring it to pass and that the hour of the Egyptian Constitution will soon be nigh.

7 | **John Bull and the Egyptian Student**

Ya'qub Sannu', "John Bull et l'Étudiant Egyptien," *L'Univers Musulman* and
Abou Naddara, fourth joint French-Arabic issue, December 1910.

This fictional dialogue was published in the last issue of *L'Univers Musulman*. John
Bull represents Great Britain.

THE STUDENT: Good morning, John Bull. You seem cheerful today. Have you
won the jackpot?

JOHN BULL: Even better! We've just received a dispatch from Paris announcing
the closure of that accursed newspaper *L'Abou Naddara* at the end of the year.
That patriotic viper's infamous tongue will soon be silenced: on that day my
friends and I will celebrate, champagne will flow like water.

THE STUDENT: Sheikh Abou Naddara is right to end his long career, for he has
been defending his homeland and his compatriots in speech and in writing
for fifty-five years. He has told you some home truths and has made you hate-
ful to all the Orient. He will soon have the satisfaction of seeing the Egyptian
Constitution proclaimed throughout the whole Nile Valley. That day is not far
off—for the Liberty Bell will soon ring out, and the sheikh will come to take
part in our celebrations.

JOHN BULL: God damn, never! We shall never let him enter and profane with his
presence our Egyptian soil.

THE STUDENT: *Your* Egyptian soil?! But you will not be there, not any longer,
you will have evacuated it. And as far the *Abou Naddara* journal is concerned,
it will reappear in Cairo, at the heart of our capital! Abou Naddara has set a
precedent, and many of our young people are fighting over the honor to be
the one to revive his organ, the organ of liberty, equality, and fraternity. Long
live Egypt! Long live the National Party!

8 | My Poor Eyes

Ya'qub Sannu', "Mes Pauvres Yeux," *L'Univers Musulman* and *Abou Naddara*,
fourth joint French-Arabic issue, December 1910.

This poem by Sannu' was written for the last issue of *L'Univers Musulman*.

Allah! While yet I am upon the Earth,
In constant celebration of your goodness,
O keep the vision in my eyes clear, bright,
That still they may contemplate the beauty
Of all the works made by thy sublime hand
Whose aspect animates me and inspires.

Thou knowest that I always have believed,
Right from my most tender youthfulness.
Thy Testaments Old and New, and thy Koran,
Have ever my wise masters, teachers been.
Oh Lord! May my eyes always be able
To read thy precious books.

If you deny the light to me I shall
Submit myself unto it, in my fashion,
E'en though my poor heart would prefer, in place
Of loss of eyesight, death itself.
For blindness terrifies me, in truth.
There you have it! Oh, 'tis menacing.

Lo! I defy it here by raising up
To Heaven this my final ardent prayer.
Deign to grant it answered, Eternal God,
And ever will my grateful, thankful soul,
Venerate, as long as I have breath,
The One True God of Abou Naddara.

9

Letter to Philip Tarrazi

Ya'qub Sannu' "Letter to Philip Tarrazi in Beirut, February 18, 1911, Paris,"
quoted in, and translated by, Shmuel Moreh in "Ya'qub Sannu': His Religious
Identity and Work in the Theater, According to the Family Archive," in *The
Jews of Egypt, a Mediterranean Society in Modern Times*, ed. Shimon Shamir
(Boulder, CO: Westview, 1987), 115.

The positive attitude that Sannu' expressed toward Islam gave the impression that
he had been born a Muslim or converted to Islam. His use of the title "shaykh" next
to his name also led some to think that he was a Muslim. As Shmuel Moreh has
shown, the Jewish "shaykh" felt obliged to clarify the matter with Philip Tarrazi, a
Lebanese historian who referred to Sannu' as a Muslim in a history of Arab journalism that Tarrazi wrote. The two corresponded about the short biographical note
on Sannu' that Tarrazi included in the original manuscript before it was published.
Having read Tarrazi's biographical note, Sannu' remarked on the mistake in the
following letter.

You said, in the beginning of the second page, "The young man then adopted
the Muslim religion." Please omit this because I did not change the faith of my
parents, although I respect the three religions [Judaism, Islam, and Christianity].
My only belief is in the omnipotence of God. This is witnessed by the conversation which took place between me and the late Muzaffar al-Din Shah when I
visited him in Contrexéville ten years ago. He asked me if I were Muslim or Shi'i?
I answered him that I am one of the Children of Israel. He said: "Since you love
our community, defend its rights, respect its law [shari'a] and praise its kings,
princes and scholars [ulama]—why don't you convert to Islam and become one
of the great men?" I answered him: "If I do that, people would say: He who is no
good for his religion, would be of no good for another religion, which he only
embraces in order to attain high position and fortune." While the Muslims now
respect and love this humble servant, because they see an Israelite raising the
banner of Islam, demonstrating his love for Islam in front of all people and trying to strengthen the ties of friendship between Muslims and Christians; and all
his life having made no mention of his own religion. In conclusion, please omit
the four or five words mentioned above.

Further Readings

Fahmi, Ziad. "Francophone Egyptian Nationalists, Anti-British Discourse, and European Public Opinion, 1885–1910: The Case of Mustafa Kamil and Ya'qub Sannu'." *Comparative Studies of South Asia, Africa and the Middle East* 28, no. 1 (2008): 170–83.

Gendzier, Irene L. *The Practical Visions of Ya'qub Sanu'.* Cambridge: Harvard University Press, 1966.

Landau, Jacob. "Abu Naddara: An Egyptian Jewish Nationalist." *Journal of Jewish Studies* 3, no. 1 (1952): 30–44.

Levy, Lital, "Jewish Writers in the Arab East: Literature, History, and the Politics of Enlightenment, 1863–1914," 142–67. PhD diss., University of California, Berkeley, 2007.

Moosa, Matti. "Ya'qub Sanu' and the Rise of Arab Drama in Egypt." *International Journal of Middle Eastern Studies* 5, no. 4 (1974): 401–33. (Reprinted in Matti Moosa, *The Origins of Modern Arabic Fiction* [Washington: Three Continents, 1983], 41–66.)

Moreh, Shmuel. "Ya'qub Sanu': His Religious Identity and Work in the Theater, According to the Family Archive." In *The Jews of Egypt, a Mediterranean Society in Modern Times*, edited by Shimon Shamir, 111–29. Boulder, CO: Westview, 1987.

Sadgrove, Philip C. "The First Experiments in Arab Drama: James Sanua." In Philip C. Sadgrove, *The Egyptian Theatre in the Nineteenth Century, 1799–1882*, 89–124. Reading, Berkshire: Ithaca, 1996.

Esther Azhari Moyal

A pioneering and daring journalist, feminist, essayist, literary translator, publisher, and teacher, Esther Moyal, née Azhari (1873–1948), was born in Beirut. She lived and worked in Cairo, Istanbul, Jaffa, and Marseilles and died, intellectually disillusioned, in Jaffa's Manshiyya neighborhood at the age of seventy-five. A graduate of Beirut's Syrian Protestant College, Moyal taught at the Scottish Church mission and, at the age of twenty, represented the Lebanese Women's League as a delegate at the International Women's Conference in Chicago. Moyal's involvement with feminism began earlier in such organizations as Bākūrat Sūriya (Syria's dawn), and in 1896 she cofounded Nahdat al-Nisā' (The awakening of women).

In 1894 Moyal married, in Jaffa, Shim'on Moyal (1866–1915)—whom she had met in Beirut—and moved with him to Istanbul. They lived there until 1896, when Shim'on earned an Ottoman certification to practice medicine. The Moyals next headed to Cairo where, in 1899, Esther gave birth to their son, 'Abdallah Nadim Moyal, and founded the bimonthly al-'Āila (The family). She wrote for al-Ahrām, a daily newspaper, and al-Hilāl, a literary journal, as well as other Egyptian and Syrian-Lebanese publications. During these years, Moyal translated into Arabic dozens of French novels and shorter dramas, as well as a biography of Émile Zola.

In the wake of the Young Turk revolution, the Moyals moved to Jaffa where Shim'on had been born. There, in 1909, Moyal cofounded an organization of Jewish women and, together with her husband, immersed herself in the promotion of liberal Arabized/Eastern Zionism, Ottomanism, feminism, and interreligious and intercommunal relations based on civic bonds. Together with Dr. Nissim Malul, the Moyals raised funds to establish Jewish publications in Arabic and in 1913–14 founded Sawt al-'Uthmaniyya (The voice of the Ottomans), a Jewish newspaper in Arabic aspiring to reconcile the sociopolitical, cultural, and linguistic aims of Jewish Euro-Zionist and Arab-Palestinian nationalisms. The untimely death of her husband widowed Moyal at the age of forty-two and left her little choice but to join relatives in Marseille. As the Nazis took over Europe in the early 1940s, Moyal managed to find her way back to Mandatory Palestine. She died there in 1948, forgotten, lonely, impoverished, and suffering from severe amnesia.

Address at the American College for Girls in Beirut

Esther Azhari Moyal, "Khitab" [Speech], *al-Hasna'*, October 1911, 24–29.

This item is a graduation speech delivered at American College for Girls in Beirut delivered in 1911.

My dear ladies,[1]

On behalf of other members of our brilliant society, I congratulate you on the great success that you have achieved after long years of hard work, learning, and inquiry day and night,[2] until attaining a high level of education and knowledge. I welcome you to the membership of our society, which welcomes you with open arms, hoping that you will pursue the great work that this school started in teaching you morals, enlightening your mind, and raising your mental capacities. Carry the flag of progress wherever your feet take you so that you can spread genuine civilization and culture throughout our beloved nation.

Dear ladies, until now you had only one task: to learn your lessons in order to see signs of pleasure and happiness on the faces of your teachers when they heard you recite them. You pleased your parents and earned the praise of relatives. Today, however, you are entering a new world and a difficult, broad arena where you will challenge each other and occupy positions for which your mental preparation has qualified you. Each of you can express your talent, skill, personality, and taste. If you can show your merits over those who surround you, you will be able to excel and outclass your peers; if you cannot, then those girls who have studied will be equal to those who have not studied.[3] If you become complacent toward the sciences that you learned in school, if you surrender yourselves to fate and circumstances and ignore books and pens—you may well

1. [The lecture was addressed to women, and most of its Arabic sentences are in the *nun al-niswa* form—that is, the sentences include the grammatical marker addressing females in the plural. That distinction cannot be shown in English, which lacks an equivalent form.]

2. [Moyal employs a Qur'anic phrase implying hard work around the clock.]

3. [Moyal employs a Qur'anic verse meaning that those who work hard cannot be equalled by those who do not work.]

find yourselves on a par with those who have never held a pen or a book. Minds are like silver cups: if you neglect them they will tarnish.

You see those who hold you back, whose hearts are obliterated by God, saying that there is no point in education and that every dirham spent on it is a waste since our Eastern traditions dictate that a woman's place is in the home, where no activity enlightens her mind and no art raises her mental capacities, nor expands the boundaries of her imagination. No, my dear ladies, you will prove these demagogues utterly wrong and [show] that life's good things are created by us, women; that we bequeath morals to the nation's sons, who are our fathers, brothers, husbands, and sons. You will appear like a fierce fighter prepared for days of danger, ready to defy and fight enemies. You will enjoy immunity by merit, and you are strong enough to repel every impudent person spurned and lost. Lend your hands to honorable work and noble causes; make use of your time productively and reap the benefits of freedom and autonomy in return—so that each one of you can return to the home from which you originated and become its right hand. You will establish the civilization that we are now in as urgent need of as the food feeding our bodies and the air purifying our blood. This is a civilization where woman is equal to man and where woman is man's partner in the battle of life, which the strongest alone wins. That is, an Arab Eastern civilization based on inherited virtues, love for labor, and excellence in everything.

We resemble now the Russian girls who awoke from their sleep decades ago to challenge men in all domains. They are now crowding the French and Swiss cities and are scattered across Europe, seeking to immerse themselves in higher education without being hindered by poverty or need. These women face the dangers of exile and knock on the doors of medicine and law. They study chemistry and the philosophy of languages and return home after they acquire a job, driving back the calamity of need and securing a well-respected position among their countrymen. This helps them to forget the hardships and suffering that they experienced during their studies. How wonderful it would be if you would look up to them and follow in their footsteps and learn the arts of engraving, photography, music, and dentistry. You would prove your equality to those men unhappy to recognize it. As Mme de Staël has written in her novel,[4] no matter how civilized a man might be, he will still be confused on meeting an intelligent,

---

4. [Madame de Staël, Baronne de Staël-Holstein, born Anne Louise Germaine Necker (1766–1817), the author of many works. The novel referred to here is *Corrine ou l'Italie* (1807).]

good-hearted woman. If he likes her, he will be jealous and wary of her; if he dislikes her, his pride will be hurt as soon as he grasps her qualities. It is not in this man's interests—nor in the interests of the current status quo—to proclaim equality between man and woman: due to this man's selfishness, he wishes this woman to remain subservient to him, like a minor to his guardian.

My sisters, God will not change a people until they change themselves, and this applies to us, the women of the East, in even greater force. We cannot avoid this advice, which weighs heavily on us, and must knock on the doors of waged employment for money to flow into our hands—a pursuit that is the pillar of modern society and a cornerstone of modern civilization. How far is the distance between those who say "give me!" and those who say "there, o souls, are your deserts." We need to obliterate this teaching as if it never existed: it is the cause of our misery and despair. May God have mercy on the soul of the poet who wrote:

Every human being can be unjust.
Those who are not must have a reason.[5]

May God bless the man aware of his limits. It is time for us to start applying the advice of this wise man so that our fate among mankind will be that of those who take, and get, as much as they give. A woman—with all pride—is the essence of life and its joy, the poetry of beauty and perfection. As our soul rises and floats in the infinite—and goes to skies of truth and evidence and imagination when we recite a poem by al-Ma'arri, al-Mutanabbi, or Abu Tammam al-Ta'i[6]—that is how we feel when we sit and talk to a well-mannered, intelligent woman who lets her female inspiration and intellectual perfection lead her. Such a woman forces her companion to think wisely and direct his imagination toward every noble, commendable thing, as the famous poet known as 'Azza[7] wrote:

I know the monks of Madyan
And I know they cry for fear of God.
But if they could hear what I heard from her,
They would bow and prostrate themselves before her immediately.

5. [A famous stanza by the well-known Arab poet *al-Mutanabbi* (915–65).]

6. [Three celebrated Arab poets.]

7. [Moyal is referring to the Ummayad poet Kuthayyir ibn 'Abd al-Rahman al-Mulahi (ca. 660–723), known as Khuthayyir 'Azza. The poem "Ruhbān Madyan" (The monks of Madyan) refers to monks who resided in the territory where the biblical Midyanites once existed.]

Nevertheless, woman has fearsome powers in this universe. Had it not been for her compassion, self-denial, and disregard for her own pleasures—there would be nobody left on earth. This fact is self-evident and requires no proof. This is her fate and identity. Her rights could not have been oppressed—and she would not have been left neglected between the walls of the house like a commodity that can be bought and sold—had not she surrendered to her emotions and weakness; had not her mother, harsh Nature, made her breasts the source of life and her loins the factory of mankind.

What could make me leave my baby to die of hunger, or allow his tender body to be exposed to the cold, while I went out with my husband every night to bars, cafes, and pleasure gardens to spend my time and money? My husband can do so with pleasure, even if we had ten children, since he does not consider himself responsible for me or for his family, except for covering expenses. I, on the other, would go crazy, and my heart and conscience would bring me to tears if I stole a minute of my life for myself and did not spend it serving my child morally and materially. I give to the family all my energy and intelligence and pledge my heart and soul to it. My husband meanwhile pays me his dirhams, yet all of his energy, intelligence, and strength are devoted to his insatiable desire for authority and glory. If I witnessed injustice or negligence from my husband, I used to look at the sky and say "that is my destiny, my fate, my luck." But no, my sisters—it is time we stopped that and pleaded with the poet. Let us cleanse ourselves of this oppression and neglect, armed with a job that we are good at and a profession that prevents our husbands from treating us like a master treats a slave, or like a judge accepting no objections. In doing so, we can survive the marital partnership, as the poet says:

I take flour from you, and I light it with my fire.
And water is from me, but butter and honey from you.

Note, my dear ladies, that marriage should not be the ultimate goal toward which we resolutely go. The girl should not follow the call by preparing herself, by spending her time and intelligence seeking that which makes her face glow and enhances her features. She makes the advertisements of Au Printemps, Le Bon Marché, and La Samaritaine[8] textbooks that teach her about clothes, brands, jewelry, and dresses. Hold on a minute, girl: like a musical instrument that does not make music unless its strings are touched, you do not express

8. [Three of the most famous department stores in Paris.]

emotions except when the discussion turns to the latest fashions. Turn your eyes to something more important than a dress that is only transitory. It is no secret that I am guilty of this like you, since it is instinctive in any individual, male or female, to try to impress other people with their art and good taste, unless they are an ascetic, Sufi, or dying elderly person. But letting fashion be our only concern and our only occupation is a humiliating thing—especially if its aim is to secure a husband, as if by gaining him you attain paradise and its pleasures. The girl makes it her ultimate goal and the center of her activities, focusing only on imaginary romances and fantasies and leaving reality to pass her like a cloud without learning its lessons. When she gets married and sees the vast difference between reality and the fantasies she fell for, she becomes depressed, surrenders to despair, and neglects herself—as if she were, until yesterday, that young girl who attracted hearts to see her and ears to listen to her nice soft voice.

Do not hang all your hopes on your husband and depend on him to make your life easy, because life is not only about happiness and fun but about duty and hard work. The happy man is the one who fulfils duties for himself, his family, and fellow countrymen with good intentions and peace of mind. The miserable man is the one who depends on others and relates his happiness only to them, even if he were richer than Qarun[9] and wiser than Iyas.[10] Be sure, my ladies: man is not born alone, and the two sexes were born together to bond and form a family and be united as partners in the ups and downs of life. Be sure that a husband will come without searching or suffering. How wonderful would it be if the modern Eastern woman could behave wisely from the time she finishes school until she gets married and masters her work, as her sisters in Europe are doing, so that she will gain the ability to protect herself from her husband's iniquity so when she faces unfairness and oppression from him—or if the days bring her a lack of love and care—she can return to work and save her children from the harshness of poverty.

Yes, my sisters, let us go and wander through the houses of the Europeans who live among us; we will find a family afflicted by fate, misfortunes, and disasters. Yet the woman learns the piano if she is a musician, or she becomes an accountant or a shopkeeper, or starts a new business if she has enough money

9. [Qarun was a rich man and a member of Moses's tribe who is said to have become arrogant due to his wealth.]

10. [Iyas ibn Mu'awiya al-Muzani, an eighth-century judge renowned for his cleverness and wisdom.]

so she can buy, sell, and finalize deals and establish companies, just like a man, even while she finds her children prosperous and flourishing, since she fulfills her duties to each of them, and puts them in school and spends as much money as she can on them. In this way, the family will not face any calamities and will continue to improve, until all of the children grow and make something of themselves, becoming men and women, citizens working in life who make one proud. I do not need to elaborate any further about the misery, destruction, and collapse that would occur if such calamities hit an Eastern house. This has always been a matter that made our tears flow on seeing it and melted our hearts on hearing of it.

If it happens to any of you that you do not find a husband on whose arm to lean, it would be natural to turn to knowledge—having spent the years of your youth and the prime of your childhood studying its laws and learning its well-kept secrets; your closest friend and companion whose planets and stars keep you company, whose trees and plants talk to you, whose minerals and soil occupy your imagination. Knowledge's book is always open, and its arms are always extended to welcome you so that you can excel in an art and find consolation and solace in mastering it. You will then leave a mark speaking for your skills and talents and preserving a praiseworthy memory of you, of which the coming generations will always speak well. Marriage honors since it allows the couple means to show a creative power fixed in them. [. . .]

Note, my dear ladies, that you are Arab Syrians and that your knowledge of English or French does not make you an Englishwoman or a Frenchwoman. No matter how hard you try to hide your nationality, your face and features will show it, and your blood will prove it, and your morals will announce it, and if you forget all of that, the Westerner will remind you through her treatment of you and take your identity away from you and compete with you over it. As the poet said:[11]

The houses of the family of *al-sha'b*[12] are always preferred
Just as spring is preferred in all times of the year.

11. [A famous poem by al-Mutanabbi.]

12. [The *al-sha'b* in Persia has been described as paradise on earth due to its abundance of water and food. When Arabs visited the place, the locals recognized and identified them as Arab. Moyal cites this to emphasize her contention that Arabs cannot, nor should they try to, escape their identity and roots because such attempts at escape will be fruitless.]

But the Arab boy among them
Has a foreign face, hand, and tongue.

Let us stop following Westerners in every situation, whether good or bad. Let us go back and learn our language, refine its expression when we talk, and make our children keen on learning it along with the poems of our poets and the proverbs of our wise men. Let us go back to giving our sons and daughters names that remind us of our great history and the poems of our significant poets, and how distant are the names of *Salma* and *Leila*, which bring together every echo of music and poetry, from the names "Halay" and "Kinikond," which mean nothing at all to us. Let us establish an Eastern Arab civilization in which the woman will make half the effort to promote and glorify it in front of civilized people, who rank us along with the Indians and the Chinese when they mention the half-savage peoples because we do not respect ourselves and [we] belittle others. For persons who do not recognize their own value are not respected.

11 | Our Renaissance

Esther Azhari Moyal, "Nahdatuna," al-Hasna', June 1912, 408–15.

Moyal delivered this address in 1912 at a celebration of the Shams al-Birr Society, a charitable society established in Beirut in 1870.

Ladies and gentlemen!

We can say that time has passed and pens have dried up. Misery is our destiny, and the West utilizes it as a tool to ensure our silence. The West manages and shapes our destiny as it sees fit—as if the West owns the East. Westerners divide lands without caring about international laws, making a mockery of all the peace treaties, so that Western states can extend their territories wherever they wish. They attacked us with their horses and soldiers and decimated our lands, spreading damage and destruction. They look down on us as lords look on their slaves, as if we were wretched animals. Time has witnessed our humiliation at their hands and has thus sanctioned our slavery.

Should we proclaim instead that we have clever minds, sound heads for planning, strong arms, and skillful hands? We need to utilize them by all possible means, as done by powerful peoples before us. Our destiny in this world is to be a clever people who will prosper scientifically and practically, who will be capable of protecting our honor and preventing the enemy's deception while repelling the greed of those avaricious toward us.

We are not going to say that we inherited ignominy from our ancestors. We are not going to say that failure travels through our veins, feeding our brains, disabling the self-reliance that drives each one of us to resist faltering and to overcome the ongoing difficulties hindering the perfection of the arts and vocations we practice. We are not going to say that the crafts we practice are only done under pressure or in order to satisfy a father or a brother. We are not going to say that they are done for meaningless glory or in order to show off. Rather, we should say that we are equal to the successful nations that had the patience and determination to make use of everything they had. We are gifted with the same talents that helped them to achieve success and greatness; all that we have to do is utilize these gifts to prove to the world that we are ready to achieve great things that will reveal the secrets of nature and all her components, and the explanations of the earth's behavior and its daily processes. Our aim for perfection is high and our desire for achieving it great. We greatly appreciate the arts and respect those who pursue them. We likewise understand true beauty as we strive to grace ourselves with it and adorn our dear nations with its manifestations—which make us happy, bring joy to sensitive hearts, and promote creative ideas and correct opinions.

Look at these Europeans flying high, owning the wind. We granted them divinity, just as the ancient Greeks viewed their Hercules and those who followed in his footsteps, making a distinction between their weaknesses and the strength of their heroes, and between their inability and the ability of those great heroes that they made their gods. They made them eternal, even though they were mortal beings. Should we despair and say: "This is fate, and nothing can stop it. People on earth are like planets in the sky. This is a great one shining in glory, and that one is insignificant and trivial?" No. Is it proper for us to anesthetize ourselves with such a drug while we have strong resolutions and clever minds, which—if utilized according to their capacity—could move mountains and turn deserts into paradise?

If our country is declining, our resources drained and our citizens forced to abandon it, then we should blame only ourselves because we are all responsible for its downfall. Whatever disasters and devastations befall our people, we should not blame our destiny—as destiny has given us our country, whose clear sky, pleasant air, beautiful places, and fertile soil are all exemplary. Look at the yellow race[13] and how they were viewed as stupid, dull, and narrow-minded. Did Japan stop there and resign itself to the fact that its ancestors were slothful, careless, and ignorant? Have you not seen how they became united as one hand [one people], thrived on education that allowed them to challenge with glory and greatness the world's most developed countries?

Did the German nations resign themselves to divisive factors and remain fragmented by a variety of dialects, political interests, and distinct provinces? Didn't they unite their interests and their languages and choose the best one among them—the language in which Schiller and Goethe expressed their eloquence—making it the language of the whole country, deriding and scorning the past? Look at these peasants of theirs who came to our countries tens of years ago and colonized the cities of Haifa and Jaffa, where they made the desert

13. [The phrase "yellow race" was commonly employed in 1912 and was not then generally regarded as racist.]

bloom[14] through their unity and hard work, making the land appear like a green paradise, pleasing eyes and opening hearts. They forged there a high standard of living and a good livelihood, whereas the indigenous peasants remained miserably poor.

Should we not be happy when we see this German peasant flourishing in agriculture, commerce, blacksmithing, and other trades, bringing comfort to his house and joy to his wife and children? In the hands of such a man there is a treasure that never ends, just like the kingdom of the earth. Should we not be surprised when we see a mother bequeath her daughter a crucial "dowry" of culinary knowledge, teaching the girl in her kitchen for two years after she finishes her education at Berlin universities? If these lessons exhaust the mother, then she can simply send her daughter off to some notable person's house where she will learn household management. Yes, my ladies—if you see Germany become noble through its female soldiers, great through its business and industry, and expansive through its colonies—they owe this greatness to the poorest peasant who sings "Deutschland über alles,"[15] which means "Germany is above everything from the planet's equator to its two poles."

Who would have thought that France could pay five billion francs to its enemy so quickly after the internecine war in 1870 and still return to lead the world and the intellectual movement through its sons in science, arts, and industry, even pioneering the art of flying? Men like Pasteur, Roux, Hayem, Hugo, and Curie, among others, brought France eternal glory. Look at the Scandinavian countries, which would have been destroyed by alcoholism had they not taken the initiative to create entertaining athletic games and suitable elementary education that revitalized the youth and gave their nations energy and strength.

Knowing all of this, we should view all aspects of our country's current situation so that we can assess the quality of our modern urbanization that requires money as its cornerstone. Or should we instead say that only those who look at things superficially will believe that we have come a long way and made many achievements since we live in massive castles, dress in nice Parisian clothes, and study European languages? We have newspapers and magazines that transmit all of our news to the poorest of our villages; we have banks, shops, and fac-

14. [Moyal refers here to Euro-Zionist immigrants to Palestine who often used the phrase "making the desert bloom" to legitimize their immigration.]

15. [The opening words of the German national anthem here are transliterated in the original Arabic.]

tories. But are these really the accomplishments that glorify the people and humble the ruler?

Gentlemen, if our values remain in this state and we continue to degrade craftsmanship and cling to our love of empty success and appearance, then it really does not matter how high we rise because we will remain stuck to the ground—low, useless, and miserable. Why are our children fond of learning only medicine and pharmacy while ignoring industry, the fire of the blacksmith, and the saw of the carpenter? They neglect the agriculture that brings them excellent food blessed by God. Without resorting to hyperbole or flattery, does not the heart burn with sorrow and sadness when we see among us a foreign girl whose fingers know only the keys of the piano and who moves hearts with her melancholic music—yet keenly devotes herself to learning the art of agriculture while this kind of pursuit does not interest our children, even though we urgently need it?

Our agricultural lands—thank God—are ample and our rivers bountiful. If they were given some care, they could enrich the country with wealth and prosperity and spread good cheer. Then what would be the point of the castles built with money from sold agricultural fields, the harvest that used to cover a family's expenses? What is the point of the factories if they only harvest the silk of the cocoon? What is the point of modern fashions if those wearing them—including the likes of our tailors, doctors, merchants, and bankers—declare bankruptcy while they find their safes full of gold, taking advantage of the money of orphans and widows? Or would they kindle a fire in their safes in order to get the insurance money?

Most of our newspapers—thank God—care only about trivial issues, and their content does not reflect the eloquence of their publishers unless they are insulting other people.[16] What is the point of the newspapers if their publishers do not have the faith and courage to speak the truth that would allow them to confirm facts and deny falsehoods? And why shouldn't they—since newspapers are the voice of the people and their defenders—raise their banners and constitute a second source of education? People learn of major events and daily happenings from newspapers. So if you do not take the position of a wise teacher who instructs souls and educates minds, or the position of a proficient surgeon who would not hesitate to use his scalpel even if it was going to hurt his patient, and if you do not take freedom, equality, and brotherhood as your

---

16. [This sentence is intended sarcastically.]

slogan—things will worsen. This will lead to discord and cowardice, where we are in urgent need of unifying our hearts and gathering them under the banner of justice so that if the people see their rulers faltering or straying from the truth, or notice any lack of qualifications for the positions they are filling, or suspect them of corruption—they will force them to follow the correct path or retire from ruling. Was it not shameful for the newspapers to engage their readers for two months with "Which is better? Hat or fez?" while Italy was mobilizing its army and preparing its fleets to send gifts to Western Tripoli[17] with which to buy the affection of the people, perhaps encouraging them to betray their countries, and then handing them over as easy prey?

What can I say about our shops? That their imports are greater than their exports and earn us our wages and nothing more? If the current situation remains as it is, it will have severe consequences, and poverty will threaten us from all sides: if we sell one pound of our raw material for ten piasters—and then buy it for ten dirhams after it is turned into household goods in Europe with the same amount of money—then we are just scraping by. True, the migrant has met a little of this annual shortfall and has spread some luxury and prosperity in the country. But how widespread would this benefit be if the generous migrant did not use all of his wealth to build a castle when he went back to his country, and maybe even borrow money to get it built? It does not matter how much he boasts about his castle to his friends, he still does not benefit the country except by enhancing its image abroad. If he thought rationally and knew what was best for himself and for his country, he would invest all of his money in the country's markets so that he could get better services in return. Or he would unite with his brothers in nationalism, agree with them sincerely and establish companies with them, or set up projects together, giving them back when taken over by well-behaved and honest people.

My people, we have had enough of this selfishness, resulting in failure and disappointment, and enough of division, disunity, and holding grudges against each other. Man is nothing on his own while much stronger with his brothers. So whenever man is selfish, goes to extremes in his love for himself, or wishes good fortune on no one except his blessed self—man will stagnate and fail to move forward. Meanwhile he watches other countries—uniting and becoming heavens on earth, reviving dying hearts, educating idle brains, providing educa-

17. ["Western Tripoli" in Arabic refers to the city of Tripoli in Libya, as distinct from "Eastern Tripoli," which is in Lebanon.]

tion to the illiterate and insights to the dull and stupid. Gardens and zoos, art galleries, historical monuments and statues made to remember great men, to refine the taste of the people and remind them of their great history and their good deeds and the fact that—when they follow in their footsteps—the doors of greatness will open before them, bringing honor and glory to the country to which they belong.

How can we answer the call of the nation—that appeals for our help against the neglect resulting from our selfishness and our racial divisions, coupled with our lack of faith in our peers—as long as we are satisfied with our situation and resigned to our fate? We should have replaced the old agriculture, one of our chief resources of livelihood, with a modern one based on education. We should have sent schools to the peasant who does not have the means to obtain education. We should have replaced the old machines with modern ones and provided peasants with chemical fertilizers that give them thirty-seven rotls for each rotl[18] of crop—equivalent to the harvest of Palestine's modern colonies.

With sons of this age—the age of electricity and aviation that scoffs at distances—we should use our strong love for our country, whose interests should be given priority over all other interests, and unite together as one hand and heart to collect enough money to establish companies and projects throughout the nation. This will give life to our dead lands and will spread energy until we no longer see a single corner that does not have hands working hard [and] directed by heads enlightened by the modern sciences, guaranteeing the means of success. People have spent long years learning the arts by day and by night[19] as they were born to do in order to discover our hidden heritage. Our hidden intellect—which whenever we begin to explore it and use it with military, industrial, agricultural, or domestic tools—will provide wealth to our country and open many lucrative and profitable fields of work for our youth. They thus will stop facing danger to leave the country in order to seek their livelihood as modern civilization demands.

It is time that we built bridges, constructed dams and aqueducts, and expanded channels and canals between our great rivers—whose waters run wasted into the seas—so we can manage irrigation and facilitate means of transportation by

18. [A rotl is a measure of weight between one and six pounds. In Palestine it usually meant between five and six pounds.]

19. [Here Moyal uses the same phrase from the Qur'an that she used elsewhere (see note 2), implying hard work around the clock.]

building more railways. It is time that we proceed with improving our harbors and ports, of which nature gave us plenty; if they had been given to Germany or Russia, their resources would have doubled. The sea attacked some of them and eroded their central features. How long are the merchants of a city like Jaffa, which is the seaport of the Holy Land, destined to throw their money into the sea with their own hands when the storms and hurricanes arrive in order to avoid the decay of the fruits that are waiting in customs in order to be shipped? How long will the Dead Sea's water continue to be high in minerals, while the neighboring lands grow only thorns, and bushes and fertile plants are turned into dead bushes? How long will the seas have no national commercial vessels that carry our commodities to their destinations—leaving us free of need of these foreign ships that go to all ports and coasts, wasting time and causing the fruits to rot? We meanwhile see ships headed to the smallest Balkan country that was, until yesterday, one of our provinces. The art of seamanship will be useful for us if we take some care over it and do not let a country such as Bulgaria, for example, gain precedence over us.[20]

We cannot be a renascent people when we do not have a social club that brings together all the artists, workers, and craftsmen in their leisure time to discuss their daily affairs and to brainstorm ways to bring success to their efforts, promote their interests, and exchange ideas about their conditions, at a time when we find the poorest city in God's wide lands full of clubs frequented daily by colleagues of the same trade. They establish associations and deputize working committees to defend the rights of the least significant member and stand as a barrier preventing any evil actions by the corrupt rulers and influential people. We cannot be a renascent people when we are afraid of the strong oppressor and curry favor with him. While we despise the weak and avoid them, we flatter the rich and praise and honor them, something they never dreamed of; if only our hearts embraced hatred and scorn for their stinginess and their strong love of this world!

Come on, gentlemen, let us fix whatever is wrong with our morals, and get rid of whatever is holding us back from a true renaissance and give priority to education, and useful jobs, with integrity as a guide, and freedom as a light il-

---

20. [Moyal's words were timely. In 1911, only a year before this speech was delivered, Bulgaria began negotiating the formation of an anti-Ottoman alliance with Greece and Serbia. This alliance was officially formed in mid-1912, and its creation was partly responsible for the outbreak of the First Balkan War in October 1912.]

luminating our homes, schools, and markets. We should implement equality of rights and duties between spouses and make the family a unit where all live for one, and one lives for all, and not treat the family home as a hotel to eat in, or a place to sleep in where the individual looks out for himself alone. Pleasure is preoccupied with its pleasures when it is happy, then throws off its burden on someone else so he can endure the hardships of his life, which is full of thorns and whose paths are not covered with roses and aromatic plants. We should bear in mind our religious duty—which enjoins us to deny ourselves for the comfort of our offspring and to improve our children, so we can enlighten their world with education and make the most of it, and of their careers, as there is no difference between males and females, and we also should arm them with persistence and patience to endure hardships, as well as give them freedom of expression and choice of profession, on the condition that their freedom not infringe on the feelings and interests of others, and teach them self-reliance.

We should also provide our children with many fields for athletics in all neighborhoods so that they can play sports that would strengthen their muscles and keep them active, give them speed, teach them how to hit a target, make their bodies flexible, and make them sharper; this is the best weapon against any hardship they may face in the future. In doing so, we are preparing the children of today to be the men and women of tomorrow who believe in the love of our country and its prosperity. If their lands provide them with an abundance of milk and honey and their projects shower them with money, then the geniuses can perfect the art that they were born to do, without preventing them from supporting themselves. Our poet no longer needs, in verse, to beg for money, and our musician need not compose a tune to flatter the rich and majestic. But for every genius that we have, his love and passion for his craft should be a powerful force to drive him to perfect his art.

We will thus have the best scientists, poets, musicians, singers, photographers, painters, sculptors, and writers to enjoy the artistic renaissance that we are going through, despite our current difficulties. Who can deny the tangible progress apparent in our poetry and song? Not too long ago, poetry was all about words and rhyme, but—thanks to the modern poet—it has become a broad realm of competition for the powerful meanings that move feelings and delight hearts. Previously our singers were dreadful and concerned only with themselves and searching for love; they now look at their love with perfection, and take pride in it and sacrifice themselves for it.

How wonderful it is when our boys and girls are perfecting Arabic music and mastering singing it, while purifying it of everything that disfigures it, so that the likes of Adelina Patti[21] will emerge from among them. Her mellow voice rings in the ears of the leaders of Europe as they roam the burning sands of Africa and its barren unknown regions, forgetting their hardships through its repetition. How wonderful it is when we can see pictures of our majestic mountains, our deep valleys, and our wide plains from the camera of the photographer with [the land's] bright colors and its ever-shining clear sky. Arab beauty decorates them, fostering intelligence and understanding.

Our sculptors have mastered the simple columns, and they are now making statues and taking an interest in the ruins that were left by the geniuses of early eras of the Greek and Roman chisels. They search these ruins and collect the best and put them in a museum, which will save and preserve their beauty so people can view them as an example and model to be imitated. Our scientists and writers can then write architectural moral, artistic, and scientific books, so that there will be nothing that cannot be set down in writing in their Arabic language, full of meanings and expressions, and that is not less important than the other powerful and well-known languages in expressing philosophic thinking. Hence, we can establish an Eastern Arab civilization based on noble inherited virtues and a love for work and achievement, and thereby take a prominent and uninfringeable place among other civilized countries. May God guide our steps toward peace and prosperity.

Further Readings

Behar, Moshe. "What's in a Name? Socio-Terminological Formations and the Case for 'Arabized Jews.'" *Social Identities* 15, no. 6 (2009): 747–71.

Campos, Michelle U. "Between 'Beloved Ottomania' and 'The Land of Israel': The Struggle over Ottomanism and Zionism among Palestine's Sephardi Jews, 1908–13." *International Journal of Middle Eastern Studies* 37, no. 4 (2005) 461–83.

———. *Ottoman Brothers: Muslims, Christians, and Jews in Early Twentieth-Century Palestine.* Stanford: Stanford University Press, 2011.

Cohen, Hayyim. "Moyal, Esther." In *Encyclopaedia Judaica*, edited by Fred Skolnik and Michael Berenbaum, 14:590. 2nd ed. Detroit: Macmillan Reference, 2007.

Jacobson, Abigail. "Sephardim, Ashkenazim, and the Palestine 'Arab Question' in pre–First World War Palestine: A Reading of Three Zionist Newspapers." *Middle Eastern Studies* 39, no. 2 (2003): 105–30.

Levy, Lital. "Jewish Writers in the Arab East: Literature, History, and the Politics of Enlightenment, 1863–1914." PhD diss., University of California, Berkeley, 2007.

21. [An Italian operatic soprano, 1843–1919.]

———. "Partitioned Pasts: Arab Jewish Intellectuals and the Case of Esther Azhari Moyal (1873–1948)." In *The Making of the Arab Intellectual (1880–1960): Empire, Public Sphere, and the Colonial Coordinates of Selfhood*, edited by Dyala Hamzah, 128–63. London: Routledge, 2012.

Murād Farag

Probably Egypt's most prominent Karaite Jew in the twentieth century and a practicing lawyer, Murād Farag (1866–1956) was a reformer, scholar, poet, essayist, translator, journalist, and editor. (His surname is often spelled Faraj, and his first name often appears as Mourad or Morad). Farag wrote some thirty books in Arabic, Hebrew, and French, starting in 1889, and he was one of the most prolific interdisciplinary Jewish authors in the modern Arab Middle East. His scholarly books, articles, essays, popular op-eds, and poems covered such diverse fields as theology and law, biblical exegesis, Hebrew and Arabic philology, medieval Arabic Jewish poetry, philosophy, psychology, interpersonal and interreligious relations in Egyptian society, contemporary legal affairs (including secular, Jewish, and Islamic law) and questions of belief and heresy. Many of Farag's writings systematically highlighted the intimate historical linkages between Judaism and Islam and between Arabic and Hebrew. Farag was the editor of the Karaite community's *al-Tahdhib* (Edification)—where his early articles were published—before becoming a regular contributor to leading Egyptian newspapers and periodicals.

In 1902 he gained some public prominence following his successful defense in Cairo's Court of Appeals of Hayyim Kahanah, a (Rabbinate) Jew of Port Said, who was accused of the ritual murder of a six-year-old Christian girl and initially sentenced to one year of hard labor. After Farag won the appeal, the judge ordered the Egyptian state to bear all the trial expenses. In 1923 Farag was invited to help write the Egyptian Constitution—for which he had passionately advocated in the preceding two decades. During the 1920s he attempted to reconcile Zionism and Egyptian Arab nationalism and also cofounded the Société Historique d'Études Juives d'Égypte.

Following his 1932 retirement from his legal career, Farag was able to immerse himself in literary pursuits and the affairs of the Jewish community. Among other activities, he campaigned (unsuccessfully) against the Jewish prohibition on Rabbinate-Karaite marriages and was elected in 1936 as a member of the Arabic Language Academy. Rather symbolically, Farag passed away in Cairo during the year of the Suez War that also marked the last chapter of the long history of the Egyptian Jewish community.

12 | The War for Our Nation

Murād Farag, "Harb al-Watan,"[1] in *Maqalāt Murād* (Murād's essays; Cairo: Ibrahim Rosenthal, 1912), 200–222.

> This essay by Farag was originally serialized in the Egyptian newspaper *al-Jarīda* during 1908. Founded in 1907 and edited by the famous liberal intellectual Ahmad Lutfi al-Sayyid (1872–1963), the newspaper was a strong voice of modern Egyptian nationalism and published essays by many liberal and secular activists like Farag. The work was later reprinted in the 1912 collection of his essays. This selection is a translation of that reprinted version, which is probably identical to the original text.

[By "war"] I mean concrete war—rather than a war of words or an incomplete war of demonstrations. I am not in denial regarding the existence of these words or those demonstrations, and neither do I deny their value, action, or influence. What I do reject is the inadequacy of their effect, benefit, and utility, which lack foundation in reason or fact. [. . .] For a national assembly to be true, it has to hold itself categorically aloof vis-à-vis any matter pertaining to religion.

A nation or [constitutional] monarchy is always in need of a bond created by nationalism, particularly when it includes people who are believers in different religions or affiliates of different doctrines. If people in Egypt were to be armed with religions or doctrines, they would kill each other. By killing I do not mean taking lives but the killing of fraternal passion and national feeling in peoples' souls; nothing is more evil than that. This engenders an inextinguishable fire or endless war. If the essence of a nation were presented, the smallest transgression from the religious perspective would be construed as a major disaster, depending on the degree of emphasis.

No one can deny that religious relationships in Egypt historically carried more weight than a rock-solid mountain and were more remarkable than the wild man plotting an ambush against a transient. Yet current representations of the national essence—or the contemporary description of the Egyptian

---

1. [Somekh translates the title of this essay as "The Struggle of the Motherland" ("Lost Voices," 13), while Levy prefers "The Struggle for the Homeland" ("Jewish Writers in the Arab East," 183).]

home or nation—transcend the dynamic of religious relations. The nation is presented in essence, yet the religious relationship is not enhanced by the same measure. [. . .] If we intend to reform our conditions from the outside, we first have to reform [ourselves] from the inside. Good internal health will be evident in one's face. We wish to have a home, a constitution, and public law. We wish to be a national community in front of ourselves and in front of others. [. . .]

As the Holy Qur'an [13:12, Surat Al-Ra'ad] decreed, "Verily God altereth not that which is within a people until they alter that which is within themselves." That is highly cherished, wisdom. Motivation to work is derived from self-will alone. If a person lacks will, he shall not function or shall work in vain. If we wish to have our own home, it can be ours only if we change ourselves to live for the nation. To become a unified, collective soul—we all must be sincere toward one another. This sincerity is seen in the expulsion from the community of anything that stands in its way in the religious realm. I cite a tangible example in the Ottoman state and its actions in every land it governs. This example is the one step taken by all Muslims, showing their progress together hand in hand with their Ottoman brothers in the same direction and declaring the following in one voice:

"Our condition will only be put right to the credit of the national general union and nondiscrimination between one religion and another or one doctrine and another in dealings, codes of ethics, and good treatment. From now on it is improper to call someone khawaja[2] or effendi.[3] Muslim or non-Muslim, each shall be called effendi to help unify sons of the one nation, to band collectively in the love of their hearts, and prevent the natural repulsion caused when someone calls another khawaja—which means either Christian or Jew."

On a special note regarding the status of the sublime Ottoman state's and Egypt's respective codes of public morals: is it the Ottoman state or Egypt that better promotes these? [. . .] The sublime Islamic State of the Prophetic Caliphate [the Ottoman state] works for public morals while we do not. We stand behind this state, which respects our religion, yet do not do so in terms of its morals. It is neither ignorant nor inferior in religious science to neglect religion by demonstrating that its codes of social ethics do not involve intellectual or scientific resistance to religion. Rather, religion preserves its integrity precisely

2. [An appellation literally meaning foreigner, in the author's era, the word was used to denote members of religious or national minority groups in Egyptian cities.]

3. [An Ottoman term denoting nobility, used in Egypt as a term of respect.]

by preventing its injury to others, exemplified in God the Almighty saying that there is "no compulsion in religion" [Qur'an, 2:256, Surat al-Baqarah].

However, the sublime Ottoman state has found itself a reference point, aware of the medication by which it was treated and cured. As for us, we are still muddling our way along and are still unable to make a breakthrough. Perhaps this is due to our lack of knowledge of how to proceed. Perhaps our ignorance results from our disregard of a fundamental holistic issue without which we have gone astray—that is, that we are like warriors for the nation. Yet this war is neither systematic nor based on a solid foundation. The worst thing about this war is the lack of confluence, meaning that we are not united in rallying around the same purpose. In so doing, we are very much like the army—convergent in body but divergent in heart. It is hearts, rather than bodies, that should first be brought together. That non-Muslim Egyptians are among, or should be, army warriors—or that they are indispensable in warfare—is an undeniable fact. Besides, being part of the national force, non-Muslim Egyptians—if ignored at home—may turn out to be more harmful than useful to this national home. [...] If we cannot draw immediate benefit from the nation by dispelling from our souls whatever is detestable about religious relations—it is beyond doubt that social benefit will be unattainable.

Nothing is greater than people from all religions and doctrines coming together in friendship to become Egyptians in the true national sense of the word. One nationality that knows for itself only one homeland shall work together to identify a nationality overruling any other national allegiance, so that we are all called Egyptians—a word of the heart that is not different from that of the tongue. It remains to be seen how damaged national and social relationships can be addressed with a view to preventing their reoccurrence as much as possible. In doing so, we appear to be forging a way forward for nationalism and public social relief. It is for our own good that we keep ourselves from doing harmful things impulsively: nothing hurts more than moral injury.

2.

My distinguished colleague, the advocate Ismail Effendi Zohdi, told me that by talking about religious relations, I am masking my real intention to exclude its impact on dealings, codes of ethics, and good treatment, or—as the French put it—"one means to forget something by remembering it." I replied: "If to forget something I must recall it, then this is a recommended remembrance."

This is analogous to prescribing therapy that is not intended to cause pain but to cure; real pain and suffering put an end to all pains. My discussion of religious relations is one of cordiality and love whereby I aim to empower cordiality and love to loom large among all Egyptians regardless of religious or doctrinal differences. When friends and family are made to experience insincerity, it disturbs serenity and all are prone to loss. Furthermore, if benefits are missed and discord and dispute are consequently triggered, it becomes imperative to have this sincerity in place, or prevent disruptive events from happening. Therefore, if a company or family member works for this sincerity—or works to purge whatever is harmful by mentioning instances of verbal harassment—this should not be taken as an attempt to draw attention to such matters. This is not intentional: the aim is to categorically put an end to these matters once and for all. If a person whose concern is safeguarding public interests lives in fear of being called a whistle-blower, he will be dysfunctional since this fear will prevent him from performing his duty. This will deprive us collectively of a genuine benefit for a temporary advantage. All public harms resulting from such caution are like the actions of an ignorant mother who hates seeing her baby crying and thus stops washing his eyes or giving him medication. This kind of actions may amount to peaceful interim caution yet one that ultimately is null. If the people of Egypt want to be at peace, they should be like one family whose members cannot be separated from each other, or like partners in an indivisible property. [. . .] It is therefore in the best interest of the homeland that its people do not harbor malice toward each other.

If Muslim and non-Muslim judges huddling in one ruling council are not clear-hearted toward each other, they will find it difficult to see clearly where their interest lies. This is applicable to the entire nation that—unless passionately united internally and externally—will not see its affairs properly run. The most important issue Egypt is working on at the present time relates to nationalism: how to make Egypt free for the sake of the people and how to liberate it from colonialism. If we wish to arrive at this end—and we have to—then we are bound to face the task of clearing the road for ourselves to walk together without obstacles or pitfalls.

3.

[. . .] The reason I write this chapter is that a man once stepped into the room where I sat. He greeted me by saying peace be with you [*alsalam aleikum*] but then stopped his salutation halfway through, changing it to "good afternoon." He meanwhile greeted others with peace be with you in full. [. . .] Similar incidents occurred several times, and I always kept quiet. This time, however, I could not take it and found it necessary to speak out. I was serving a twofold purpose: self-relief and service to the National Assembly—ultimately attempting to mitigate the harm done to the feeling of human and national fraternity.

The exclusive use of a particular greeting means being conscious of who is Muslim and who is not. This consciousness grows out of the fact that Muslims are ordinarily found grouped together in one place, while non-Muslims—who are people of the same nation—sit together elsewhere. It has rarely happened that a council does not group together the Muslim, the Christian, and the Jew. Harm is not implied in the mere consciousness of someone's religion but instead points deep down to some kind of estrangement or antipathy or at least inequality in terms of public morality. Any morality—common greetings included—should be applied equally to all citizens: just as you say *alsalam aleikum* a thousand times, you should do it also in the presence of a Jew or a Christian: there is no need for differentiation.

If the sublime Islamic State of the Prophetic Caliphate, in the course of its social policy, regarded Muslims and non-Muslims as equal by authoritatively prohibiting the use of the term *khawaja* and generalizing the term *effendi* to apply to all, then we should take this as an example to be emulated concerning equality of titles.[4] Isn't this salutation a synonym for security? Could it be to the satisfaction of Islam that non-Muslims are denied security by its people? Aren't we all placed together under the protection of the sentry of one God? Can't we consider "good morning" or "good night" or "happy day" as involving a request for happiness by the person who greets us? Is there anything better than happiness during this lifetime? If "peace be with you" as a greeting is not applicable to non-Muslims, then they are not worthy of being greeted. [. . .] If those who greet with "peace be with you" want to prove their contribution to the service of the National Assembly, they will have to greet all equally. If all or some of them find this obligation too difficult to discharge, this greeting must be mandated by law in order to uphold public morality. Greetings should neither be linked to the presence/absence of a non-Muslim, nor be changed halfway through their utterance.

---

4. [Farag himself held the honorary Ottoman title of bey.]

4.

Many equate the "peace" in the phrase "peace be with those who follow true guidance" with the peace of greeting and thus do not consider the Christian or the Jew an adherent of true guidance. To them, neither the Christian nor the Jew qualifies to have peace bestowed on them. They are disqualified from being told *alsalam aleikum*, and whoever utters the greeting in their presence will be viewed as a wrongdoer who will have to ask for forgiveness. Furthermore, the term "peace" in the phrase means safety or salvage; rescue for the followers of true guidance.

[. . .] Consult, for example, the interpretation of Imam Mohammad al Razi Fakhr al-Din on page 46, Part 6, of his 1306 book.[5] According to Islamic law [*sharia*], the phrase does not mean that the greeting of "peace" should be bestowed or not on different groups of people. In his interpretation, following true guidance represents a metaphor for the Christians' and Jews' recognition of God, and also in pursuance of the Holy Qur'an—as he cites "When you are greeted with a greeting, greet in return with that which is better than it or (at least) return it equally." Imam Fakhr al-Din's interpretation of the phrase reads "when believers were commanded to embark on the jihad, they were also advised that if enemies were inclined toward peace, they would have to react with contentment." Likewise, the phrase "When you are greeted with a greeting, greet in return with that which is better than it, or (at least) return it equally" is similar to "But if they are inclined toward peace, you too should incline toward it."

In the jihad, man faces his enemy in war and greets him; the latter may not pay attention to the greeting and thus kill the former. Perhaps he is a Muslim whose blood is ordained by God not to be shed by his fellow Muslim. [Muslim] believers are also told that they will not be discredited by reciprocating the generosity of whoever greets them and is generous to them, even if he is a nonbeliever. Part 3, page 287, of Imam Fakhr al-Din's book cites: "if we tell them 'peace be with you,' is it permissible to mention mercy? El Shoaby was quoted as telling a Christian 'peace and mercy of God be with you.' When asked why, he replied: 'Isn't he living in God's Mercy?'" Even if Egyptian Christians and Jews were described

5. [Farag refers here to the great medieval scientist and Qur'anic exegete Fakhr al Din Razi (or Abu Abdullah Muhammad ibn Umar ibn al-Husayn al-Taymi al-Bakri al-Tabaristani Fakhr al-Din al-Razi, 1149–1209). The book Farag mentions here is Razi's multivolume *Tafsir al-Kabir* (The great commentary), which was written before 1209. The year 1306 in the text is therefore a mistake.]

as enemies [. . .] and the Christian or the Jew judged as infidels—non-Muslims were still qualified to be greeted in return with a greeting better than theirs, including a mention of mercy. [. . .]

5.

If there is, among Egyptian constituents, estrangement, antipathy, or inequality with regard to codes of social ethics, it may be explained by the fact that we lack a constitution of our own. A constitution would be a contract sealing a healthy partnership between all of us in Egypt. It would be representative of our shouldering of responsibility on the basis of serving the public interest and preventing any injury to which it might be exposed. We would consider ourselves members of the same house working together, running our affairs, and giving due consideration to our social relief. The only hierarchy would consist of delegates to be directly in charge of the nation and its population with a bond joining them together to progress toward one destination—that is, public service for the ultimate benefit of all, irrespective of religious affiliation. We are currently wanting in this regard and have no assembly. If one group of us wants something from another, the former is in a state of confusion about where to go, or with whom to lodge its request. As we know, the government has no time to be engaged in the interests of the people in general and is in fact removed from their concerns in such domains as literary and social affairs.

[. . .] Egypt—supported by a constitution—would be far better off than it would be without it. If, notwithstanding different religious affiliations, this constitution could impartially secure the benefit of bringing people together in terms of nationalism and association, this would be fairly successful. The constitution would also envision development in the scientific realm, in all its manifestations, in order to shine light all over the country and assist people in finding their way through the darkness in which they now find themselves. [. . .] If we continue to bury our heads in the sand, then when will we have our constitution and when will our state of fatigue be terminated? Are we not truly drained? Are we not continuously struggling in an unabated jihad? Do we not need a truce to have mercy on ourselves in this unnecessary internal war that casts a pall on many of our interests? We would do better to address these interests directly by engaging in the formation of a constitution.

My discussion of a constitution is justifiable since it both serves, and has a bearing on, every theme I have thus far discussed. I have talked, among other things, about social morality and how we all should be regarded equally in this respect; a case in point is the peace greeting. Is there a possibility that this aim will attract more public interest? The answer could have been affirmative if we had managed to have a constitution of our own. Granted, I sometimes meet cherished friends and colleagues who smile at me, laughingly saluting me with *alsalam aleikum wa rahmat allah wa barakatu*—peace be with you, and God's mercy and blessings. How much I wish that this love had instead been geared toward public service to help persuade individuals such as myself about the host of themes raised in sections 4 and 5 above. If a constitution is the key for remedying this grievance, I hope God will accelerate its arrival.

6.

I now wish to ponder whether there could be in Egypt any opponents to a constitution and what their position in the argument might be. I am not referring here to the British but, rather, to the Egyptians. I am not oblivious to the fact that what the British say on the issue is influential. What concerns me most is that nearly all Egyptians be satisfied with a constitution, accept and demand it rather than view it as subject of contestation. [...] While it is true that everyone is free in thought and opinion, it would be surprising to have Egyptian opposition to a constitution. As is well known, a constitution is a public law regulating the affairs of the country—internally, scientifically, literarily, and socially. Its benefit is for the country itself, for its people in general—whether Muslims, Christians, or Jews without discrimination. Why would Muslims harbor fears when it comes to the constitution? And, if they did, why wouldn't they speak up? If one was a civil servant and considerate of his beliefs, then let him first and foremost be cognizant of the fact that he is free, that human freedom is above natural rights, and that without such freedom, one is bound to miss the gist of the argument from the humanist point of view.

Whereas freedom is a property that can never be taken away, its owner is the party responsible for its loss. I am not recommending revolt or action in conflict with discretion, sobriety, and deliberation. All I am advocating is that one shall not imprison his natural freedom in his chest. If someone disapproves of a constitution or opposes its very formulation, he must be reminded, as mentioned before, that a constitution is intended for public interest. It is therefore inappropriate for any citizen to be opposed to a constitution. We are left with the Christian and the Jew who—as civil servants—may temporarily feel uncomfortable about the security of their posts. This theme again brings us to the issue of the rule of their Muslim brothers. If opposition by a Christian or a Jew arises from fear of injustice on the part of their Muslim brothers, they are then misled and mistaken: the Islamic nation in Egypt, armed with a constitution that provides for nondiscrimination between Muslims and non-Muslims against the backdrop of its civilization, would not accept the idea of religion governing its dealings.

This is particularly important since independence is a public consultative process bringing in, together with Muslims, those in charge, whether Christians or Jews. All work hand in hand with one intention: fidelity to the same country and its people, without regard for religious differences. Otherwise, no project will ever be functional in any country comprised of citizens of diverse backgrounds. It is perhaps different elements that prompt the call for independence and advise all people of the same nation to gather under the justice of one brigade—namely, fraternity, freedom, and equality as is the case in France, for example. So do not be appalled by a constitution, you people, and do not fear freedom or its claims. You should, rather, be united into one whole and see to it that your vote is counted toward your country's commitments to science, literature, association, love, fraternity, freedom, equality, and peace.

7.

[. . .] I still recall that Egyptian newspapers do not mention the term "mercy" in connection with the passing away of a Christian or a Jew. They instead deplore his demise by calling him "the regrettable" [al-mu'sif] rather than "the late" [al-marhum]. I also remember that Coptic newspapers—in their bid to retaliate—have stopped short of referring to mercy for the Muslim dead, repeating again the appellation of "regrettable" rather than "late." Newspapers strip the dead of mercy: Muslim publications take it away from non-Muslim deceased, while non-Muslim publications retaliate in kind. In my view, the latter party did wrong in their retaliation. Withholding mercy is not within their realm of competence. Other papers are not in a position to withhold mercy by not mentioning it, nor to validate it by making reference to it. It is merely an obligation of a literary and social nature. It would have been much more consistent and appealing if non-Muslim papers had maintained a mention of mercy and meanwhile blamed their sisterly Muslim papers with a tone of propriety. If they reverse their position that would be well and good, but if not, it is not a problem to keep mentioning mercy because it is improper to do that which you deny others the right to do.

The *Gazette* has a reconciliatory role to perform in this regard by failing to differentiate between Muslims and non-Muslims when affixing the term "late." According to Fakhr al-Din's interpretation, the Christian and the Jew are not denied mercy when they are alive; why then should they be denied this more urgently needed mercy when they are dead? If they are, then the label "regrettable" as used in these papers will be synonymous with the term "doomed" that some employ when accompanying for burial a deceased Christian or Jew. This evokes unfavorable feelings among decent Muslims as well.

Furthermore, if agitation is aroused on hearing the word "regrettable" on the road, then there is a parallel resentment generated on its writing in newspapers. This is because it is a deliberately uttered omission with reference to mercy—and thus necessarily involves harm. As stated above, we are living in an age where social welfare should not be confused for religious sectarianism. Social welfare is not purely materialistic in form but also involves—and even more importantly—literature. Humans are prone to change and dissonance. We are working on loving each other as much as possible. What I request is to end blasphemy. Otherwise, we will never have a National Assembly. If there is infidelity involved—which I think there was, and which I would not tolerate—Islamic newspapers are not speaking on behalf of religion, believers or Muslims in general; they are instead speaking on behalf of themselves, being papers circulated to Muslims and non-Muslims alike, markedly national, literary, social, and ethical in their public interest. It is my point of view and belief that codes of social ethics constitute the public interest's most important dimension.

8.

Some have told me that what I write in my articles and essays alerts Europeans to the intolerance, as they call it, that we are experiencing. We need to obliterate this impression from their minds. I replied that if it was possible for me to whisper what I write to all my Egyptian brothers for this effort to materialize, I would have done that and would not have to publish it in the *Gazette*. Yet newspapers still serve as our only possible and useful forum. We did not have much choice and we had to have recourse to publishing. What else could we have done? Publishing should not be our intention; the hoped-for benefit from the act of publishing is what really matters. If publishing is to be forbidden, its benefit will be barred accordingly. Yet publishing is essential and what is essential is indispensable. It is likewise far better to tell me directly what I hate to hear than to feel rancorous and remain dissatisfied with me. We have to be sincere toward each other: why can't we listen to what each other has to say?

If we are unhappy about the foreigner's knowledge of our deficiencies—and this was unavoidable—do we need to miss the opportunity of reforming our conditions merely for the sake of this foreigner? Can't we find in this reform a way of silencing and keeping the foreigner at a distance? If he is of any significance to us, then let's ensure that he will cease having a reason for arguing with us. Again, if we were to reverse our status, this should not be done exclusively out of concern for the foreigner but for our own sake. This, in turn, will help us win the respect of foreigners. Is it shameful to talk about our drawbacks and flaws in order to set them right? If we were to keep silent about them, when would they be addressed? Do we have any remedy other than to converse? Doesn't talk serve to exercise due diligence as far as duties and obligations are concerned, as well as to indicate what is essential and what is not?

Had we succeeded in establishing an indigenous public—or rather national communities—that would have replaced the *Gazette*, what would we be writing about ourselves today? We would have arranged get-togethers with lecturers to address us, yet we have none. It is even harder to put such communities in place in the absence of a constitution. That is the reason why whenever I seek any kind of reform, I realize that it is within reach only by virtue of a constitution. How many times have I stumbled across the need for a constitution in the course of my writing? I am wondering how we can have access to this cherished constitution for the fulfilment of our aspirations.

Openness and sincerity are better than reluctant concealment. I suggest that we are all nationalist Egyptians. We have to act truly as such by calling each other to account and by pledging what should be and what should not be. Each one of us will have to examine himself against the current interest to reconcile ourselves with each other in all domains. This kind of interest is not in contrast with religions or religious doctrines. I am not asking anyone to give up his religion for another. My request is that we take one another to task to clear our souls of unfavorable mutual feelings. We should discard words and deeds that inspire hatred in order to live in permanent peace. By peace, I mean peace of consciousness. If neighbors do not get along peacefully, they will be in trouble. We are members of the same home and nation. We deserve, and are entitled to, love and serenity. I do not claim the existence of hostility among us but do want to make the point that it is in our interest to express grievances with one another so that hearts can relax and serenity can reign. God knows that had it not been for my determination that we should all come to terms and learn to love each other, I would not have written these words. I am guilty only of sincerity and love, and I ask God to forgive me but not to expunge these qualities from me. [...]

10.

[...] Public interest is certainly not considered to be so unless its exterior reflects its interior, meaning that it should be holistic and not piecemeal in approach. It should deal with a larger whole and not only a part, even though this part may seem to its people like a whole. If Muslims in Egypt, for example, have a relevant public interest—it shall not be deemed public by all Egyptians and non-Muslims in the event of Muslims giving consideration to their private interest at the expense of public interest. This is because, in doing so, Muslims will be working for the private rather than the public good. In a country with a disparate population, private and public interests may run parallel; a case in point is the care people give to raising and educating their children. But private and public interests are surely in sharp contrast when, for example, some want a constitution while others are skeptical about it on the ground that it will be viewed by the latter as serving a private interest. Those skeptical of a constitution maintain that the other group, who will be in control of the constitution, is larger in number and more powerful and "we can get lost because we are weaker and form a minority."

This, in my mind, is Egypt's condition. I believe that Muslims generally favor a constitution and this is their right. A constitution is not a priority for some non-Muslims as many among them have concerns about it and tend to resist it, even if only subconsciously. They believe that their private interests are not commensurate with the public interest. Therefore, the two interests should be reconciled to balance each other in the public interest. How to ensure this coalescence? By preventing it from harm. [...] The nation should not hear with its ears or see with its eyes anything that is injurious to it in connection with religion. A nation or home is for all its people and its people are all for it. My words are not addressed to one category of Egyptian in particular but to all Egyptians generally—myself being one of them. While newspapers still talk about Christianity and Islam, let us Egyptians dismiss this kind of talk and keep it away from nationalism. This will help to free the nation to be shared by all and will also facilitate the making of a constitution.

Further Readings

Al-Gamil, Yosef. *A History of Karaite Jewry: The Karaite Community's Life in the Diaspora and in Israel* [Hebrew]. 2 vols. Ramla, Israel: National Council of Israel's Karaite Jews, 1979.

El-Kodsi, Mourad, *The Karaite Jews of Egypt, 1882–1986*. Lyons, NY: Wilprint, 1987.

Gamill, Albert. "The Commemoration of Mourad Farag." June 2007. http://www.hsje.org/pdf/mfarag.pdf, accessed May 31, 2012.

Cohen, Hayyim, "Faraj, Murad." In *Encyclopaedia Judaica*, edited by Fred Skolnik and Michael Berenbaum, 6:711. 2nd ed. Detroit: Macmillan Reference, 2007.

Levy, Lital. "Edification between Sect and Nation: Murad Farag and al-Tahdhib, 1901–1903," in *Intellectuals and Civil Society in the Middle East*, edited by Mohammed Bamyeh, 57–78. London: I. B. Tauris, 2012.

———. "Jewish Writers in the Arab East: Literature, History, and the Politics of Enlightenment, 1863–1914." PhD diss., University of California, Berkeley, 2007.

Nemoy, Leon. "A Modern Karaite-Arabic Poet: Mourad Farag." *Jewish Quarterly Review* 70, no. 4 (1980): 195–209.

Snir, Reuven. "Faraj, Murād (Morad Farag)." In *Encyclopedia of Modern Jewish Culture*, edited by Glenda Abramson, 252–53. London: Routledge, 2004.

Somekh, Sasson. "Lost Voices: Jewish Authors in Modern Arabic Literature." In *Jews Among Arabs: Contacts and Boundaries*, edited by Mark R. Cohen and Abraham L. Udovitch, 9–20. Princeton, NJ: Darwin, 1989.

———. "Participation of Egyptian Jews in Modern Arabic Culture, and the Case of Murad Faraj." In *The Jews of Egypt, A Mediterranean Society in Modern Times*, edited by Shimon Shamir, 130–40. Boulder, CO: Westview, 1987.

Nissim Ya'acov Malul

Dr. Nissim Ya'acov Malul (1892–1959) was born in Safed to a family that had emigrated from Tunisia to Ottoman Palestine 200 years earlier. Shortly after Nissim's birth, his father, Moshe Hayyim Malul, was appointed rabbi of the Jewish communities of Tanta and Cairo, and the family moved to Egypt. Nissim Malul was educated in Jewish schools in Cairo and Tanta and later attended the American College of Tanta, studying Arabic literature, journalism, and philosophy. Malul began writing for the Egyptian newspaper *al-Muqattam*.

In 1911 he returned to Palestine and began to write regularly in Hebrew and Arabic for journals in Palestine, Egypt, and Lebanon. He was part of the public discussion about the nature of Zionism and also responded to articles published in the Arab-Christian newspapers *Filastin* and *al-Karmil* that he deemed extremist in their opposition to Zionism. Malul simultaneously tried to establish a Jewish newspaper in Arabic, *Sawt al-'Uthmaniyya* (The voice of the Ottomans). His partner in establishing this newspaper was Dr. Shim'on Moyal; the work of his wife, Esther, is also featured in this volume. *Sawt al 'Uthmaniyah*'s main goal was to elaborate on Zionism to Palestine's Arab readers. In Jerusalem in 1913, Malul, Shim'on Moyal, and other Arabic-speaking Sephardim founded Ha-Magen (The shield), an organization that aimed to respond to writings in the Arabic press that were hostile to Zionism.

During World War I, Malul was expelled by the Turkish authorities to Damascus, and from there he escaped to Cairo. He renewed his journalistic career in Palestine after the war. A believer in, and advocate of, Arab-Jewish understanding and cooperation, Malul wrote essays for both Arabic and Hebrew publications. With financial assistance from the Zionist movement, Malul established two newspapers in Arabic—*al-Akhbar* and *al-Salam*—and wrote in Arabic for another Zionist-supported workers' newspaper, *Ittihad al-'Umal*, attempting to raise class consciousness among Arab workers. In Hebrew, Malul published articles in the newspaper *He-Herut* (Freedom), where he debated the place of the Arabic language and culture within Zionism. He was adamant that knowledge of Arabic is a necessity for all those who honestly aim to foster understanding with Arabs. An advocate of semitic Jewish nationalism, Malul viewed Arabic as inseparable from Jewish culture, which in his view was Oriental. Odd as it may seem to contemporary observers, Malul's conviction was that Arabic is vital for the building of Hebrew culture and that European culture—in contrast—leads to the death of Hebrew culture. In 1927, Malul left Palestine with his wife, Aliza (b. 1895, of Tunisian descent), and spent two years in Iraq teaching Arabic and Hebrew in the Jewish elementary school in Hila named after Menahem Salih Daniel (whose work is also featured in this volume). Aliza Malul published essays on Jewish life in Iraq in the *Do'ar Hayom* after the couple returned to Palestine in 1929. Less publicly active after his return, Malul dedicated the remaining thirty years of his life to the study of the Arabic lanaguge and the history of Iraqi Jewry.

Our Status in the Country, or the Question of Learning Arabic

A. Nissim Ya'acov Malul, "Ma'amadenu ba-Aretz: She'elat Limud 'Ivrit-'Aravit" (The question of Hebrew teaching of Arabic), *Ha-Herut*, June 17, 1913.
B. Nissim Ya'acov Malul, "Ma'amadenu ba-Aretz: Hishtatfut ba-Ta'amula li-Drishat Zekhuyot ha-'Arviyyim ve-Yisud 'Iton 'Aravi-Yehudi" (Participating in the struggle for Arab rights and establishing a Jewish-Arab newspaper), *Ha-Herut*, June 18, 1913.
C. Nissim Ya'acov Malul, "Ma'amadenu ba-Aretz: Sof" (Our status in the country: end), *Ha-Herut*, June 19, 1913.

This essay was published in three consecutive issues of *Ha-Herut* in 1913. Malul was then involved in a heated debate about Jewish and Hebrew culture, Arabic, and the (Jewish) question of assimilation. The debate began with an attack on Malul's activities to promote the study of Arabic among Jews. On May 16, 1913, Ya'acov Rabinovitch (1875–1948) — a prominent playwright, poet, and essayist — published a lengthy article in *Ha-Po'el Ha-Tsa'ir* (the labor movement's newspaper), in which he addressed several cultural threats such as Christian missionary activities. Defining missionary work as an "external threat" (*sakana hitsonit*), Rabinovitch went on to deal with the "internal threat" (*hashash penimi*) — Malul's activities. Rabinovitch chastised Malul for fighting for Arab rights and for teaching Arabic in Jewish schools. He was particularly angry because Malul was trying to form a special union of Jewish Arabic teachers — people whom he defined as "pushers of foreign culture into our midst" (*makhnise kultura zara le-tokh mahanenu*). Rabinovitch specifically pointed out that the Arabic teachers were "mostly Mizrahi Jews" (*yehudim mizrahiyyim*) who did not know Hebrew well enough, and who did "not learn anything from Hebrew culture." "For them and for their leaders, a modern Hebrew book is like a book sealed with seven seals," he declared. "These people" — the Mizrahi Jews — "live among us," he said, "but they are to us like strangers." Turning back to the question of the teachers, Rabinovitch intensified his tone: "These are the people that we let into our schools — and we do not know how dangerous they are, particularly if the natives ['*am ha-Aratz*, the Palestinians] will be given any national rights." Instead of their teaching us Arabic, he concluded, these teachers need to learn Hebrew and perhaps other European langagues. This way, he concluded, we will all become one national division (*hativa le'umit ahat*). Rabinovitch also paid specific attention to the activities of Ya'qub Sannu' and Rahamin Bivas (an Egyptian Jewish actor and singer who sang in Arabic), calling them "Jews who left their people and submitted themselves to the service of that people [the Arabs] and now urge us to follow their lead and all of this in the name of [the values of] nationalism, racial assimilation, patriotism, etc." Malul's response to these accusations was published soon thereafter in *Ha-Herut*. The debate was apparently so intense that *Ha-Herut*'s editors intervened in Malul's essays several times, inserting notes such as the first one below and other comments.

A. THE QUESTION OF HEBREW TEACHING OF ARABIC[1]

Mr. Ya'acov Rabinovitch expressed bitterness about my work in *Ha-Poel Ha-Tsa'ir*. I proposed: (1) the formation of one union for all Jewish Arabic[2] teachers; (2) to help those who advocate for Arab rights; and (3) to establish a Jewish journal in Arabic.[3] Rabinovitch objected to all the items in my proposal and considered them inappropriate.

Here is my response:

With regard to the issue of a union for Jewish Arabic teachers, an article also appeared in *Ha-Or* rejecting this idea and utilizing the same arguments as Rabinovitch. At the time I sent a response to *Ha-Or*, but apparently they already had too much material to publish so my article was condemned to concealment.[4]

Concerning the first question, then: this union, what is it for? Indeed there are many foreign-language teachers among us—French, English, German, Turkish—so what is so special about the Arabic language that we should form a special union for its teachers?

To this question my answer is: Arabic is not like other languages. There is a big

1. (Note by *Ha-Herut*'s Editors: We have made room to publish the words of this author although we clearly do not agree with them and we will respond to them in a later issue.)

2. [In the original, Malul says "Hebrew-Arabic teachers," by which he means Jewish teachers of Arabic.]

3. [In the original, Malul says "Arab-Jewish journal," by which he means a Jewish journal in Arabic.]

4. [*Ha-Or* was another Jerusalem-based newspaper. Malul uses the term "*le-Geniza*," which in modern Hebrew would mean "to be archived." But his clear sarcasm and the fact that he mentions this incident suggest that "concealment" is a better term.]

difference since Arabic has two branches: the literary language and the vernacular. It is hard for our children to learn Arabic because they are considered foreigners, and thus the accent and pronunciation are difficult for them. Until this day—despite trying to teach Arabic in our schools for some time now—we have been unable to attain the desired result despite all our efforts and investments.

Therefore, we are left with two options. The first option is to cease teaching Arabic, since we have failed to attain any benefit from learning it, and rather to become a Jewish nation in our own right with our own unique language [Hebrew], customs, and public and private affairs. In this way we will become an isolated nation, separated from all other peoples living under Ottoman rule.[5] We will not engage with the existing nation [of Palestinians] in any way, thereby destroying this [linguistic] connection with the outside world, and our situation will become similar to that faced in the past by Spain, Portugal, and now in Russia (? The Editors).[6]

The other option is to fortify ourselves through the Arabic language and redouble our efforts in teaching it to our children, the younger generation, through both private lessons and in our schools. In this way we can avoid the strong current [of ignorance and isolation] that is threatening to drown current and future generations. For this purpose we must unionize the Jewish Arabic teachers so that we can create a new method of instruction that will make it easier for the students to learn. We should also create and compose Arabic textbooks that will strengthen our cause and that do not harm our sense of nationality.

The need for this is especially felt now that there is a new Ottoman law decreeing Arabic as the dominant language rather than Turkish in all government institutions. We have already witnessed the government removing all officials who do not have a good command of Arabic. Thus if we want to settle in this land, the land of our past and our future, we must learn its language.

5. [Ironically, when writing in Hebrew, Malul uses the grammatical formation "Ottomania," which linguistically equates the Ottoman Empire with other states, such as Hungary, Germany, Italy, Lusitania, and Iberia.]

6. [The editors placed a question mark after this sentence since it is difficult to understand precisely what Malul intended to say with regard to the Iberian and Russian precedents. However, it is clear that he was concerned about the isolation that would inevitably result from stopping instruction in Arabic. He is probably also highlighting the fact that ignorance of the Arabic language of the region on the part of Palestine's emerging Jewish community was likely to result in some new ghettoization of the community, repeating the pattern of some locations in Europe before the twentieth century.]

It is clear that it is criminal to teach our children all those European languages that *push them to leave the country* and live in the Diaspora [in Europe] and build their future there, as many of us do these days. If this is what we want, we should return to the practice of our ancestors—they only made *aliya* when it was time to be buried here . . . As for the fears about learning Arabic and assimilating with the other people of this land, and losing our sense of nationality, they are all nonsense. Those who make this claim forget the purpose for which we came here; forget why each one of us left his country and his ancestral home to invest our strength here in this country to raise it from its ruins. They forget that we came here to build a new nation (? The Editors), remove the cold stone heart and replace it with a beating, flesh-and-blood heart. We came to repair and not to break, so how could the Arabic language penetrate our hearts and make us lose our own precious literature? It is unimaginable and impossible that such a toddler ["undeveloped"] culture could push us back.

Thus all those complaints about the teaching of Arabic, and a union of the Jewish Arabic language teachers, are just nonsense that influence only the naive, or those who understand the significance of being a nation in name only . . .

There is no requirement for a nationalist person to know his language (! Sic, The Editors). The nationalist is one who experiences feelings of nationalism (!). He is a nationalist through his nationalist deeds. And if we agree that there is no nationalism without a national language then we should—according to Mr. Rabinovitch—tell our brothers in Europe who invest their power and fortunes in our nation, first among them Dr. Max Nordau, that they are not nationalists since they do not know the Hebrew language.

It is not true—as Mr. Rabinovitch says—that I call for merging [with the Arabs] and assimilation with them. Those who read my articles in the Arab press know that this is not the case. My purpose is pure and simple: to strengthen the internal foundations of the Yishuv by bolstering it from the outside.

B. PARTICIPATING IN THE STRUGGLE FOR ARAB RIGHTS AND ESTABLISHING A JEWISH-ARAB NEWSPAPER

Anybody who is more or less familiar with this assembly, particularly those who read the Arab press, won't deride me for joining the Assembly of Advocates for Arab Rights. It is clear that this is not the right time or place to explain the reason why I joined this movement and the benefits that my connection with this assembly could potentially bring to the Yishuv.

I revealed a bit of my thinking in my article in *Ha-Herut* entitled "The Arab Movement and the Jews" and in other similar articles. But I am constantly ridiculed for stating that the Jews demand from the Turks rights for Nassar and Shukri Al-'Assali . . .[7]

With regard to the third question, concerning the establishment of a Jewish newspaper in Arabic, I must confess that during the famous debate between Mr. Ludivpol and Dr. Moyal, I did not chime in, and I have no intention of doing so in the future since everyone is entrenched in their position and insists that only they are right and refuses to listen to other opinions.[8] The majority of our Ashkenazi brothers are opposed to this initiative, and the Sephardim are in favor. Therefore I have decided that even if a discussion on this issue is a good thing, it is preferable for me to remain removed from the debate. I shall express only my opinion concerning the narrower issues relating to the press in general and not about the newspaper in particular.

Who does not know that our brothers in Syria, Egypt, Tunisia, Algeria, Morocco, and the rest of the countries of the Orient do not really care about the movement to settle Eretz Yisrael, and in general are very removed from all this business of our national movement?

These brothers of ours do not know any language except Arabic. So how, I ask, can one approach these masses of tens of thousands of our brothers without being able to speak in their language, Arabic?

In my opinion, the best means to draw their hearts toward us is by creating a journal—perhaps a monthly at first—in Arabic. In this journal we can speak to our brothers about the benefits of the national movement and present them with episodes from the history of the Jews, biographies of our sages in the past and the present, and news from the Jewish world and particularly from Eretz Yisrael. The literary style should pull at their heartstrings. In this way we can enfold our Oriental brothers within the wings of nationalism.

I do not present these thoughts as mere suggestions, but as a decision that I am prepared to undertake in the immediate future; that is, when the new laws of publishing are finalized and the old laws have been nullified—particularly

---

7. [Najeeb Nassar (1865–1947) was a Palestinian journalist and founder of *al-Karmil*, the first anti-Zionist Palestinian newspaper. Shukri Al-'Assali (1868–1916) was a Syrian nationalist executed by the Ottoman Governor Jamal Pasha on May 6, 1916. He was an outspoken critic of the Ottomans and Zionism.]

8. [Avraham Ludivpol (1886–1921) was a Russian-born journalist who had been active in Palestine since 1897. Dr. Moyal was an associate of Malul's, as mentioned above.]

the law that demands that the publisher and the editor pay a large sum of money as a guarantee. If this project of creating a Jewish journal in Arabic is achieved, I believe that it will be the best way to attract our brothers who do not know Hebrew and are thus alienated from our great national movement.

C. OUR STATUS IN THE COUNTRY: END

Mr. Rabinovitch suggests that Abou Naddara destroyed Hebrew nationalism. Nobody except the Egyptians, and the Orientals in general, appears to understand the great merits of this man. Abou Naddara raised the banner of Judaism in Egypt during the time of the Khedives Sa'id Pasha and Ismail Pasha.[9] He supported and helped every Jew in Paris while he resided there. He never worried about his own health or old age and traveled wherever he was needed in order to help a Jewish youngster enter one of the Haute Ecoles. He relentlessly labored for the Jews until his last day, even during the last twenty years of his life when he was nearly blind.

It is true that his nationalism was based on foreign cultures and foreign languages, but his major project was carried out when Hebrew was considered a dead language in Egypt. The same was [true] when he moved to Paris, the very same city where Dr. Nordau, who does not know Hebrew, resides.

Mr. Rabinovitch is wrong in his assumptions. If we, the heirs of Rabbi Ye-hudah Ha-Levi and Maimonides, wish to follow in their ways, we must know Arabic well and merge with the Arabs (?! The Editors) the way they, the great sages, did (?! The Editors).[10] As a semitic nation we must reinforce our semitic nationhood and not blur it within European culture. By utilizing Arabic we can create a real Hebrew culture, but if we blend it with European elements we will simply be committing suicide.

This is what I thought worthy of clarifying. May Mr. Rabinovitch and all those who think like him listen.

9. [Sa'id Pasha (1822–63) was the *wali* (governor) of Egypt between 1854 and 1863. His nephew Ismail "the Magnificent" Pasha (1830–95) became khedive of Egypt in 1863 and went into exile in 1879 in the wake of British interference in Egyptian politics. Ismail's reformist reign was heavily oriented toward Europe.]

10. [The signals and notations of disagreement and question in this sentence were inserted by the original editors and appeared in the printed version.]

Further Readings

Campos, Michelle U. "Between 'Beloved Ottomania' and 'The Land of Israel': The Struggle over Ottomanism and Zionism among Palestine's Sephardi Jews, 1908–13." *International Journal of Middle Eastern Studies* 37, no. 4 (2005): 461–83.

———. *Ottoman Brothers: Muslims, Christians, and Jews in Early Twentieth-Century Palestine.* Stanford: Stanford University Press, 2011.

Gorni, Yosef. *Zionism and the Arabs, 1882–1948: A Study of Ideology.* Oxford: Clarendon Press of Oxford University Press, 1987.

Jacobson, Abigail. *From Empire to Empire: Jerusalem between Ottoman and British Rule.* Syracuse, NY: Syracuse University Press, 2011.

———. "Sephardim, Ashkenazim, and the Palestine 'Arab Question' in Pre–First World War Palestine: A Reading of Three Zionist Newspapers." *Middle Eastern Studies* 39, no. 2 (2003): 105–30.

Ben-Zion Meir Hai Uziel

Ben-Zion Meir Hai Uziel (1880–1953) was the Sephardi chief rabbi of Mandatory Palestine and the first Sephardi chief rabbi of the State of Israel.

Born in Jerusalem, Uziel descended from a notable family of rabbis. His father, Yoseph Raphael Uziel (d. 1894), was the head of the Rabbinical Court (Beit Din) of the Sephardi community. Ben-Zion Uziel received his rabbinic education first from Rabbi Yihya Tsarom (b. 1842 in Sana'a, d. 1917), head of the Yemeni community's Rabbinical Court. He later studied at the Tiferet Yerushalaim Yeshiva with Rabbi Abraham Cuenca (1867–1937), one of the most prominent Sephardi rabbis in Jerusalem. Uziel was appointed as a teacher at Tiferet Yerushalaim at the age of twenty, and in 1911, when he was thirty-one, the Ottomans appointed him Sephardi rabbi (*hakham bashi*) of Jaffa.

During World War I he was exiled by the Ottomans to Damascus, but he returned to Jerusalem even before the arrival of the British in 1917. In 1921 he replaced Yaacov Meir (1856–1939) as rabbi of Salonika, and in 1923 he returned to Palestine to serve as chief Sephardi rabbi of Tel Aviv. In 1938 he became the Rishon Le-Zion (chief Sephardi rabbi of the Yishuv), and in 1948 he was appointed chief Sephardic rabbi of Israel.

Uziel held numerous positions in political organizations as well. He was one of the leaders of the Mizrahi—a Zionist party of Orthodox Jews founded in Lithuania in 1902; its name is not related to Mizrahim—and was a member of the National Executive representing the Jews of Mandatory Palestine. As an active Zionist, he represented the movement in numerous international venues. In 1927 he spent time in Iraq spreading the Zionist message among Jews there.

Unlike his more famous counterpart, the chief Ashkenazi rabbi of the Yishuv—Rabbi Avraham Yitzhak Ha-Kohen Kook (1865–1935)—Uziel did not understand Zionism and the modern Jewish state in messianic or mystical terms. Throughout his career his approach to Zionism was rationalistic, and he tended to see it only as a political movement dedicated to Jewish national revival and to the creation of an autonomous Jewish society. Uziel also disagreed with Kook over the issue of women's suffrage. Kook was strongly opposed to women's participation in elections within different organizations, including the representative body of the Yishuv. Uziel, together with most of the Sephardi rabbis and some other Mizrahi rabbis, was in favor of women's suffrage: "The mind cannot accept that women be denied this personal right [the right to vote] ... [how can one] pull the rope from both ends—see women as bound to obey those elected yet deny them the right to elect them?"[1]

Uziel was a prolific jurist as well as the author of many works, mostly unpublished, of Jewish thought and poetry. His most important work on Jewish law is *Mishpetei Uziel* (The laws of Uziel), a six-volume collection of *responsa*. Some of his other writings were collected in *Sefer Mikhmane 'Uzi'el* (Hidden treasures of Uziel).

1. [Quoted in Zohar, "Traditional Flexibility and Modern Strictness,"1120.]

14 | Angels of Peace

Ben-Zion Meir Hai Uziel, "Mal'akhe Ha-Shalom," in *Sefer Mikhmane 'Uzi'el: ma'marim kelaliyim, mikhtavim tsiburiyim u-le'umiyim, ne'umim yesodiyim li-tehiyat Yisra'el u-vinyan artso* (1939, Jerusalem: ha-Va'ad le-hotsaa't kitve Maran, 2003), 435–38.

This item is a speech that Uziel gave to members of the American King-Crane Commission to Palestine in 1918. The investigation commission visited Palestine in May and June of that year as part of the deliberations concerning the future of the country after World War I. Already known as a leader in the Yishuv, Uziel was asked to address the members of the commission.

My esteemed peers:

For many years we have awaited your arrival on our soil. We waited, as we believed that your arrival fulfills our eminent, longing of millennia. To our great pleasure, the joyous day has arrived wherein your feet walk on the holy soil. Your eyes shall see the flourishing community of the People of Israel in our Land, and your ears shall hear the soul's longing of the People of Israel dwelling in the Land, the dream of the entire People of Israel that has dwelled in the Diaspora, in all its avenues and tributaries. It is with boundless pleasure that I am so honored to present to you on behalf of the People of Israel its welcome of peace, and I say, "Welcome, thou angels of peace."

My esteemed peers, I see in you not only emissaries of the peace conference, but emissaries of all humanity. The inspiration for peace in one land and for one people is the inspiration for peace the world over. I look on you as the emissaries of the supreme stewardship that by supreme grace has bestowed absolute triumph, and [that] admonishes our benevolent and beloved government—that of Great Britain over the Holy Land—the land about which our Torah says: "It is a land the LORD your God cares for; the eyes of the LORD your God are continually on it from the beginning of the year to its end" [Deuteronomy 11:12], and which shall emerge from our lips first and foremost, and from the mouths of the covenantal kingdoms who shall come after, heralding to the People of Israel, the oppressed and tortured, exiled and wandering, dispersed and scattered over the earth for these millennia, a heralding, I say, according to which the establishment of a national home and safe haven for the People of Israel in the land of our ancestors is a necessary provision for the continued national existence of the People of Israel, as well as the Jewish soul's uplifting since we became a nation and unto this day.

Our longing—the longing of all Israel to establish for ourselves our national home in this, our ancestral Land—is not a longing that stems from love of the [British] rule and the government, but rather a longing hidden in the depths of our hearts since God took us from our Land with a strong arm until today. This necessary longing that our history of Diaspora persecution and the murders committed in our day and before our eyes in various lands, is the clearest and most reliable testimony that the People of Israel cannot continue its existence without a safe haven and national home wherein it will continue its political, civil, and spiritual life in full freedom and autonomy.

We want to return and to live our political and spiritual lives in our Land, to return and to build the Land, to return and to fulfill Torah law, which abounds with mercy and compassion for all who are created in God's image, and which treats one and all with the same law, as it is written: "The community is to have the same rules for you and for the foreigner residing among you" [Numbers 15:15]. God forbid we constrain any individual; God forbid we offend the religious and national sensitivities of any of the nations, or negate the rights of all citizens.

We want to join hands in productive work with all communities and nations, to make the land flourish and to live therein in freedom, love, and peace; and we want to plow the desolate land by means of large-scale, commercial, and faith-based agriculture, and to revive the land from its desolation; to employ therein thousands and tens of thousands of hands that shall earn a livelihood from the fruits of their labors, that will make the land flourish, that will increase its industry and its produce, and will show the world all its merits; to restore Israel from the Diaspora and its wanderings, that its soul shall yearn to water the land of our ancestors by the sweat of its brow, to invest all its skills and qualities therein, and to bury its bones therein. And we always aspire to return to our Land, wherein every stone, every corner, and every clod of soil is holy to us for eternity.

I am certain that all the military governors who have governed here will testify to our upright conduct since the occupation until this day: not only have we not committed any offense nor offended the sensitivities of our neighbors who dwell here, but we also know how to turn the other cheek. Many tales are told against us, and many have spoken against us verbally and in print. And what have we done to counter this apart from the groan that bursts forth from our hearts and is heard by the government?

Upon my word, I say: Our Jewish striving is for peace, and if others say otherwise, I state in advance that their words are incorrect. Many peoples have dwelt in this land, and many after us but passed herethrough. Have any sought and seen any national writings that they left behind? Where are the records of the kings of Canaan in literature, art, and science? Many peoples dwelt here after us for centuries, and aside from individual records for personal purposes, what can you see here?

In addition, since our coming to dwell here, aside from that same prophetic spirit that sparks therein that shall be a light and a merit for all humanity forever, there remain here ancient records and remnants of fortresses standing in their holiness, entire cities that still bear their Hebrew names, and cities built by Hebrew labor that exist until this day. Masses [of people] descend on these historic places of ours, over which shall unfurl our Holy Temple that the People of Israel hallowed and dedicated until this day for all nations. Masses [of people] descend on these visible and known places, both those that have been discovered and others that will yet be uncovered in the near future. From border to border is this land soaked with the blood and sweat of our ancestors, and has been hallowed for us by the Torah and its special commandments. Many are the national institutions that Israel has established in its Land, even during the Diaspora; go forth and see our dwellers, our buildings in Jerusalem and all the cities that Israel has managed to populate, as well as the colonies from Dan to Beer Sheba, wherefrom you'll see and prove that our task is a national one to which individuals have enlisted by the hundreds in the shared task of reviving this Land from its desolation, a revival that will benefit to the maximum the entire Yishuv. Let us look for work, permanent settlement that will be fully autonomous [with] absolute security for [an] eternal existence, and our neighbors will be better, more reliable friends to the People, the Land, and its inhabitants; and [they will be] good friends to have, [both] for humanity and for the development and flourishing of the Land.

Travel the land, esteemed friends, and your eyes will see in every corner and city, every street and school and workshop, factories, industry, and commerce, as well as yeshivas that are raising the next generation of Torah, law, and science prodigies. These institutions will increase and expand, and we shall be able to say that they will be paragons, from which the Divine prophecy of Israel's prophets shall emanate.

Esteemed guests,

Recognize our feelings, the expression of our souls, the soul of the entire People of Israel, and you are filled with faith that Divine supervision has been placed on you, and the God of the heavens shall comfort you with His guidance and shall lead you on the path of truth and eternal peace, and your name shall remain as a blessing among the builders of Israel and the pillars of world peace.

In the name of the God of Israel, in the name of all the peers of the sages, in the name of the entire People of Israel, I hereby greet you again: Welcome.

15

A Speech in the Celebration of My Jubilee

Excerpt from Ben-Zion Meir Hai Uziel, "Ne'um be-Neshef Yovel ha-Hamishim,"
in *Sefer Mikhmane 'Uzi'el: ma'marim kelaliyim, mikhtavim tsiburiyim u-le'umiyim,
ne'umim yesodiyim li-tehiyat Yisra'el u-vinyan artso* (1939, Jerusalem: ha-Va'ad
le-hotsaa't kitve Maran, 2003), 473–78.

In 1930 Uziel delivered a speech during a celebration of his fiftieth birthday (apparently held against his explicit wishes). In this speech, he made several autobiographical comments placing himself within the greater narratives of Jewish and Sephardi history and spoke about his vision of Ashkenazi-Sephardi unity.

Mr. Chairman, dearest and most esteemed rabbis and teachers, I am speechless; you have bestowed much love and effection on me in your words.

[. . .] And in seeing you all here tonight convened together, pleased with the event that vis-à-vis my mere personality is trivial, and [yet is] precious regarding my public stature in your giving honor to the Torah. In my eyes, I am hereby filled with comfort and encouragement, and draw renewed strength for our future task. I'm not [feeling] fifty today after spending time in your company, but rather twenty, and ready to enlist in the task, and for this I again thank you.

And now a few words directed at our welcomers. First of all I want to say that to tell you the truth, the descriptions and praise that you've heaped on me out of love are undeserved. While I am an offshoot of two large families in Israel—Uziel on my father's side, may he rest in peace; and Hazan on my mother's side, may she live long—I cannot state that I inherited the entirety of the holy treasure stored in my father's soul, nor all the noble attributes. Our sages teach us the duty to tell the truth, wherein if one says to an individual that he is learned in two Talmudic tractates, and he is learned only in one, the individual must reply, "Do not say of me more than is actually in me." As it is said: One who studied only one tractate, then went to another locale, where he is held in esteem for the fact that he had [as it were] studied two tractates, is obligated to tell them, "I studied only one tractate."[2] Based thereon, I say that while I am neither a genius nor great among Israel, I try to train myself toward that so that I shall be worthy

2. [Talmud Yerushalmi (Palestinian Talmud), tractate *Shevi'it*, p. 30/b ch. 10, halakha 3.]

of being called by my father's name, and worthy of the seat of honor that I now occupy. And now to return to what was said by one of the speakers, who said that whenever he runs into me I am carrying the book [the Torah]. This [always carrying the Torah] in itself is not something that needs to be praised, but it is imperative to note [because] in the original [rabbinic] literature [the Torah is] the people's soul and its hope, and [it is essential to be] a loyal son thereof.

My good friend and peer, the esteemed Rabbi Fishman,[3] touched in his speech tonight on the Sephardic and Ashkenazic, about whom I have stated at other times that I do not understand the difference. The great ones of Israel gave us neither a Sephardic country nor an Ashkenazic one, but, rather, the Torah with its many branches and tributaries—the Torah that accompanied us to all corners of our misery [diaspora], from the Land of Israel to Babylonia, from Babylonia to Spain, and from there to France, Germany, and beyond—the Torah is what reared the great ones of our people, generation after generation and country to country, in whose glorious footsteps we walk. All these are likened unto the creeks that split off from the sea and then return thereto. From the days of my youth, I drew all that I could from the Torah of our rabbis, who handed down rulings in locale after locale, and from them I feel my soul always.

I now appeal to the friend of my youth, the esteemed writer A. [Avraham] Elmaleh, and I say to him: I am a lover of the unity of our people, and I wish to see unnatural rends, formed against our will in the wake of our dispersion, healing and returning [us] to our single, unified source. I loathe this schism with all my heart, and condemn in the strongest terms any schism formed under the mantle of religion.

At the same time, I seek to differentiate between the concepts of unity and idleness. I strive to see brothers dwelling together in the field of work and in the field of literature. May God grant that from the descendants of the great ones of Sepharad shall emerge great arbitrators and commentators on the Law, researchers and poets, interpreters and Kabbalists. This is my longing and this is my prayer. Will I live to see it in my lifetime? I hope that God grants it. Yet by the same token I despise idleness on both the individual and the tribal levels.

From this viewpoint, I have lent my hand and my soul to the world unity of the Sephardim, yet from the first moment I stated that its center of gravity

3. [Rabbi Yehouda Leib Fishman Maimon (b. 1875 Bessarabia, d. 1962 Jerusalem) was the founder of the religious Zionist movement Ha-Mizrahi (the name has no connection to the word "Mizrahim") and later became the first minister of religions in Israel.]

must be in service to culture and Torah. More than once have I sought [for the Sephardim] to establish a rabbinical seminary. Torah and enlightenment are the healthy foundations of peace and unity, [as it is said]: "All your sons will be taught by the LORD, and great will be your children's peace" [Isaiah 54:13].

I hope that we will yet reach the shared task of the entire people fulfilling this goal, wherein many blessings lie.

Further Readings

Ratzabi, Shalom. "Zionism, Judaism and Eretz Israel in the Thought of the Rishon le-Zion Rabbi Ben Zion Meir Hai Uziel" [Hebrew]. *Pe'amim* 73 (Fall 1997): 60–83.

Uziel, Ben-Zion Meir Hai. 1939. *Sefer Mikhmane 'Uzi'el: ma'marim kelaliyim, mikhtavim tsiburiyim u-le'umiyim, ne'umim yesodiyim li-tehiyat Yisra'el u-vinyan artso*. Jerusalem: ha-Va'ad le-hotsaa't kitve Maran, 2003.

Zohar, Zvi. "Traditional Flexibility and Modern Strictness: Two Halakhic Positions on Women's Suffrage." In *Sephardi and Middle Eastern Jewries: History and Culture in Modern Era*, edited by Harvey E. Goldberg, 119–33. Bloomington: Indiana University Press, 1996.

Joseph Aslan Cattaui Pacha

Joseph A. Cattaui (1861–1942) was Egypt's most prominent Jew between the two world wars, tracing his family's residence in Egypt back to the eighth-century Umayyad period. His surname is often spelled Cattaoui, and he is also known as Yusuf (or Youssef) Qattawi. A graduate of the world's oldest engineering school, the École Nationale des Ponts et Chaussées in Paris, Cattaui authored books on Egyptian and world history as well as of scientific articles, writing in Hebrew, French, and Arabic. He was also an entrepreneur, a wealthy businessman, financier, agricultural industrialist, and hydrologist. Reasonably sympathetic to women's causes, from 1924 until his death, Cattaui was the avidly non-Zionist leader of Cairo's Jewish community.

A practicing Jew, he began his public life and career by taking a position in the Egyptian Ministry of Public Works. In 1912 he was made a pasha; in 1916 he was elected to the Legislative Assembly; and in 1916 he joined the Committee of Trade and Industry. Cattaui then left Egypt to study the sugar refining industry in Moravia. After his return he became the director of the Egyptian Sugar Company and president of the Kom Ombo Company, which developed a sugar industry in Aswan Province, cultivating sugar cane on 70,000 acres of what had been desert land. Building on this base, Cattaui established industrial and financial enterprises, often in partnership with other Egyptian Jewish families. Following the 1919 Revolution, Cattaui was sent to London to help negotiate Egyptian independence. During this same period he was also the founding director of Bank Misr and the chief mentor of Tala'at Harb (1867–1941), a leading Egyptian economist and founder of the Bank of Egypt.

In 1922 Cattaui was appointed to the Constitutional Committee that drafted the Egyptian Constitution. He became minister of finance in 1924 and minister of communications in 1925. At this time Iraq also had a Jewish minister of finance, the legendary Sasson Heskel Effendi, (later Sir Heskel Sasson, 1860–1932). In 1927 King Fuad appointed Cattaui to the Egyptian Senate, where from 1931 to 1935 he chaired the Finance Committee. Amid the tumultuous concurrent rise of Zionism and Arab nationalism, Cattaui did as much as he could to help Egypt's chief rabbi, the scholarly Haim Nahum Effendi (1872–1960), manage the affairs of the Egyptian Jewish community. Both men kept as low a profile as they could.

16

On Solidarity and on Diversity

Excerpts from Joseph A. Cattaui Pacha, *Pour Mes Enfants* (For my children),
ed. L. Carteret (Paris: Ancienne Librairie, 1920), 141–147 (on solidarity) and
41–50 (on diversity).

> In 1920 Cattaui wrote a long book that was designed as an "open letter" addressed
> to his children and was titled *Pour Mes Enfants*. In this letter he addressed several
> issues he considered vital, among them the questions of solidarity and diversity.
> The following two sections are the excerpts on these topics from the book. The
> titles of the sections and of the selection as a whole are ours.

On Solidarity

All societies should be founded on the core principle of the equitable and
continual exchange of rights and duties that go to make up Solidarity, thanks
to which an individual attaches him- or herself to the rest of humanity. To be
part of a body, an atom must be animated by a cohesive force just as powerful
as that which emanates from the other atoms. Within a society, Solidarity is this
cohesive force. It begins with the family and broadens its scope little by little
until it finally embraces the whole of humanity. To disconnect oneself from the
obligations imposed by Solidarity is to condemn oneself to live selfishly, that is
to say, to live as a stranger in the midst of a society and a family, who do not take
any interest in the stranger, since the stranger is not interested in anyone else.

To be useful to no one is really to be worthless (Descartes).

The selfish man, shut up in the narrow confines of his lonely existence, is like
a prisoner lost in oblivion. By the just forces of the laws of nature—of which
he is ignorant—the indifference that he professes toward everything that is not
himself destroys within him all sentiment regarding others. [. . .]

To render us insensible to pain we must forfeit also the possibility of happiness (Sir John
Lubbock).

The selfish man shuts his heart to urges capable of nurturing this precious
flower of friendship, whose delicate perfume scents the lives of a privileged few,
and causing it [the flower of friendship] to bloom; by so doing he forbids himself
from fully developing his life. This can only be achieved either by the intimate

exchange of all consciences, or by the total sharing of all in the same idea of progress, with each aiding the other.

Life can be maintained only by being spilt (M. Guyau).

When the feeling of Solidarity is elevated to the level of sacrifice, it creates great prophets, masterly teachers, and heroic martyrs. Their names attract legends; their dazzling actions lend their image a supernatural sheen. But in truth the events that tradition attributes to such individuals represent only a few moments in their moral activity, and if their sublime actions are forever etched in the memory of generations, it is because their intense lives were profoundly human and they had lived and thought as all people ought to.

Moses and Mohammed are the two great prophets of Light, not because they both evoke an image of gentle geniuses gathering up, in the solitude of the desert, the Law of Justice and Fraternity, nor because they call to mind the image of the hardy chieftain leading the chosen people in the conquest of foreign lands. Moses and Mohammed are instead the two great prophets of Light because by struggling to awaken a previously obscure conscience, they knew how to turn into reality the ideal of Solidarity of which their dreams had given them a glimpse.

Socrates is the Sage of Sages not because he is represented as holding discourses at his memorable feasts or receiving the hemlock with a stoic serenity. He is, instead, the Sage of Sages because by accepting death out of respect for his beliefs, he has given an example of probity that has become one of the highest accolades of human reason. Jesus is proclaimed as God by his faithful not because he appeared on the mount spreading the good news, nor on the cross blessing his executioners. Jesus is instead proclaimed as God because by pronouncing out loud his words of charity on Golgotha, he enriched humanity's moral heritage with an incomparable diamond.

And they were happy, each one of them, to an extent that not even the most daring imagination could wish for, in the profoundest, most exalted sense of the word. They were happy because they succeeded in drawing from their inner life enough light to lighten the world and to give it the eternal formula of the *religion of duty*, with the love of one's neighbor as its worship and a clear conscience as its temple. The work of union that they wished for with all their strength is, without doubt, still far from being completely realized. Perhaps the cause must be sought in the overly exclusivist zeal of successive generations that, one after the other, have created a fossilized, irreducible dogmatism with its long parade of credo, mystery, and revelation whose effects have only too often engendered superstition, intolerance, and fanaticism.

No matter! They nonetheless remain the purest witnesses to the human conscience. Great men to the greatest of men, they lived above all these prejudices. Holding short shrift with the morality of the Pharisees, full of terror and seductiveness, threats and promises, each as unclean as the other, they knew how to bear the ideal of Good to the level at which they had found its greatest expression, reserved for certain chosen ones: to renounce the self for the good of all.

On Diversity

Within each one of us there is a reserve of clear ideas and a reserve of obscure ideas. From a general viewpoint, they both gradually become clearer as one's conscience broadens. Yet at the same time, and very often, an obscure idea may emerge from the shadows of one's mind as a consequence of one word, or gesture, from outside. An idea—even if it might seem false—will prove capable of revealing another idea in total opposition to it that will develop bit by bit within your soul, finally emerging to take its place among the ensemble of your own ideas.

If you go into a dark room behind a friend who, candle flame in hand, wishes to show you an object to which he attaches a particular interest—your gaze, indifferent to this object, may neglect to rest on it and instead prefer to seek out another object that interests it immediately, although your friend has not given it the least thought. You will then not pay any attention to the first object, even though it is thanks to it that you will have been able to discover the second. From a wider viewpoint, diversity of opinion—far from being a weakness—must on the contrary be considered an agent of progress. The human mind, which is always in need of clarity, is ceaselessly at work thanks to diversity.

The light of knowledge is born from the clash of ideas (French proverb).

[. . .] In the first instance, diversity of different individuals creates diversity of strengths and abilities. This, in turn, creates a role for these individuals within the field of employment. It also permits them to find the necessary energy to fulfill their role for the common good. It next creates diversity of wants and aspirations that, in turn, spurs individuals to follow their initiatives and blaze new paths in life.

Individual diversity is a necessary ingredient of human progress. The more there are individual rivalries, the more fertile will be the field of work (E. Lavisse).

By this it is to be understood that although—on the one hand—your reason and conscience must be your only advisors, this same reason and conscience—on the other hand—will be so much the stronger, and you will be better aware of how to observe and study what you see and hear around you.

The communication of others is one of the best schools that may be (Montaigne).

What is more, the importance of this diversity of opinion cannot be stressed enough, particularly from a moral perspective. There are lofty moral principles whose essence lies beyond the realm of personal appreciation, beyond the circumstances of time and place, which every honest person ought to ascribe to utterly and unyieldingly, whatever his circumstances or locality.

True law is right reason conformable to nature, universal, unchangeable, eternal, whose commands urge us to duty, and whose prohibitions restrain us from evil. Whether it enjoins or forbids, the good respect its injunctions, and the wicked treat them with indifference. This law cannot be contradicted by any other law and is not liable either to derogation or abrogation. Neither the Senate nor the people can give us any dispensation for not obeying this universal law of justice. It needs no other expositor and interpreter than our own conscience. It is not one thing at Rome, and another at Athens; one thing today, and another tomorrow; but in all times and nations (Cicero).

Morality is fundamentally the same for everyone, albeit found in different forms according to locality. It must be hoped that one day these will be united in an atmosphere of Truth and Justice and where all issues that arise will be resolved, if not definitively, then at least on the basis of sound Reason. The search for Good and Evil has always preoccupied thinkers, and each century has brought another grain of truth. Doubtless, the hour will come when—in a greater state of illumination—human conscience will see the shining dawn of peace and harmony so long wished for by good men of all ages.

While waiting for this golden age, let us be content with the relative truth as currently perceived by our reason, and let us drive it forward methodically, thus bringing us closer (as far as it is within our power) to the ideal of which we dream. If all men would think like this they would be truly ready to listen to one another. However great an error might be, a thoughtful man can always extract from it some grain of truth that will come to enrich his conscience.

I spent the remainder of my youth in traveling, in visiting courts and armies, in interacting with men of different dispositions and ranks, in collecting varied experiences, in proving myself in the different situations into which fortune threw me, and, above all, in making such reflection on the matter of my experience as to secure my improvement (Descartes).

The greater will be the profit you will thus draw from your reflections and the firmer will be the ground on which you tread. You will at the same time be guided in the practice of the two virtues the civilized person values most: (i) tolerance, that is, the respect of the opinions of others when they are given in good faith; and (ii) leniency, that is, the good will to know how to excuse—and how to defend oneself—against partisanship and prejudice.

The most critical time for you is when—leaving the realm of theory—you find yourself in the clutches of reality. Out of necessity you will take as landmarks the lessons and examples your teachers have provided. Your first surprise will be when you notice that people are, in general, far different from the ideal that you have formed for yourself. Do not lose heart. Think, instead, that—like you—many of them have received lessons and examples from which they too have drawn an ideal perhaps loftier than your own. If people you meet are not all that you have imagined, it is because life has shaped and adapted them according to their own realities. Some, the weaker ones, have come up against difficulties which it was beyond their ability to overcome: due to these tribulations—which they did not know how to predict—they have come crashing down. There are, conversely, others who—better instructed by their duty toward themselves— have adapted and developed themselves normally, in the path of truth and light, that they chose in the first instance.

The chief factor that will have caused some to rise to the challenge, and others to become lost, will have been this school of all moments that we call "experience." It causes happiness for those who know how to learn its lessons, and misery for those who become discouraged by it. Do not regret that for the moment—through lack of experience that will only come in time—you do not have any other guide than your ideal. In the first stages of your journey, ignoring the difficulties of the road, listening only to the voice of your dreams, you walk with an unconscious happiness. You have youth, you have the enviable privilege of resolute impetuosity, bursts of spontaneity and carelessness in the face of danger. At certain times these can give birth to great things, things that wiser men of mature age would be incapable of.

You are like a young bird who has not yet taken flight. Just newly hatched, he dreams of wide open spaces, and the thought of the new things that await him gives him a *frisson* of pleasure. As soon as he is able to take to the wing, he will cast himself from the nest and, without concerning himself in the slightest as to which branch he will land on, he will go ever higher in conquest of the unknown. He may come to perceive far-flung horizons that he will see no longer once his wings are weighed down by experience, which has taught him reflection, which calculates, and prudence, which moderates.

Further Readings

Badran, Margot. *Feminists, Islam, and Nation: Gender and the Making of Modern Egypt*. Princeton: Princeton University Press, 1995.

Beinin, Joel. *The Dispersion of Egyptian Jewry: Culture, Politics, and the Formation of a Modern Diaspora*. Berkeley: University of California Press, 1998.

Davis, Eric. *Challenging Colonialism: Bank Misr and Egyptian Industrialization, 1920–1941*. Princeton: Princeton University Press, 1983.

Goldschmidt, Arthur, Jr. *Biographical Dictionary of Modern Egypt*. Cairo: American University in Cairo Press, 2000.

Gorman, Anthony. *Historians, State, and Politics in Twentieth Century Egypt: Contesting the Nation*. London: Routledge, 2003.

Krämer, Gudrun. *The Jews in Modern Egypt, 1914–1952*. Seattle: University of Washington Press, 1989.

Mizrahi, Maurice. *L'Egypte et ses Juifs: Le temps révolu, XIXe et XXe siècle*. Geneva: Avenir, 1977.

Vitalis, Robert. *When Capitalists Collide: Business Conflict and the End of Empire in Egypt*. Berkeley: University of California Press, 1995.

Hayyim Ben-Kiki

A Sephardi intellectual of North African descent—son of Rabbi Shmuel Ben-Kiki (chief rabbi of the Tiberias rabbinic court, d. 1919)—Hayyim Ben-Kiki (1887–1935) was born in Tiberias and lived and worked there most of his life. During the 1920s he served as the secretary of the Sephardi Union in Haifa and as correspondent in Tiberia and northern Palestine for *Do'ar Hayom* (Palestine daily mail). He passed away in Aden, Yemen, on his way to India on a mission on behalf of the rabbis of Tiberias. The circumstances of his death and the purpose of his mission are not clear.

Sadly, there is little reliable information about this fierce critic of European colonization in the Middle East as well as of European Zionism in Palestine. We know that Ben-Kiki was suspicious of "modernity" while concurrently criticizing "traditionalist" views and religions. An advocate of "Jewish pride," he viewed Oriental Jewry as the custodian of the old "Hebrew" mentality. Ben-Kiki's writing was all-encompassing in its approach. He also often moved abruptly from an insight about history and culture in one context to an insight in another place. His writing was clearly polemical, and he often attacked— even ridiculed—political, cultural, and religious movements in the Middle East, whether they were Christian, Muslim, or Jewish. Ben-Kiki's lengthy articles were chiefly published in the Hebrew newspaper *Do'ar Hayom*, which was edited by two well-known intellectuals in the Zionist Yishuv: Itamar Ben-Avi (Ben-Zion Ben-Yehuda, 1882–1943) and Ze'ev Jabotinsky (1880–1940). Both men disagreed with Ben-Kiki's analyses yet were sufficiently open to print them.

European Culture in the East

Hayyim Ben-Kiki, "Ha-Tarbut ha-Eropit ba-Mizrah," *Do'ar Hayom*,
October 12–15, 1920.

> This long analysis of the impact of European culture and Europe in general on the
> Middle East was published in four consecutive issues of *Do'ar Hayom*. In it, Ben-
> Kiki analyzed the ways in which the Muslim, Jewish, and Christian communities in
> the region had responded since the nineteenth century to the European influence
> in the region.

OCTOBER 12, 1920

The Orient has a unique culture and unique customs and religion that greatly distinguish it from the West. This difference is profound and is based on the *Weltanschauung* of the great oriental sages and prophets and their opinions concerning life and death, good and evil. In ancient times, Western nations feared Eastern expansion into their lands, so they used armed force against the Orient, and they succeeded in pushing the onslaught westward and saving their countries. Yet at the same time they perceived that a constant threat to their lands existed as long as the Orient remained culturally and spiritually intact.

When the human and social sciences prevailed [over other modes of thought], forces inside the kingdoms and among nations came to realize that just as one cannot weaken a certain substance except with another substance and with armed might—so one cannot weaken the spirit, except with spirit. When one tries to subjugate the spirit with might, the opposite outcome prevails, that is, the spirit's strengthening. This was the genesis of the idea of spreading Western culture to the Orient. The Europeans thought that by presenting to the natives their culture and its essence, the Easterners would come to appreciate it. Yet they hardly managed to accomplish even a small measure of this goal. Sometimes they even worsened things since many in the Orient came to loathe European culture precisely as a consequence of their exposure to it. Europe still profited from other elements of this endeavor. The venture of spreading European culture to the East helped Europeans to acquaint themselves with this region. Most importantly, this project weakened the national culture of the Orient. The Easterner got baffled by the diverse education, fashion, beautiful new customs, and so on and so forth. All of this caused Oriental people to forget their identity, until they gradually internalized the notion that they were weak, inferior creatures.

Europe employed a variety of means to arrive at its goals. These included Turkey's economic and spiritual weakness, the penetrating influence of foreign governments in the Ottoman Empire or large amounts of money poured into schools, hospitals, and charitable institutions. All such means made Europe—and anything originating from abroad—appear formidable in the eyes of the natives. Love and submission to the rich is not just something occurring at the individual level alone; it is also—and even more intensely—a national trait. This is even truer among acculturated commoners. Yet the most effective instrument Europe found in the Orient was religious difference.

The Jews and Christians—who are distinct collectivities within the Orient's body of nations and subjects—proved to be an excellent tool for helping Europe fortify its position in the [Ottoman] Empire. Europe utilized Jews and Christians as a vehicle through which to push new ideas and worldviews onto the empire. This resulted in the Orient's weakening of national unity. The Christians never had any national sentiment; even though their language is Arabic, their character and mentality—even more than in the case of the Jews—are very divergent from [those of] the Muslims. This situation is conditioned by the Christian religion itself, which is incompatible with Islam and the spirit of "Muslimhood." Europe reinforced this situation through its schools and its influence on the government. Thus, both sects—the Jews and Christians—evolved separately without any internal or mental desire to make contact with the larger society: the only ways in which they are part of the people are through their language and simple habits.

Language—the foundation of racial unity—was the only thing that could hold back the expansion of Europe's influence. But Europe conducted herself with savvy and wisdom even in this realm. She did not disregard Arabic, or try to eradicate it by investing in the teaching of foreign languages. Instead, Europe tried to keep the Arabic language alive, teaching it with enthusiasm and rigor. She only did one small thing to Arabic. Using its teachers and students, both in Europe and abroad, she changed the character of the language, giving it a new European essence and style, thereby effacing Arabic's original character. The new writers and teachers injected European literature into Arabic literature. When one reads the new Arabic literature alongside the old one, they appear to be written in two different languages.

This state of affairs is not the outcome of natural internal developments. Evidently, the Muslims—notwithstanding being stylistically influenced by Christians—still retain some linguistic elements that distinguish them from the Christian Syrian[1] style of writing. An essay written by a Christian author does not resemble one written by a Muslim author. The latter writer has respect for the ancient dignified style of the Arabic language. He enjoys peppering his writing with old idioms. He always bears in mind Arab and Islamic history when he writes, treating their heroes with awe. Thus his writing commonly springs out through these two great prisms. Conversely, the Christian writer can only utilize the [modern] language as such: all the creative innovations that he introduces to Arabic drift strongly toward the European style and, thus, as a whole result in the deepening of the latter's impact. The modernization and standardization of the Arabic language following the European style was a lofty ideal for the Syrian Christians as a consequence of foreign influence. One can posit that they carried out this project with great devotion for the purpose of cutting Arabic loose from the old Islamic moorings that anchored this rich and poetic language. I fail to see originality in more than half a generation of [the most recent] literary work. Original literature can spring only out of a national sentiment and a sense of history; the Christian Syrians lack both. They were therefore unable to produce original literature in Arabic. These Syrians relinquished their national sentiment when they became Christians and ceased to acknowledge the Islamic forefathers as their own forebears.

This expansion of education brought great development to the country. But it is a general human development that ultimately weakened greatly the Arab national sentiment that did not evolve with it. And so, not only did the Arabic language not resist European culture; on the contrary, it became its biggest assistant. In this way Syria's vast Christian public became a tool of Europe as well as the advocate of European modes of thinking and spirit. Lack of national sentiment, coupled with hostility toward [Muslim] Turkey, stirred public attention toward Europe that, in turn, courted this affinity in both Syria and Egypt. With any political question or problem that Europe stumbled across in the Orient, it used the Christian community as its advocate and voice. Both Europe and the

1. [For Ben-Kiki, "Syria" means the territories comprising the modern states of Lebanon, Syria, and Israel and Palestine. This is particularly so when he discusses the Christian community. When he speaks of "the Land" or "the country," he refers to Palestine. While here he uses the term "Arab" mostly in reference to Arab Muslims, it is clear that he thinks of "Arab" as a cultural category that includes Jews and Christians as well.]

local Christians did not consider Syria their home; the latter saw themselves only as residents, and their sole demand was for [European] protection and rights.

When European armies conquered the Land, the situation was reversed. The most important European interests required that this instrument—the Christians—become [Arab] nationalists, and this occurred with no preparation or any mental qualms. Christians now instantly became enthusiastic nationalists, shouting "We are Arabs! Racial brothers of the Muslims!" One would really think that this indeed was the case: that those Christians were oppressed and tortured under the Ottomans and could not express their feelings for their homeland because Turkey did not encourage them or because the Ottoman government would accept their demands only if they did not express their Arab national sentiments openly. One could believe this line of argument, yet [empirical] events and reality proved it erroneous. The country, released from Ottoman rule, did not come under one government but under many different ones. Thus the cries of those Syrians followed the spirit of the ruler in each country. Syrian newspapers in the Land of Israel sang a different tune than those in Beirut. The Christians welcomed the French in Beirut with glee, while the Muslims stayed rock solid in their demand for a united Syria.[2]

OCTOBER 13, 1920

In this regard, Jewish trajectories took a very different shape. Syrian Christians could not envision giving up the Arabic language, which obviously was alive as well as used in all walks of life, be they secular or religious. Despite the instruction and teaching of foreign languages, few people partake [in that education], and indeed the masses would become alienated if they did. Therefore, European culture had put new wine into old vessels and infiltrated the Arabic language. With Jews the story is different. The Jews did not have a special common language. Hebrew was considered a holy language, the exclusive realm of the learned clergy. The masses needed it only for liturgical readings. Arabic, on the other hand, was a spoken language, used out of habit and simply for getting by in everyday life. Thus, the Jews had no language that the foreigners had to pay heed to. Consequently, when Europeans began disseminating European culture among Jews, they did not have to take the linguistic aspect into account at all.

2. [See the previous note. In contemporary terms, the vision that Ben-Kiki describes here would most likely be called "Greater Syria."]

To be sure, Arabic and Hebrew both remained in the newly devised European programs—Hebrew for religious studies and Arabic for secular studies (as was customary in the traditional Jewish schools). It would therefore seem, in the first instance, as merely a minor modification, that is, solely limiting Hebrew studies while not changing the program altogether—just trimming it a little. In reality, however, former Jewish education was smothered and dwindled into feeble flame that ultimately would lead to its complete demise.

The rabbis understood instinctively where things were heading and protested these changes. But they did not study the issue in a sufficiently profound manner and limited their resistance to religious matters alone. In other words, they argued that this curriculum would cause Jews to drift away from keeping the mitzvoth. This protest was of course weak and could not resist the culture that pretended to be speaking in the name of life, since it is well known that life overrides religion. It is not only that the rabbis failed to understand the question of European cultural penetration, or to express the wrongs this penetration was perpetuating. It can even be argued that the rabbis' protestations actually assisted Europe to win over Jewish minds. The rabbis framed their protests as a demand that spiritual life and study be strengthened at the expense of worldly life and secular teaching—an argument that remained unpersuasive to the Jewish public, which saw, in European education, prospects for a future filled with success and dignity for their sons.

In this way Western culture spread among the Jews in a manner altogether different from that of the Christian case. The Jews were unfortunately on the losing side of things. The Syrian [Christians] encountered European influence while sensing neither ambiguity nor rapture. This new culture needed their language, and they therefore accepted it on their own terms. The new culture served as a vast platform on which they were able to develop their distinct identity. Because the whole project was conceived of as transferring European culture into Arabic, it required the vigorous dedication of all mental powers and therefore could mobilize a mass movement to carry it out. While the educators of the Syrians envisioned the Syrian public, the educators of the Jews had in mind only the individual Jew. Whereas the Christian was educated so he would become a Syrian European, the Jew was cultivated to cease being Oriental at all. The curriculum imposed on the Jew was a carbon copy of the education found in European schools. Only those who were motivated enough and prepared to work in European institutions were able to understand and inhabit, more or less, the European culture. The [Jewish] masses were left empty-handed. All they have acquired is European chatter and pretensions, a bit of external propriety in conversation and in life, and simplicity, or internal mental rudeness when it comes to aspects of social life. This new education is an atrophied organ, not in the body of the people, but in the body of all humanity.

The root of the mistake and the failure was in the nature of the curriculum given to the Jews. Since it was written in a European language entirely, it had to be nationalistic—as all educational European books are nationalist. In this way, the Europeans wanted to make the Jew part of the same nationality as the education he was receiving, yet that was impossible to achieve. National sentiment is neither learned nor acquired; it springs from historic and racial love. One can respect and admire history that is not "one's own," yet one cannot love it. And when love is absent, devotion is absent as well, and the impact of such education on the student remains artificial, weak, and shallow. As such, it does not generate sufficient respect. It is possible to say with certainty that—during their first months out in the real world after graduating from school—90 percent of the Jewish students forget the foreign geography and history they were taught with rigor and vigor. This happens because they do not need this material and they do not value it emotionally. The [Christian] Syrian education, on the other hand—which was not based on a foreign language—was not injected with any nationalistic purpose. It was therefore designed just as a general humanist education. Even the teaching of Arab ethics, poetry, and science—which are part of its foundation—was done in a free scientific fashion, and its impact as a modern education was therefore deep and complete.

The [Christian] Syrians, a religious sect cultivated and strengthened by European culture, indeed lack any organic or concrete unity. Such unity cannot come into being unless it is nationalistic, that is, linked with the past and the future. But there remains a unity based on understanding when it becomes necessary, or during times of danger. Conversely, the Europeanized Jewish student who receives a foreign education does not know at all what unity is because from the very beginning of his education he considers himself a son of the world, a son of all of this world. Therefore, unity for the Jew is meaningless and impossible to achieve even with his fellow students learning with him in the same classroom. This is because this [Jewish] student—who lives in Oriental surroundings—is forced to acquire, whether or not he wants them, virtues, ideas, and norms that are incompatible with the education he receives. This mixture of Western ideas and Oriental norms gives rise to an awful result: each student comes up with his own worldview, his own opinions about life, his own beliefs and ideas.

Each student differs in this regard from his peers. Each student is a world unto himself.

One can thus imagine a unity of opinion among the Christian Syrians, while it is impossible to find it among the Jews. The latter are like isolated stalks—as far from each other as the East is from the West. Indeed we heard that in Turkey there is a "Society of Alliances Israelite Alumni," but this is not a popular movement calling for reform in life. This society is merely an association for the sake of pleasant conversation, clarifying certain local political questions, or for the sake of just being a member of some society. The word "society" already has its strong appeal among the young in the Orient, whatever purpose it might serve, or no purpose at all. It is nice and pleasant to be a member of such a society. We have thus created a private Jew who can form attachments to any community, any environment, and has no feelings of social obligation or rights. This person's sole wish in life is to fill up his stomach and rest his mind and body. Such an education does not produce courageous moral heroes, but only people with bare and hollow souls. One cannot hope for a writer or a poet to emerge from this education, even in the language in which the students are educated.

This is the Oriental Jew who is the product of Western culture.

OCTOBER 14, 1920

The influence of Europe on the Muslims was weak. Here they [the Europeans] could not barge in, as if Islam was like a city whose walls were breached, since in Islam's case there is an ancient historical culture that one cannot easily dismiss. European influence on Islam was therefore indirect. Like the Jews, the Muslims have a national religion. National unity originates for them with and through religious unity. During Ottoman rule—and especially before the "constitution"[3] —their nationality was amalgamated with their Turkish coreligionists. There was no perception that these were two different nations, whether inside the schools, in the press, or even in the marketplace. Since these two elements—the Muslim Arabs and the [non-Arab Muslim] Turks—did not live together, they did not have any frictions, whether economic or class-related. Governmental and religious unity mandated that they should see themselves as one nation.

3. [Ben-Kiki is probably referring here to the 1908 reforms that aimed to institute constitutional monarchy under Abdul Hamid II. An earlier attempt to create a constitutional monarchy took place in 1876.]

The education of Muslims in Syria is Arab nationalist,[4] both in private and public schools. Muslims who have acculturated in Western culture are few and are by and large acculturated only in a scientific professional sense—as doctors, lawyers, engineers. They entered Europe's cultural shrine after being sufficiently immersed in their own language and culture. For many, acquiring European culture proved to be vital: not only did it not weaken their national sentiment, it strengthened it. Originally, this was the case both with the Turks and with the [Muslim] Arabs[5] who were united under the [Ottoman] Empire. The Arabs were even more loyal to the Ottoman government than the Turks [were] and considered the wars of Ottoman rulers as their own. But the Young Turks— who were educated in Europe—came up with their own national "European style" demands on rising to power. They wanted to create a new curriculum for education—one language for an entire country that was obviously nothing but Turkish. Moreover, the Young Turks tried to emphasize Turkish superiority over Arabs. This gave rise to envy and hatred toward the Turks among the prominent Arabs, while also opening their eyes to the profound differences between them and the Turks.

At that point, Arab nationalist societies were established. They instigated a fierce debate in the press that in turn gave rise to a distinct—that is, anti-Turkish—form of Arab nationalism. This development was rather easy. For the Arabs are far more distinguished than the Turks. They have wonderful moral and religious values, a glorious poetic and philosophical history that had had a great impact on the world of science—whereas the Turks have nothing of this kind. That is how the Turks themselves created this rift between the two and within a large part of their own empire. What Europe could not do during the days of Abdul Hamid [II, 1842–1918]—the Young Turks, students of Europe, managed to do. They noticed that the sentiment of Ottoman "nationalism" among the Arabs was flawed, and when they started "messing" with it with coarse hands, the consequence was that they spoiled it completely. Nationalism is a fragile sentiment that one cannot just change—but only deepen, praise, and improve as long as its natural original qualities remain unaltered. If this national sentiment does

4. [Ben-Kiki's use of the term "nationalist" is loose and should be understood as such. Nationalist movements and tendencies in the region were in an embryonic form at the time he wrote.]

5. [Ben-Kiki's use of the word "Arabs" here is intended only to distinguish between two Muslim groups.]

not fit others' vision of nationalism,[6] it does not really matter. This is history's decree that one cannot simply resist.

As mentioned above, the European impact on the Middle East's Muslims was indirect. The contacts with Europe—by land and by sea—exacerbated European commercial activity in the region and nearly destroyed completely the local, national [native] industry. This expansion brought European tastes to the region in clothing, furniture, and architecture (Arab architecture has disappeared from Syria during the past few decades, and only in Egypt they are still insisting on building government buildings according to the ancient Arab style).

The European presence in the region and the exposure to a European lifestyle opened the eyes of the Arab, and he could see that he had had no sense until now of what life is all about. These European qualities began penetrating the Muslim domain without being perceived as a threat to Arab mentality and culture. The Arab was happy to welcome the [technological] innovations—since they made life easier and more pleasant—and he tried hard to acquire them. The more, the merrier. This way European culture entered only superficially, touching just the surface without causing an overriding change in Arab mentality and virtues. A mixture of Western tenets (such as love of life and its intensity) and Arab values (such as quietism, modesty, and frugality) began to govern Arab mentality. It weakened the religious sentiments among Arabs—as well as their national sentiments (since the latter are founded on the former). Hitherto the Arab was emotionally offended when foreigners touched his domain. Now, when he saw how beautiful the world is, his regard for holy matters of the world to come and the afterlife diminished, and he considered himself a distinct individual with nothing to worry about and fight for.

This new trait especially affected urbanites, since it was in cities where the European life of pleasure and indulgence were seen most frequently. That is why in Turkey's recent wars, the Arabs tried any legitimate or illegitimate way to rid themselves of army duty while only reluctantly providing financial support to the military effort. All the rich with a measure of political power avoided helping the government, while concurrently becoming even richer by taking advantage of the government during the war.

When the war ended and Turkey was off the political stage, Arab leaders awakened; that seed of resisting the Ottoman government in the name of Arab

6. [Ben-Kiki refers here to the incompatibility he perceives between the Arab sense of loyalty to the Ottomans and the nationalism of the Young Turks.]

nationalism and unity, sowed during late Ottoman days, came to life. But it must be emphasized that Arab nationalism is not yet sufficiently sound and does not come out of mental necessity. The reason is that the Arab people—like the Jews—have long forgotten their political independence and must therefore be reeducated to think about it anew. Prior to the war, the nationalist movement was not a mass movement but was created by some Arabs with influence and power. Nor did the nationalist movement intend to redeem the Arabs for the same self-rule. It only aimed to relieve the Arabs of the Turkish yoke and replace them with other rulers—French or English—whom they considered better. This idea was quite well known and was publicized by the press all over Syria.

The idea of Arab political unity is the product of the previous war's politics. The Arabs identified a window to become free with self-rule; they could not reject such a good gift. In the interim, however—in order to arrive at this level of self-rule—one must direct the national demand toward external powers, as well as internal forces, and express it only in the "negative" way. Put differently, the Arabs are nationalist because they cannot tolerate foreign rule. Even the Jewish movement—which is only a movement of safe settlement—is utilized by Arab nationalists as a material means of filling their ideological void. The resistance to foreigners in general and to Jews is understandable. It provides a vast space for further thinking, talking, and writing. There is enough in that to excite the already enthusiastic Arab imagination.

Even our new [Zionist] institutions and press helped to fan the flames of the misunderstanding between the Arabs and us. These institutions do not take into consideration anyone but the Jews and Europe, and totally ignore their neighbors. They treated Arabs prejudicially and dismissed them—imitating the prevailing Western attitude toward the Arabs, even though the strong Europeans actually use different methods here in the region. It is two and a half years now that the Balfour Declaration has been on our mind. It is always present in our newspapers, meetings, and festivals, and it is entirely out of control. The many celebrations should not have taken place and the many [self-congratulating] articles should not have been written. The noisy articles and carnivals that are not coming in the right time or place only undermine the leaders' actions while muddling up their "perspective."

The unity of Christians and Muslims that we see today does not have any solid foundation. We, Jews, are closer to each of these two groups than they are to each other. With regard to the question of resisting foreign rule, the Christians will not offer a helping hand to the Muslims. They will do it for the sake of "peaceful relations" with their stronger neighbors. As for the question of anti-Zionism, it was created among the Christians, and from them migrated to the Muslims. Yet this is not a superficial migration of ideas. Anti-Zionism first interested some educated Muslims who were in contact with Christians for business and private matters, and then anti-Zionism spread among other Muslims who do not know much about the issue and are indifferent to it.

This is how anti-Zionism works among the Muslims: some smart talkers come and say that this Jewish movement brings catastrophe to the country. Since it is shameful to object to their claims, no one does. On the other hand, who really cares if the Jews succeed or not? This is the Muslim-based anti-Zionism. The Christians, on the other hand, are not indifferent. They oppose Zionism out of jealousy. They cannot bear to see the Jews succeed. The Christians are active anti-Zionists. While the Muslims would talk for a short while, they hardly act on their words. Each Muslim smart talker finished his prophecies against Zionism and then left the stage. The Christian newspapers, on the other hand, remain filled with envy, and to this day their screams and innuendos fill the air.

OCTOBER 15, 1920

There is only one element that remains untouched by European influence: the [old] Jewish community. Despite the great expenditure and effort of foreign educators pertaining to the Jews, they failed to transplant their education into this community. European influence weakened the Jews only in a quantitative manner—by spreading some tens of its sons here and there. But the picture of the Jewish presence in the land is still the traditional old one. The community—wrongly labeled "Arab" in the derogatory way—has nothing to do with the national aspirations of [Muslim] Arabs and nothing to do with the ambitions of the Christians. It is situated in the center in the sense that it is close to both communities. Each of the two considers the [old, linguistically and culturally Arabized] Jewish community as a close relative and a secret partner. One of the reasons for this is that Judaism is the mother of Christianity and Islam. So each of these religions is influenced by it and maintains a constant affinity to it. Thus, despite all the contradictions, the Jew has a certain partnership with each community.

Those who accuse the old Jewish community—especially the Sephardic community—of "Arab assimilation" indicate, if they truly believe what they are saying, that they do not know what assimilation is. Assimilation means using the country's language and manners; it is the total submission to its culture. In Europe—following the ghetto's destruction and after the emancipation—the Jew found himself facing high culture in every regard: science, poetry, philosophy, the affairs of state. Compared to all this, Judaism appears as only one-dimensional, its influence and greatness notwithstanding. The values of Judaism did not evolve and develop with this European life, and thus the Jew came to view Judaism as old and limited. Perhaps there are a few isolated Jews who are still strong in their national pride, but the sentiment of the masses is of succumbing to the greatness and power of European culture, both in terms of matter and of spirit. When such sentiments take over the individual and govern his life, the result is that he assimilates. Assimilation is a sense of smallness, of mental submission before the strong. The mentally assimilated person does not remember that Israel is unique, the "chosen people."

This kind of attitude cannot be born with Oriental Judaism and Jewry.

Here the Arabs' ancient culture remained intact as it was in the days when Islam was spreading, and it underwent no fundamental changes. Islam cannot tolerate any change in the worldview it inherited from its inception, since such change will destroy the Arabs. Islam accepts progress only when it takes places within and under the patronage of religion. Christian peoples did not experience this kind of burden—or at least did not feel that such was the case—for Christianity itself is one step in the development of these peoples. Progress in the Orient is so slow that one cannot really sense it. Intellectuals or poets criticizing the Arab worldview never existed in Arab history. If one expressed certain ideas out of fear and horror, one did not leave any mark or legacy. In Egypt there was a literary movement calling for the liberation of women.[7] Not, God forbid, for actual equality, just to remove the veil and uncover women's faces. Books and essays were written about this, [and] there is even a newspaper dedicated to this cause. The movement itself made a great deal of noise in its time in the Arab world but eventually failed. Today this issue is merely a literary subject for writers—in theory and never in practice.

Religions, with all their habits and traditional views about their own eternity, still reign in the East as a force above nature. Judaism, therefore—which is the basis and the foundation of these religions—retained its dignity and respect. The Jew feels his culture is superior to all others and patronizes them. The others

---

7. [Ben-Kiki is probably referring here to the Union of Educated Egyptian Women, founded in 1914 by the legendary feminist Hoda al-Sha'arawi (1879–1940).]

sense this Jewish feeling "instinctively." Israel—while in the Orient—was always spiritually superior, as it was throughout the world before our generation, when religion ruled and the Jews were inside the ghetto. The Jews in the Orient did not assimilate. This is because Islam is not designed to, and is not capable of, "engulfing" other peoples. Islam protects the religion and traditions of other peoples because this is how it keeps its own identity intact. This is why Israel survives in the Orient.

Unlike all that mishmash of education and foreign influence playing with the spirit of the Orient for its own pleasure and good, Hebrew education comes to redeem Hebrew's external picture by providing the Jew with the Hebrew language and morals as the foundation for his education and learning. This educational movement is undoubtedly good but—I must add—not entirely original. It was not created out of other gradual developments from within the people, but instead came as a revolution in the way in which we observe others. To be sure, our first nationalists were people who knew all the light that is in Judaism but who additionally grasped the beauty of Japheth [Europe].[8]

This duality was perplexing. On one hand, Judaism left its mark on Europeans and does not allow self-dismissal in face of others; on the other, European culture and its creations are already rooted in the soul of Jews. So what did these Jews do? They made Europe and Judaism compatible. They did not like the earlier Jewish thinkers, who insisted that Judaism will avoid absorbing new ideas and views. They also attacked the notion that one can be either an old traditional Jew or a European Jew while declaring, instead, that it is possible to be both. It is possible to be a cultivated person with beliefs and ideas without any restrictions, and at the same time it is possible also to be a good and faithful Jew.

By articulating these ideas and trying to advance them, such Jews sought to rectify their own souls. Thus we are familiar with the new educational textbooks insisting on love, diligence, and learning. These Jewish intellectuals saw how the other nations teach their children—how they transmit their histories and their morals—and they strove to emulate them. Assimilation mandates "let us Jews be like the rest of nations"; nationalism declares "let us Jews be as one of the other nations." I am not an expert authorized to say anything about this dilemma. Maybe this is how things should be. But I must comment that we should

8. [Ben-Kiki here makes a nice pun in Hebrew: "Yefeyfiyuto shel Yafet" (Japheth's beauty).]

be careful with this culture coming to us in new vessels. We must be watchful that it does not ruin the feeling of Jewish pride that is prevalent particularly in the Orient. We must stay alert that our culture maintains its old character and spirit and does not become a Hebrew-speaking European culture.

On the Question of All Questions Concerning the Settling of the Land

Hayyim Ben-Kiki, "Al She'elat Ha-She'elot be-Yishuv Ha-Aretz," *Do'ar Hayom*,
August 30, 1921.

This essay was published by Ben-Kiki nearly four years after the British had issued
the Balfour Declaration and at a time when the rising Palestinian-Arab national
movement was becoming increasingly hostile to Zionism. Ben-Kiki wrote this essay
in response to hesitant calls from various Zionist quarters to reach out to the Arabs
in Palestine. His title was pointedly almost identical to that of an essay published
in 1919 by Yitzhak Epstein (1863–1943), an educator and advocate of the use of
Hebrew, and Ben-Kiki's essay was framed as a direct response to that earlier essay.
The origin of Epstein's work was a speech he had delivered at the Zionist Congress
of 1905. In 1907 he had published an essay in the Odessa-based journal *Ha-Shilo'ah*
titled "She'ela ne'elama" (A hidden question). That essay warned the leaders of the
Zionist movement about what Epstein saw as dangerous "writing on the wall" — that
is, the Yishuv's disregard of the Arabs of Palestine and its disgraceful treatment of
them. "The existence of the Arabs in Palestine is invisible because the leaders do
not want to see them," exclaimed Epstein. Praising the Arabs' love of Palestine,
he continued: "We must not cause any harm to any people, particularly to a great
people whose hatred toward us [might be] very dangerous." Jewish ignorance
about Arab life and culture, Epstein maintained, was a "shame" [*herpa*]. He urged
the Zionist leaders to change their policies toward Arabs and to take measures
"that no Jew" had thus far undertaken to learn and teach the Arabic language and
culture. Epstein was not alone in voicing such criticism, yet his was the fiercest
of his day. Consequently, he was widely attacked for "encouraging assimilation
between Jews and Arabs" as well as "weakening the national Jewish standing." In
1919, after tensions between Jews and Arabs had worsened, Epstein published his
essay in a longer format, this time with a new title: "The Question of all Questions:
Concerning the Settling of the Land." This time the essay was published in the
Land of Israel (then Palestine) itself. By this time, attitudes had changed somewhat, and Epstein's ideas were better received than in 1907. Yet during this entire
period, the debate over this crucial Arab Question was situated exclusively within
European Zionist circles — first in Odessa and then in Palestine.

Ben-Kiki's intervention, in response, emphasized that something crucial was missing altogether from Epstein's analysis. Ben-Kiki was in agreement with Epstein's diagnosis and proposed policies that urged Arab and Jewish "integration." Ben-Kiki also warned the new Zionist migrants that their harsh treatment of the Palestinian peasantry was inflaming the situation. Yet Ben-Kiki's response to Epstein's essay was chiefly triggered by the fact that Epstein had utterly ignored the presence of a large Middle Eastern Jewish population — in Palestine and elsewhere in the Middle East — that was already culturally integrated with the Arabs and knew them and their culture. Ben-Kiki found Epstein's thinking lacking, since it betrayed insufficient understanding of the deeper problematic that governed the Zionist attitude toward Arabs. Ben-Kiki felt that what lay at the core of this attitude was outright hubris — arrogance (*yehirut*) — toward everything, and everyone, non-European.

The Arab Question — with which the youngsters born in this Land [the Sephardim of Palestine] have been familiar for many years, and because of which they were subject to disgrace and ridicule by the prominent men within the Yishuv — has now settled in the minds of the higher echelons of the Yishuv's leaders, who see it as most crucial. More are now of the opinion that the deliverance of the Yishuv is entirely dependent on the solution to this Question.

Before the War [the Great War, World War I], the Nationalists [Zionists] viewed our Land as destroyed and deserted, awaiting our industrious hands. They believed that the Land's inhabitants, whether they wanted to or not, would have to accept us. The desolate Land must be built on. Humanism itself demands it! And we, only we — can carry out this task, and only we have the right to do so. No maligning or criticism could override this historical human claim. It did not occur to the leaders of the [Zionist] movement to consider the possibility that such criticisms could become so strong as to acquire a national value potent enough to impress the nations of the world [that is, could become the basis for a national Palestinian movement].

True, before the Great War it was impossible to imagine that the Question would develop into such a complicated matter. But still, the [Jewish] natives of this Land [the Sephardim] felt that matters were not being well organized and that all the noise — accompanied with that ringing arrogant tone that came at us from outside — was inappropriate for both the time and the place. The [older] Sephardic Yishuv, a community that came from the lands of the East to an Eastern country — whose soul was forged and formed along several generations with the Arab peoples—sensed that something unpleasant was taking place here, and that all this movement [activity] was not carried out decently. But the admonitions, criticisms, and warnings [of Palestine's Sephardim] were considered meaningless. They stirred only ridicule and gave rise to accusations of assimilation. The new [European] settlers say that any Jew who speaks the language of his native country is assimilating.

The leaders now see that the seed of evil that they have planted is beginning to produce fruit and thus see their mistakes. Mr. Itzhac Epstein thoroughly discusses this issue in *Do'ar Hayom* and describes and accentuates the danger to our hopes in this Land. Epstein arrives at the same conclusions that were published in the journal *Ha-Herut* well before the War.[9] He demands the establishment of an Arabic newspaper, the publishing of pamphlets in Arabic, the organization of concerts in Hebrew and Arabic, and the provision of moral and material support to the Arabs.

Although Epstein, the esteemed author, endeavors to encompass all aspects of the Question, we are still of the opinion that the main issue at stake remains unaddressed by him and is absent altogether from his writing. Epstein accuses the Yishuv of being negligent and for not initiating any action concerning the Arab Question. From his tone it seems that the [Zionist] settlers did all of this intentionally and maliciously—as if they were fully aware of all the bitter consequences—yet deliberately and wickedly ignored them. Yet neither we—nor, for that matter, Mr. Epstein himself—really consider such a claim to be true. We thus come to pose a most fundamental question: why did the leaders of the Yishuv ignore this crucial [Arab] Question—a Question that today is seen as the single most dangerous one to all of our past, and future, work? Epstein did not touch on this at all. It is thus clear to us that the various elements in his essay do not fit together very well. We find his description of the danger powerful and riveting; his charge about our negligence does touch our heart. But we do not see that the remedies Epstein offers—at this point in our movement—are useful and practical, so that we can say with certainty that they will deliver us. From reading between Epstein's lines, we suspect that even the author himself is not certain about his own words and has doubts about the success of our project. But this is our duty and we cannot just rid ourselves of it.

9. [Among others, Ben-Kiki is referring to Nissim Malul's proposals—one of which is included in this book.]

What, then, is the reason that we thus far have not been able to understand the way our neighbors think and talk? This lack of understanding was intentional. Our expert diplomats—who flooded the world with their journals, speeches, interviews, and books, trying to show how just our cause is—were certainly not incapable of doing the same thing here [in Palestine], had they only found it necessary. But they deliberately ignored the necessity [to explain their cause to the Arab people of Palestine].

To begin with, they thought that the Arabs—who until recently were not the Land's de facto rulers—were not important enough to be considered. Second—and this is the crucial part—they thought that taking the inhabitants into account was not something that should be prioritized among the national and educational principles that the new literature [new Jewish thought] and Zionism—with all its strands and concepts—sought to achieve. The failure lies in the fact that the settlers did not bring the Jew, as he is, to reside in the country, but placed him within the purgatory of exile and redemption and stuffed him with spiritual phrases about Judaism and its lofty and exalted ideals. These foggy ideals—that other people develop over generations—are the burden that the new settler has to bear. When we [the Zionists] come here we do not want just to live in the country, cultivate its land, and be present in it. No, we want to carry out an entire national program so that all the Jews and all the nations of the world can see the new well-rounded Jew, who is complete in body and spirit and whose soul is not torn [. . .].

And what about the poor Arab who does not have all these nationalist ideologies? Who is he to place obstacles on the road to carrying out this program? When the new [European-Zionist] settler comes to the Land, he does not come to accommodate and adjust. The precise opposite is the case: he comes to make others adapt to him. He does not come to learn, but to teach. Our tragedy is that the guides of the Yishuv conceived of all aspects of the life of a free nation in its homeland and tried to implement them all at once in a single blow. They did not follow the path of historical development and move forward gradually—from the easy task to the harder one, from the simple to the complicated. All this new organization of life, which goes forth from the new literature [Jewish thought], is a complete contradiction to Epstein's call for "descending to the culture of the natives of the Land." Epstein complains bitterly that we did not do anything in terms of utilizing popular diplomacy. With great agony he calls this behavior "social-political stupidity." But truly, no one is to blame for this—not politicos and not the committees. The problem is hidden within the foundation of the national movement itself. Paying attention to the mind of the Land's native residents and taking it into account is something that no one can imagine because it runs against the very basic general law of the national movement that considers such acts as assimilation.

Epstein is furious that "our diplomatic work is rotten" . . .[10] Yet the actual fact is that our culture is rotten! The root of evil in our work that produced the rupture with the Arabs is that we deserted our Oriental [Mizrahi] culture, whose basis is Arab culture, and brought in Western culture in its place. This new culture is completely opposed to the culture and mind of the people of this country—it turns us into a foreign, alien element that threatens to destroy the foundations of their [Arab] culture. It is that which makes them angry. All the other complaints about occupation and [the threat of future Jewish] domination are nothing but "politics," they are at best secondary. The principal condition for being good neighbors, as well as for mutual [Arab-Jewish] trust, before we come to propose to the Arab people what Epstein wants to offer to them (etc.), is one: return to our Oriental culture! [. . .]

In everything we do, we must think of building the country—creating a national Jewish home in this Land. We must neither think how this home should be, nor think who should dwell in it, whether these people or others. We need to do all that is easy and [all] that will hasten the building of the country. We thus need to stir up a "pioneer movement" from the lands of the East—Turkey, the Balkans, Morocco, Tunisia, Algeria, and elsewhere.[11] This Jewry is ready to respond to the first call to come to the Land, and there is no limit to the benefit that it would bring to it. The settling of such Jews costs considerably less money and would also cause a lot less noise. As many as these pioneers are, the Land's native residents will be immensely happy when they come. The Sephardim were the pioneers of the Old Yishuv, without which no one would have even imagined setting foot in the Land; they should likewise be the pioneers of the New Yishuv. We must help the Sephardi person to come, provide him with comfort-

10. [Epstein complained about the lack of outreach toward the Arabs of Palestine via what he called "popular diplomacy."]

11. A note by *Do'ar Hayom*'s Editors: the proposal of the esteemed author [Ben-Kiki] is very true. Yet he does not know that the main opposition to such a movement [of Eastern Jews to Palestine] came from Mr. [Menachem] Ussishkin [1863–1941]—Head of the [Zionist] Council of Delegates—who is vehemently opposed to the idea that such Jews will come to the land; Ussishkin said so explicitly and unequivocally to one of our Editors.

able loans, and leave him by himself. He will enter the Land on his own without any supervision or care, and his presence alone will bring peace between the Hebrew Yishuv and the inhabitants. [The Sephardic person] will know how to pave the road that Mr. Epstein says is "long and hard" and even impossible; to him [the Sephardic person] it will be easy.

One of the measures that would also pave the road to fulfill Epstein's proposals is to make room in the leadership for important elements from among the children of this Land.[12] Not as clerks and panderers but as leaders and supervisors of departments dealing with settlement, or departments in charge of general projects that have public value or require direct contact with the Land's inhabitants in such domains as buying land, organization of *aliya*, etc. These leaders will be responsible for their actions in front of both the Yishuv's highest leadership and the public. Such forces exist in the country, and once we decide we need them, we will find them.

This road forward is easy and comfortable simply because it is natural. It fits the culture of the Land, and with simple, peaceful, and calm work our Yishuv shall grow and prosper and we will acquire a "national home" in the Land, walking a road that is free from any sense of enslavement—not of ourselves and not of others. This natural road is humanist and is nationalist without any artificial intention or program. It likewise does not require any "patience" [with Arabs] because our actions will not look as if they are designed to change the conditions, norms, and customs [of the people]. The great code for our work should not be "descending to the culture of the Land" but instead working with it.

Further Readings

Campos, Michelle U. *Ottoman Brothers: Muslims, Christians, and Jews in Early Twentieth-Century Palestine*. Stanford: Stanford University Press, 2011.

Epstein, Yitzhak. "A Hidden Question" (1907). In *Prophets Outcast: A Century of Dissident Jewish Writing about Zionism and Israel*, edited by Adam Shatz, 35–52. New York: Nation, 2004.

12. [It is not inconceivable that Ben-Kiki's language here is deliberately vague, as there were after all serious limitations to the tolerance of his otherwise liberal European-Zionist editors. It is thus unclear—perhaps particularly during this even pre-Brit Shalom period—whether Ben-Kiki is referring here to Palestine's native Sephardim, non-Jewish Arabs, or both groups. For details about who advocated for institutional cooperation between Jews and Arabs in Palestine, see also in this context the selection in this book by David Avisar, who wrote precisely a decade after Ben-Kiki.]

Gorni, Yosef. *Zionism and the Arabs, 1882–1948: A Study of Ideology*, 61–63. Oxford: Clarendon Press of Oxford University Press, 1987.

Jacobson, Abigail, "Sephardim, Ashkenazim, and the Palestine 'Arab Question' in Pre–First World War Palestine: A Reading of Three Zionist Newspapers." *Middle Eastern Studies* 39, no. 2 (2003): 105–30.

Menahem Salih Daniel

Menahem Daniel (1846–1940) was one of the most prominent leaders of the Jewish community in Baghdad. He served in the Ottoman Parliament and was in the Iraqi Senate from 1925 to 1940. In the first half of the twentieth century, he was one of the highest-ranking Jewish politicians in the Arab Middle East. His son, Ezra Daniel (1874–1952), succeeded his father as a member of the Iraqi Senate.

Menahem Salih Daniel to Chayyim Weizmann, September 8, 1922,
English Central Zionist Archives, Jerusalem, Z 4/2101.

The following letter is part of Menahem Daniel's correspondence with Zionist leader Dr. Chaim Weizmann.

The Secretary
Zionist Organisation
London
Baghdad, 8th September 1922

Dear Sir,

I have the pleasure to acknowledge receipt of your letter of the 20th July 1922. It is needless to say that I greatly appreciate and admire your noble ideal, and would have been glad to be able to contribute towards its realization.

But in this country [Iraq] the Zionist Movement is not an entirely idealistic subject. To the Jews, perhaps to a greater extent than to other elements, it represents a problem the various aspects of which need to be very carefully considered. Very peculiar considerations, with which none of the European Jewish Communities are confronted, force themselves upon us in this connection.

You are doubtless aware that, in all Arab countries, the Zionist Movement is regarded as a serious threat to Arab national life. If no active resistance has hitherto been opposed to it, it is nonetheless the feeling of every Arab that it is a violation of his legitimate rights, which it is his duty to denounce and fight to the best of his ability. Mesopotamia has ever been, and is now still more, an active centre of Arab culture and activity, and the public mind here is thoroughly stirred up as regards Palestine by an active propaganda. At present the feeling of hostility towards the Palestinian policy is the more strong as it is in some sort associated in the mind of the Arab with his internal difficulties in the political field, where his position is more or less critical. To him any sympathy with the Zionist Movement is nothing short of a betrayal of the Arab cause.

On the other hand the Jews in this country hold indeed a conspicuous position. They form one third of the population of the Capital, hold the larger part of the commerce of the country and offer [have] a higher standard of literacy than the Moslems. In Baghdad the situation of the Jew is nearly an outstanding feature of the town, and though he has not yet learnt to take full advantage of his position, he is nevertheless being regarded by the waking up Moslem as a very lucky person, from whom the country should expect full return for its lavish favours. He is moreover beginning to give the Moslem an unpleasant experience of a successful competition in Government functions, which having regard to the large number of unemployed former officials, may well risk to embitter feeling against him.

In this delicate situation the Jew cannot maintain himself unless he gives proof of an unimpeachable loyalty to his country, and avoid with care any action which may be misconstrued. This country is now trying to build up a future of its own, in which the Jew is expected to play a prominent part. The task will be of extreme difficulty and will need a strained effort on the part of every inhabitant. Any failing on the part of the Jew will be most detrimental to his future.

On the other hand, the large majority of the Jews are unable to understand that all they can reasonably do for Zionism is to offer it a discrete financial help. We have had, since Dr. Bension's arrival to this country,[1] a sad experience of the regrettable effects which an influx of Zionist ideas here may have. There was for some time a wild outburst of popular feelings towards Zionism, which expressed itself by noisy manifestations of sympathy crowded gatherings and a general and vague impression among the lower class that Zionism was going to end the worries of life, and that no restraint was any longer necessary in the way of expressing opinions or showing scorn to the Arabs. This feeling it is needless to say was altogether unenlightened. It was more Messianic than Zionistic. To an observer it was merely the reaction of a subdued race, which for a moment thought that by magic the tables were turned and that it was to become an overlord. Very few stopped to think whether the Promised Land was already conquered, and if so how long it would take till all the Jews of Mesopotamia repaired to it, and whether any reasonable policy was in the meanwhile desirable. In this state of raving the Jews could not fail to occasion a friction with the Moslem, specially as the latter were then high up in nationalist effervescence, and a feeling of surprise and dissatisfaction ensued, which caused a prominent member of

1. [Ariel Bension was the representative to countries in the Middle East of Keren ha-Yesod (United Israel Appeal—literally, the foundation fund—the central fundraising organization for Israel).]

the Cabinet to remark to me reproachfully that after so many centuries of good understanding the Moslems were not at all suspecting that they had inspired the Jews with so little esteem for them.

During my first interview with Dr. Bension at a time when the internal political situation was particularly critical, I explained to him my anxiety as to the effect of the rather sonorous success of his mission on the political difficulty of the Jews at that juncture and requested him to postpone his mission, if possible till the political outlook should be more reassuring. I am not aware that he actually took any steps in this direction but the enthusiasm of the Jewish population has never abated since then.

In view of the above circumstances I cannot help considering the establishment of a recognised Zionist Bureau in Baghdad as deleteriously affecting the good relations of the Mesopotamian Jew with his fellow citizens. As stated above some misunderstanding has already occurred which if allowed to take root, might well lead to a breach, which will have for the Jews grave consequences. The Jews are already acting with culpable indifference about public and political affairs, and if they espouse so publicly and tactlessly as they have done lately, a cause which is regarded by the Arabs not only as foreign but as actually hostile, I have no doubt that they will succeed in making of themselves a totally alien element in this country and as such they will have great difficulty in defending a position, which, as explained above, is on other grounds already too enviable.

I hope you will fully understand the point of view which I have tried to set forth. I am the first to regret having to take it, because, I repeat, I have, on principle, great sympathy with your aims and warmly appreciate the devotion of your distinguished leaders of the Jewish cause. But you will realise that in practical policy the Jews of Mesopotamia are fatally bound to take for the time being a divergent course, if they are to have a sound understanding of their vital interests. I am not qualified to speak for them. The opinions expressed above are my own personal opinions. The Community is unfortunately too helplessly disorganised to have any co-ordinate opinion, and that is indeed why it is the more exposed.

For Dr. Bension personally I have nothing but high esteem, but I regret that his mission having had the practical consequences described above, I am forced to regard its development here with some misgiving. He is regarded both by Moslems and Jews as representing the Zionist Mission as nobody here, is realizing the distinction between that Mission and the Keren Yesod.

I again express to you my deepest regrets at being unable to respond to your call [to support Zionism], and at the unfortunate difficulty of our position vis-à-vis your Movement.

I am, Dear Sir,

Yours faithfully,

(SGD) [signed] Menaham S. Daniel

Further Readings

Behar, Moshe. "Nationalism at Its Edges: Arabized-Jews and the Unintended Consequences of Arab and Jewish Nationalism, 1917–1967." PhD diss., Columbia University, 2001.

Kazzaz, Nissim. Ha-Yehudim be-'Irak ba-Me'ah ha-'Esrim (The Jews in Iraq during the twentieth century). Jerusalem: Hebrew University Press, 1991.

———. Sofa Shel Gola: ha-Yehudim be-Irak aharei ha-Aliyah ha-Hamonit 1951–2000 (The end of a diaspora: The Jews in Iraq after the mass immigration 1951–2000). Or Yehouda, Israel: Babylonian Jewry Heritage Center, 2002.

Meir-Glitzenstein, Esther. Zionism in an Arab Country: Jews in Iraq in the 1940s. London: Routledge, 2004.

Shiblak, Abbas. The Lure of Zion: The Case of the Iraqi Jews. London: Al Saqi, 1986.

David Avisar

A teacher, educator of teachers, author, playwright, and Sephardi politician, David Avisar (1888–1963) was born in Hebron and grew up in a religious Sephardi environment. He was educated at the yeshiva of the great rabbi and kabbalist Eliyahu Mani (1818–99), who arrived in Hebron from Baghdad in 1856. Avisar also studied with Hizkiyahu Medini (1833–1905), who was Hebron's chief rabbi as well as the author of the *Sede Hemed* Talmudic encyclopedia. Around 1900 Avisar moved to Jerusalem, where he completed his studies at the Ezra Education Seminary. Shortly thereafter he founded the first elementary school for children in the Old City. During World War I, Avisar was exiled to Turkey, yet he managed to smuggle himself back to the Galilee, where he worked teaching the Bible and Hebrew. He was able to return to Jerusalem around the time that the Balfour Declaration was issued, and after the British occupation of Palestine he was able to resume his teaching career.

Avisar was a strong advocate of Sephardi and Mizrahi political activity and involvement, particularly within Socialist Zionist movements and parties, and he tried to form bridges between the labor movement and Sephardi workers. In this regard he was quite different from other Sephardi activists, who were more concerned with Sephardi and Mizrahi elites. Avisar also immersed himself in various Sephardi cultural projects. In 1933 he and other Sephardim founded Halutse Ha-Mizrah (Pioneers of the East), an organization that advocated for Jewish unity, the promotion and support of Sephardi culture, and the integration of Sephardim into institutions of the Zionist movement and the Yishuv. Avisar himself was a member of several Zionist institutions and a delegate to five Zionist congresses. After the founding of Israel, he was appointed head of the Teachers' Union in Jerusalem and wrote numerous essays on education. During this period, he was a member of the ruling Mapai Party. Avisar worked tirelessly to commemorate the Jewish community in Hebron, after its destruction during the riots of 1929, and to collect and preserve Sephardi culture and Mizrahi music. An ardent Zionist, Avisar was nonetheless known for his deep connections with the Arabs of Jerusalem.

20 | A Proposal Concerning the Question of Understanding and Reaching an Agreement with the Arabs of the Land of Israel

David Avisar, "Hatsa'a lishe'elat Havana ve-Heskem 'im 'Arvie E," in Shlomo Alboher, *Identification, Adaptation and Reservation: The Sephardi Jews in Eretz Israel and the Zionist Movement during the "Bayit Leumi" (National Home) 1918–1948* [Hebrew] (Jerusalem: Hasifriya Haziyonit, 2002), appendix 5.

In October 1930, a year after the deadly clashes in Jerusalem and the killings in Hebron, Avisar published this document as a pamphlet in Jerusalem. He hoped it would serve as the foundation for comprehensive political, institutional, cultural, and linguistic Arab-Jewish cooperation in creating a modern state in Eretz Yisrael and Palestine.

For days and years we have been talking—in [Zionist] Congress meetings and in various other assembly meetings—about the need, the desire, and the possibility of reaching an understanding and agreement with the Arabs of the Land of Israel concerning the building of our national home. Leaders and politicians, together with trade unions and political parties, periodically declare this ambition. Yet to date not a single person or group has offered a comprehensive proposal, constitution, or practical program for either studying the question or negotiating its resolution.

In times of anger this question becomes more acute. All sorts of declarations and partial propositions are thrown into the air and do more harm than good. A comprehensive proposal that takes into account the present and future is yet to be delivered. As a result, the trust between us [the Jews] and the Arabs has been weakened. No one believes or pays attention to our declarations. Fears are increasing, resistance is rising, and we are always standing in front of a blocked wall and confronting the danger to our existence.

I therefore think that only a clear, complete, and comprehensive proposal and a wide-ranging political program can provide a basis for discussion between us and the Arabs. It is better for the Oriental to hear the whole truth, even if it is cruel and harsh, than to continue wondering what the intentions of his rival are.

I shall try, herein, to deliver my proposal as points for discussion:

1. The Foundation—the Land of Israel, on both sides of the Jordan River, from Litani and the Hermon to the Red Sea bays, is the motherland of the people of Israel, who currently comprise more than three million households outside the Land and a million people who live in it.

2. The Purpose—the purpose of the people of Israel is to build the Land of Israel, to prepare it and turn it into a safe haven for any Jew who wants to come and settle in it to live a life of independence, freedom, development, and safety. We also want to turn the Land into a center for the rest of the people of Israel, who remain in the Diaspora. The purpose of the Arabs in the Land of Israel is to build the Land and to live a life of development, safety, freedom, and independence.

3. The Agreement—three million Jewish households scattered around the world and the million residents of the Land come to an agreement by forming a constitution—say for a hundred years—that will protect and help to fulfill the goals of the people of Israel and the Arabs of the Land of Israel.

4. The Budget—for the sake of building the Land and for the development of its residents, and for preparing it to always be able to absorb Jewish immigrants, a large budget is required. Three-quarters of this budget shall be paid by the Jewish people, and one-quarter shall be paid by the [non-Jewish] residents of the country as taxes (as the situation is now).

5. The Government—the national and municipal governments, the Parliament, and the city councils, will be made up of 50 percent Jews and 50 percent Arabs. Positions shall be divided according to their ranks and income.

[...]

8. The Language—the two official languages, Hebrew and Arabic, shall be equally displayed in all official documents. They should appear on each document interchangeably: Hebrew-Arabic and Arabic-Hebrew. All residents are obliged to learn both languages. All decrees and documents, notices and signs shall appear in both languages. All members of the military, police, and bureaucracy must have a good command of both languages. The government is obliged to provide language courses for officials. Every official shall be given five years before taking a mandatory exam testing his linguistic proficiency.

[...]

It would not be an exaggeration if I were to say that one of the reasons behind the wild outbreaks [of Arab violence] is the insult that we did not take them [the

Arabs] into account and that we did not negotiate with them when we started building the country after the Balfour Declaration.

Therefore, we must turn to the East and commence with decisive propaganda:

1. First we must convince the Arabs to *strongly believe* in the return of the people of Israel to their Land. It will happen! And there is no force in the world that can resist this, just as there was power in the world that was able to annihilate the people of Israel and end their existence. This is a divine decree to which all should submit.

2. It is our duty to teach them *the history* of the people of Israel and the history of this Land. It is known we ruled this Land and lived here a life of freedom and dignity for 1,500 years from the time of the conquest of Joshua until the destruction of the Second Temple. Until the Arab conquest we were the majority in the land and an important economic power, and the connection between the people of Israel and the Land of Israel never ceased to exist. In every generation there were Messianic movements, and the best of the nation came to the Land to live and to die in it. We come here today with fresh and new creative forces.

3. During this long period, we received *five to six declarations* from the gentiles. The declaration of King Cyrus of Persia; the declaration of Lulianus Caesar of Rome; the declaration of Salah al-Din al-Ayubbi, king of Egypt; the declaration of Don Joseph Nasi with the agreement of the Ottoman Sultan Selim I; the Napoleon Declaration; and the Balfour Declaration. All responded to the providential decree, and the League of Nations, which consists of more than fifty-two nations, gave its blessing for the return of the people of Israel to their homeland. [. . .]

4. While here and abroad and up to this day, we have created *high culture*: prophecy, supreme ethics, a law of justice, social views, relations with nations and kingdoms, diverse literature, etc., whose fruits many nations enjoy. The other nations who came to the Land after us did not create anything, and even the 1,300 years of rule of the Arabic language does not show any creation to be proud of.

5. *Hebrew demographics* as well as censuses taken during the Roman period show that during the time of the Second Temple, the land had more than six or seven million Jews, living mostly as farmers. The whole country was tilled, planted, and fruitful. The wine presses and the wineries, which are quarried in stone, bear witness to this. The pits and pools, the bushes and caves on every

hill and valley, the terraces of mountains and lone wood trees testify as 1,000 witnesses to the vigorous work of the Jews and the capacity of the Land to absorb people.

6. Today there are fewer than two million people living in poor conditions and in poverty on both sides of the Jordan River. The country is ruined, desolate, and must be rebuilt, and only a people whose belief and existence are connected to this wilderness can and have the skills to restore it to its previous days of glory. The return of the people of Israel to their Land is what *saved and will save* it and its inhabitants from further destruction by *foreign nations* who want nothing but to exploit it. Without the Jewish success in securing the Balfour Declaration, etc., other people would have entered the Land, causing further destruction. The local residents of this country would have continued to live as serfs and slaves to strangers. Our small amount of work so far has already revived the spirit of the Arab nation and improved its life a great deal.

7. The Land of Israel is very poor today. Its imports exceed its exports by five to six million Mandatory pounds a year, and there is an urgent and pressing need to develop its production, both agricultural and urban—otherwise it will forever be bound to others.

8. We need huge investments, gifted people, experience, and science in order to increase production. Above all, we need faith in our success. And which nation has all of this but the nation of Israel, who longed for this Land throughout history and will do everything for all who settle in it and inhabit it.

9. *The Arab nation* will eventually understand that the *Hebrew nation* is the one returning to its land. It is returning to its brethren who share its race, language, history, faith, and hope. It is returning to the residents of the Land of Israel who have Jewish blood in their veins, not by might or by power, but by spirit, the spirit of Hebrew ethics, to create a kingdom of justice and peace that will be an example for all the nations.

Further Readings

Alboher, Shlomo. *Identification, Adaptation and Reservation: The Sephardi Jews in Ertetz Israel and the Zionist Movement during the "Bayit Leumi" (National Home) 1918–1948* [Hebrew]. Jerusalem: Hasifriya Haziyonit, 2002.

Avisar, David. "Eastern Jews in the Zionist Congress" [Hebrew], *Davar*, November 3, 1935.

———. "Sephardic Jews and the 19th Zionist Congress" [Hebrew]. *Ha'aretz*, June 16, 1935.

Patai, Raphael. *Journeyman in Jerusalem: Memories and Letters, 1933–1947.* Lanham, MD: Lexington, 2000.

Elie (Eliyahu) Eliachar

Born to a distinguished Jerusalem Sephardic family of rabbis, leaders, and entrepreneurs, Elie Eliachar (1899–1981) had a long career as a Sephardic leader, politician, businessman, and writer. He was a member of the first and second Knesset, initially representing the Sephardim and the Edot Ha-Mizrah Party and later the liberal Tsiyonim Klaliyim Party. With David Sitton (whose work appears below), he was one the founders of the World Sephardic Federation and served as head of the Sephardic community in Jerusalem for many years, before and after the founding of the State of Israel.

Eliachar was educated in the Lemel Elementary School in Jerusalem and then in the Alliance School. In 1913 he went to the University of Beirut to study medicine, but he returned to Palestine before completing his studies during World War I. He worked in several hospitals and served as a medical officer in the Ottoman Army. Following the war, Eliachar returned to Beirut, where he studied until 1921. Shortly thereafter he moved to Cairo, where he studied law for a year before returning to Jerusalem in 1922. He completed his legal studies between 1932 and 1935 in Jerusalem. From 1922 to 1935, Eliachar served in the Mandatory government and was the editor of its *Commercial Bulletin*. He was elected head of the Sephardic community in Jerusalem in 1942, and in the same year he founded its journal, *Hed Ha-Mizrah* (Eastern echo), which collected a great deal of ethnographic and historical material from Sephardic and Mizrahi sources. He also wrote for *Do'ar Hayom*, the *Palestine Weekly*, and other Hebrew newspapers. Eliachar's extensive papers, containing numerous historical documents on Sephardic and Mizrahi life, are now housed in the Israeli National Library in Jerusalem. In 1967 Eliachar wrote the powerful *Hovah 'alenu Limno'a Giz'anut Yehudit Bi-Medinat Ha-Yehudim* (We must prevent Jewish racism in the state of the Jews). He is noted especially for two pioneering books: *Israeli Jews and Palestinian Arabs* (published first in Hebrew as *Living with Palestinians*) and *Living with Jews* (published in Hebrew in 1970).

21 | A Jew of Palestine before the Royal Commission

Excerpt from Elie Eliachar, *A Jew of Palestine before the Royal Commission* (Jerusalem, 1936).

> Eliachar appeared before the Palestine Royal Commission (known as the Peel Commission), which visited Palestine in 1936 in the wake of the outbreak of the Arab revolt. The commission is famous for its report, in which it proposed abolishing (eventually) the British Mandate almost entirely and partitioning the land into two states—one Jewish and the other Arab. Soon after his appearance before the commission, Eliachar published his testimony, prepared in writing before he delivered it, as a small booklet.

I am Jew born in Palestine. My family has resided in the Holy Land for Centuries without interruption and there are few even among the present leaders of the Arab movement who can boast as long and direct a connection with this country. Were I to appear before the Royal Commission my evidence would therefore be concentrated [focused] not with theory but with facts derived from personal knowledge and the experience of generations.

As one whose Arab friends in Palestine and aboard are numerous, I may say with satisfaction that notwithstanding these trying disturbances Arab-Jewish friendship has in many ways continued unchanged.

If I now take pen in hand and hypothetically put the case before the Royal Commission it is in the hope that both Arabs and Jews may join in an effort to find a solution to the present calamitous conditions, for love of the country so dear to us.

As no cure is possible without careful diagnosis so no solution could be found to our difficulties without a fearless and honest analysis of the situation.

I trust that my Arab friends will not misunderstand or misconstrue my statements of fact. We Jews must also understand that though the truth may be unpleasant to the ear we must face facts boldly if we want to cure our wounds and continue rebuilding Palestine to the advantage of both Jews and Arabs.

Long before the [world] war, Arabs and Jews in Palestine lived and labored under the same oppressive regime. Few Arabs and still fewer Jews enjoyed any measure of prestige and all were ruled, and ruled with a mailed fist, but the Turk.

Those who dared voice independent opinion, to say nothing of national sentiments, were crushed mercilessly.

Foreign intrigues, aiming at the partition of the territories of the "Sick Man of [the] Sublime Porte,"[1] led to a movement of the liberation of Syria and Palestine immediately before the [world] war. This movement, however, had no real national background.

During the war, the Jews of the world, and later [those of] Palestine, assisted the Allied Armies in their relative measures to conquer Palestine and Syria. So did the Arabs of the Hedjas[2] but not of Palestine. It is sufficient to read Lawrence[3] to ascertain the weight in gold of the then "nationalistic" feelings of his Arab followers. No such charge could be leveled against the group of young Jews led by Aaronsohn of Zichron Jacob, who assisted the Intelligence Service of the Allied Armies.[4] During the war I happened to be in Nazareth, closely connected with Hassan Bey, the Arab military "Sir Tabib" (Chief Medical Officer) who conducted the investigations against members of the Aaronsohn Group. Scores of Jews were imprisoned and tortured. Not one of them gave up his secret, and the leaders, men and women, preferred death to the betrayal of their ideal—a liberated Palestine.

The martyrs of the Arab cause, Syrian[s] and Lebanese hanged by Djemal Pasha during the war had their counterpart in the Aaronsohn group of martyrs some of whom died as a result of torture at Zichron Jacob while others were hanged at Damascus.

The Bedouin levies that helped in the conquest of Syria were counterbalanced by the Jewish battalions composed of determined volunteers from abroad and later from Palestine itself.

The entry of the British Armies into the country was hailed with joyous relief by both Arabs and Jews. The suzerainty of the late King Feisal over Damascus

1. [The Ottoman Empire was often called "the sick man of Europe." The Sublime Porte was the name of the Ottoman sultan's court.]

2. [The Hijaz region in Arabia known since 1925 as Saudi Arabia.]

3. [Eliachar refers to Thomas Edward Lawrence (1888–1935), the British officer famous for his involvment in the Arab Revolt against the Ottomans in the Hijaz during World War I.]

4. [Eliachar refers to the Netzah Israel Lo Yeshaker ("The Eternal One of Israel will not lie," Samuel I 15:29), known as "Nili." The organization, led by Aaron Aaronsohn, spied for the British in Palestine during World War I. The organization was mostly based in the early Zionist colony of Zikhron Ya'acov, here referred to as Zichron Jacob, where the Aaronsohn family lived.]

and Syria was greeted everywhere with joy, and there were a tacit if not expressed acceptance by the Arabs of the fact that part of bounty should fall to Jews in the form of the Balfour Declaration.

Unfortunately the field was open for political and religious intrigue. So many interests cross each other in this holy country that peace could not last long. And from intrigue to intrigue, from one misunderstanding to another, we have come to these disastrous days.

What is really the situation? Is there a way out of it?

[...]

THE JEWISH CASE

Are the Jews an Alien race to Palestine as pretended? Is not every corner, every stone in it pregnant with Jewish history whether dating back to the Old or the New Testament? Has there been any period, even the shortest, when Jews did not live somewhere in Palestine and has there ever been any stoppage of Jewish immigration, no matter what the temporal rule of the country may have been at the time? For two thousand years, scattered throughout the world, we have turned our faces towards the East, to Palestine the birthplace of our race.

The Messianic ideal of a return to this country never left us and our history is rich in movements aiming [at] the re-establishment of the Jews in their ancient homeland. The Talmud says that a Jew living outside Eretz Israel is deprived of the Divine Grace.

Our religion is in direct relation with the natural conditions that distinguish Palestine from other countries. Our blessings and curses do not and cannot apply to any other country but Palestine. Our prayers are meaningless if not connected with Palestine. In our prayers we look towards Palestine and in death we are buried with our faces turned towards Palestine.

Over 16,000,000 Jews throughout the world, more than all the Arabs of Palestine, Transjordan, Syria, Iraq, Yemen, Hejaz, Oman, Nejd, Hasa and the rest of the desert, estimated ([by the] *Encyclopedia Britannica*) to total less than 14,000,000, crave for a refuge, a home in Palestine, the cradle of their race, the home of their history, the source of their religion, the centre of their culture, the spring of their prophetic messages which spread the world over.

No Nejdian or Iraqi has yet left his domicile to dwell in and rebuild Palestine at a sacrifice. But millions are the Jews ready to sacrifice all for the sake of their ancient fatherland.

Persecuted and humiliated in a multitude of countries, we have nowhere to turn to but Palestine. After two thousand years of suffering it is only right that a place should be allotted to us in which we can settle in peace. The nations of the world have recognised our right to "reconstitute" our ancient homeland and what the Jews demand is to be allowed to rebuild it without prejudicing in the least the interests of the existing non-Jewish community. Can then a nation that for two thousand years has kept alive such a longing for a particular country—with what they have achieved in that country in a few decades—be treated as alien to that country just because a few hundred thousand people who at present inhabit it declare themselves the owners of that country?

After the war, as Dr. [Chaim] Weizmann has said in a recent address "they with their millions were thrown out of gear, suspended between heaven and earth, the countries of the world have come to be divided into two categories: countries where Jews could not live, and countries where Jews were not permitted to enter."[5]

To enlarge the misery of the Jews in so many countries in the West and East is superfluous. Conditions are well known. Dispossessed two thousand years ago by the strongest empire and dispersed to the four corners of the earths, they have kept alive their aspiration for a return to their Land. Throughout all these years the have never despaired. Three times a day during the principal prayers, and after each meal, Jews pray for the return of [the people of] Israel to the Promised Land. Persecution, inquisition, expulsions, could not deter them from belief and whenever opportunity offered they used temporal means to reestablish themselves in Palestine.

The Jewish historical and moral rights over Palestine are older, much older, than the Balfour Declaration or the Mandate and [even] if the latter fail us our connection with this country shall continue unabated. With the Balfour Declaration Jewish hopes took on new life. Strong with the promises given, and "assisted" by anti-semitism, they have accomplished in no more than two decades what may be looked upon, without false pride, as an astounding achievement in agriculture, industry, commerce, culture, sanitation and social work. Why then have the Jews not won over the goodwill of the Arabs?

5. [Eliachar refers to Chaim Weizmann's speech "Palestine To-Day" (*International Affairs* 15, no.5 [1936]: 671–83).]

Intoxicated by the pledges contained in the Balfour Declaration, and the Mandate, the Jews devoted all their energy to the country, attending with superhuman love and devotion to its material and spiritual needs. Lack of colonisation experience and the fever to turn into reality the pledge given made them ignore all existing difficulties, the particularities of place, the mentalities of inhabitants. Due to their own mentality acquired in totally different environments they failed to understand and win over the indigenous population.

Lacking tradition in statesmanship our leaders failed to gauge at its true value the Arab factor in Palestine and—which is regrettable—to take advice of the pre-war Jewish inhabitants of the country who offered it time and again. There is truth in the oriental saying that "a blind man in his own house enjoys better vision than a newcomer with full sight." The overflow of energy of the younger immigrants, the constant propaganda in the local press, at meetings, or displays, kept the attention of our neighbours focused on our activities. On the other hand the failure to establish, from the start, direct contact with them, mutual interests in education, social work, economic matters etc., estranged us completely from the Arab community.

More than the lack of employment of Arabs by Jews which is a myth, thousands of Arabs are employed in every field of Jewish activity whereas seldom does any Jew find employment with an Arab, the campaign for the *employment of Jews by Jews* was detrimental to our interests.[6] If from a Jewish point of view the picketing of Arab labour may be explained and understandable, it created a wrong impression on the Arab population and was used by their leaders as a successful argument to incite the masses.

Jews all over the world have a mouthpiece, a journal, to speak to their compatriots in their own language, to explain their aims and defend their cause. In Palestine, surrounded by Arabs as we are, we were discouraged at the first failure to keep adequate Arab periodicals, leaving the field open to all our opponents and to their poisonous anti-Zionist and anti-Jewish campaign. To these early hours and moods we owe many blunders.

6. [Eliachar refers to the Zionist "Hebrew Labor" ('Avoda 'Ivrit) campaign of the early Yishuv, which called for hiring Jews only in Jewish workplaces and settlements. One of the outcomes of this campaign was the creation of two separate economies—Arab and Jewish—in Mandatory Palestine.]

True, the task before the Jewish leaders was gigantic and the pressure of persecution in Europe and elsewhere demanded, and continues to demand imperatively, the concentration of all efforts upon the transfer to Palestine of as many Jews as possible in the shortest possible time.

It is also true that the uncompromising attitude of the Arab leaders rendered futile any tentative [attempt] at a rapprochement.

My statement may be unpleasant to the ear of many a Jew. But when I set out to voice my opinion I promised myself to analyse as truly as I could, the entire complex [nature] of the problem. To admit our mistakes with the intention of correcting them is in itself the best excuse and apology, just as a surgical cut is useful though painful.

THE SOLUTION

We Jews are of Eastern origin notwithstanding our prolonged stay in Western countries. Palestine is in the East and our first duty when returning here is to regain the best Eastern attributes, retaining by all means such good traits as we may have acquired in the West.

Both Arabs and Jews are Semites, therefore cousins; our languages are the same stock, so are our religions, and much of our character is the same.

Must we give up all hope of bringing both our communities to an understanding for a harmonious development in the general interest of the country in which we both live?

Mistakes were made by Jews and Arabs alike and they must be corrected!

Jews have vehemently decried the accusation that they aim at ousting the Arabs from Palestine or dominating them in the future. They have declared that Palestine is and shall remain a common fatherland for both communities. Even Jabotinsky, the Zionist Revisionist leader whom the Arabs have learned to quote profusely, said to the Shaw Commission that "there is not one Zionist who really dreams of ousting the existing rural population."[7]

On the other hand Arab domination over Palestine is impossible, first because Great Britain has vital interests here: her Imperial routes are at stake; second, because if Great Britain retires some other colonising State would step in; third, because the Jews of the world also have a say in the matter. A community

7. [In 1930 the Commission on the Palestine Disturbances of August 1929, chaired by Sir Walter Shaw, investigated the outbreak of violence in 1929.]

400,000 strong (about 30 percent of the population) with age-long connection with Palestine and supported by international pledges, economically stronger than the Arab majority, cannot be turned into a subject minority at the mercy of a hostile majority.

Let all concerned be reasonable and accept the invitation to sit round a table under British guidance and discuss ways and means for the welfare of our common fatherland. Palestine would not be alone to benefit from an understanding between Arabs and Jews; it seems to me that all the neighbouring countries would benefit as well.

ARAB-JEWISH COOPERATION

The Arab world is awakening after centuries of oppression. Under British guidance and with Jewish cooperation adjoining Arab countries could grow and develop and eventually unite in a Federation under the aegis of Great Britain. Palestine—and the Jewish National Home—should figure in such a Federation.

It may be retorted that this is a farfetched probability. Take a longer view of prevailing conditions in neighbouring countries and throughout the world to-day and it will be realised that not only is this possible but that it should be the earnest concern of Great Britain, the leaders of the younger Arab States and the Jews, to foster [it].

Jewish hopes, as at present expressed, rise or fall with British support or failure. A Jewish Nation owing gratitude to Great Britain and friendly to the Arab world is a negligible pawn in any game.

For Great Britain, Jewish gratitude and a friendly Arab-Jewish Federation under her control could help a lot in her Imperial Policy.

A strong British Empire is the only security for the existence of self governing Arab countries, whether it be Egypt or Iraq.

No other interests could be so well intermingled and all that [we] require to bring happiness to all concerned is moderation and goodwill in every camp.

How can this be achieved?

SOME SUGGESTIONS

1. The Arabs of Palestine should recognize the Mandate and its implications for the establishment of a Jewish National Home in Palestine.

2. With the consent of Great Britain, the Arabs and the Jews, an agreement should be concluded declaring the absolute equality of both Arabs and Jews in

Palestine at present and in the future notwithstanding the numerical importance of either community at any time. Such agreement is to be duly endorsed by the League of Nations and the United States of America and incorporated in the Mandate.

3. In view of the agreements that have been concluded between certain Arab countries under British influence, it should be the policy of the Palestine Government to enter into similar agreements with the adjoining Arab countries, whereby, customs and other barriers should be dropped gradually in order to strengthen economic and friendly relations between them. In all such agreements between Palestine and adjoining Arab countries, the status of the Jewish National Home and the equality of the Arab and the Jewish communities should be emphasised. This may serve as an additional guarantee by self-governing Arab countries to Arabs and to Jews alike, and also as a forerunner of the Federation of Arab States and Palestine under the aegis of Great Britain.

With the settlement of the international political aspect of the Palestine problem both communities should turn their attention to the joint development of their common country.

4. A Legislative Council with an equal number of Arab and Jewish members [who] appointed or elected and a number of officials nominated by Government should be constituted.

The president of the Legislative Council should be appointed by the [British] High Commissioner.

Resolutions to be passed by majority of votes.

In the event of an equality of votes a casting [determining] vote should be exercised [cast] by the senior official member.

To secure the fulfillment of the international obligations of the Mandatory, [and] to maintain law, order and good government, the High Commissioner should retain for a number of years of the prerogative of veto over all matters passed by the Legislative Council. All decisions of the Council should require the approval of the High Commissioner before being enforced.

The determination of the labour immigration schedules[8] would depend solely on the economic absorptive capacity of the country, due consideration and encouragement being given to the creative effort of the Jewish immigrants and Jewish capital.

8. [Eliachar refers to the quotas imposed on Jewish immigration to Palestine during the 1930s.]

The High Commissioner would retain the power to agree to or dissent from the findings of the Council, and to allot such immigration schedule as in his opinion would be adequate for any given period.

5. There should be no restriction on the sale of land in urban areas throughout Palestine. The sale of agricultural land should be regulated to safeguard the interest of the Arab agricultural community and to protect their tenant-cultivators. [It should be p]rovided that no restrictions should be imposed where a landlord and/or his tenants consent to move elsewhere in Palestine or Transjordan, on the basis of an exchange of land within limits to be foreseen by law for their upkeep.

6. In agriculture and in industry, both Jews and Arabs should cooperate to complement each other's requirements to their mutual advantage. For example, the Jewish industry for extracting vegetable oils should encourage and assist the Arab and Jewish cultivators to produce the seeds required instead of importing them. The Jewish silk weaving industry should foster the planting of mulberry trees and the rearing of silk worms in those Arab villages which at present take [only] an amateurish interest in the industry.

7. Jews are coming to Palestine to build their National Home. It is only right that their energies and efforts should be devoted to reach this goal. For two thousand years they have been ousted from agriculture and their greatest effort is now concentrated to reestablish contact with the soil of their homeland. Only by the creation of new undertakings can they increase the country's absorptive capacity for additional immigrants. This is our excuse for employing as many Jews as possible. Otherwise the Jewish effort shall be futile and would only help to increase the number of "illegal immigrants" from adjoining countries. Thousands of Syrians, Hauranis, Beduins, Egyptians and others have entered Palestine during recent years. Neither the Mandatory [government] nor the Jews are bound by any pledge to promote this immigration. The indulgent attitude of the authorities to such "immigration" is contrary to all provisions of the Mandate.

On the understanding that Arabs and Jews agree that the labour market shall be open only to local Arabs and to Jews, a percentage of labour of each other's communities should be employed in all new undertakings, whether in agriculture, commerce or industry. The estates of the Jewish National Funds,[9] the basis of Jewish agriculture, should be excluded from such an agreement.

9. [The Jewish National Fund (Keren Kayemet Le-Yisrael, founded in 1901) was, and still is, in charge of buying and developing land in Palestine/Israel.]

8. All new public limited liability companies should offer a percentage of their capital share issue to members of both communities in Palestine which [issue] if not raised by one, may be completed by the other community, after the lapse of the prescribed period.

9. All new public cooperative societies (such as saving societies, transport etc.) should reserve a certain percentage of their membership to members of the other community which if not filled during the prescribed period may be completed by members of the founders' community.

10. Arab and Jewish education must forcibly continue independently until their requirements are adjusted. But Arabic should be a compulsory subject in all Jewish schools, and Hebrew in all Arab schools. Admission of Arab students to Jewish schools and vice versa should be encouraged in order that eventually one official system of education might suffice for both communities.

Let the Jews publish periodicals in Arabic and the Arabs issue Hebrew journals to exchange views, to get to know each other better, and let Government severely censor the entire press of the Holy Land. Freedom of speech and expression should always be a sacred thing but freedom of the individual should stop when it endangers the freedom of his neighbour. Constructive criticism is a blessing but poisonous attacks on religious or racial grounds should be discouraged mercilessly, if Palestine is to have rest and peace.

11. The knowledge of Arabic and Hebrew should gradually be made compulsory in the Public Service and new applicants to the Service should be required to know both languages. Members of both communities to share equally in the Service.

12. With the consent of the Governments concerned a number of Jewish immigrants should be encouraged to enter the adjoining Arab Countries annually. These immigrants being chosen from the liberal professions, manufacturers, investors and skilled labourers may be of considerable assistance in the development of the countries adopting them.

13. Palestine and Transjordan should be united in the interests of Arabs and Jews alike. This union may be the forerunner of an Arab-Jewish Federation.

CONCLUSION

The attitude at present adopted by the Arab leaders is unflinching and irreconcilable [with Jewish attitudes]. But I do not lose faith in an alternative understanding once it becomes clear to them [the Arab leaders] that it is impossible to brush away the Jews and their claim over Palestine.

In mutual understanding between Arabs and Jews, with the good will of great Britain, lies the solution for all the difficulties of this beloved country of ours. Murder, arson and terror cannot frighten even the British Empire with all their interests in the Holy Land, nor can they move the Jews empirically experienced in every kind of difficulty.

The Arabs are and will remain in Palestine.

Jews are returning to Palestine on the strength of sacred international pledges upon which they have staked all their future and they [the pledges] will not prejudice the Arabs [against the Jews]. For either community to persist in looking upon the other as enemy to be eliminated or muzzled would only mean continuous warfare with consequent disaster.

On the other hand, by mutual concessions, Palestine may progress towards cultural and economic leadership in the Near East. It may form the nucleus around which the union of all Arab states under the guidance of GB [Great Britain] could develop.

The safety of the interests of the British Empire may thus be assured for many generations to come and a great and powerful British Empire is the best safeguard for extended Peace.

Elie Eliachar, "Yehudim ve-'Aravim," *Ha-Mizrah*, September 11, 1942.

Eliachar was known for his critique of Zionist attitudes toward Arabs and Sephardim. In this article, he discusses the question of Jewish-Arab relations in Palestine and the newly formed organization called the Union (Ha-Ichud), led by Dr. Yehudah (Judah) Leon Magnes (1877–1948), founder of Hebrew University in Jerusalem. Magnes and his associates in the Union called for the establishment of a binational state in Mandatory Palestine founded on strict Arab-Jewish parity. Magnes was also a member of Brit Shalom Society. This society has entered history as a noble attempt by several enlightened (mostly German) Jews, including Martin Buber (1878–1965) and Ernst Akiva Simon (1899–1988), to reach a compromise with the Arabs over Palestine. In contemporary memory and historiography, the attempt is commonly invoked as the only serious effort from within Zionism to reach a compromise with the Arabs. In this essay, Eliachar reminds his readers that the Sephardic perspective, similar to that of Brit Shalom and the Ha-Ichud, had been expressed—but ignored by European Jewish intellectuals—for decades.

There has been unrest in the Yishuv in recent days in the wake of the public appearance of a new political body—the Union [Ha-Ichud]—established by Dr. Magnes and others who share his views. The Union's platform is promising in that it is linked to the Zionist movement while also seeking to address the pressing problems that our evolving country faces through unity between the Arab and Jewish peoples. Coupled with the Union's creation, Dr. Magnes's recently published articles in [the Hebrew publication] *Problems of the Day* have awoken the national press. Thus, authors with divergent opinions have once again started to address the question that we call, pointlessly and distastefully, "the Arab problem." One must add that only a few in the Yishuv support the Union, while many more are opposed to it for various reasons.[10]

10. May I note that already in the first issue of *The East*—published on June 10, 1942—I addressed some of these issues. In an article titled "Our Podium" I wrote:

We are standing at the gateway of our newly founded Hebrew homeland that is emerging in our ancient land—the same land for which the right to settle was given to the people of Israel at Mount Sinai. There is enough room for tens of thousands of newcomers

The following words do not aim to discuss the Union and its methods specifically. I would instead like to open a discussion in *The East* [*Ha-Mizrah*] about the larger question we all face. In *The East's* first issue, the editorial board declared that the question of the relationships with our Arab neighbors—both in this country [Palestine] and in neighboring [Arab] countries—is a question that we cannot ignore. I am therefore confident that members of the board will allow the space needed for an open debate on this issue from various perspectives to all of those who wish to express and share their opinions.

It must be stated in the clearest terms possible: our leaders committed an unforgivable sin in the immediate aftermath of the [1917] Balfour Declaration and the British conquest of the Land [of Palestine] when they refused unwisely to come to grasps with reality. When the first [Zionist] Board of Representatives began taking action, it ignored the Arabs who had been living here for centuries; who viewed this place as their home; and who have past, present, and future rights in this land. Our leaders' attitude vis-à-vis this question was blind. Intentionally or not, they also ignored the even more challenging reality—namely,

---

from among the tortured and persecuted in the Diaspora's inferno who are yearning for Zion. We shall cooperate with anyone who helps to increase migration to our Land—for it is the only way to save the torn and tortured Jewry from the hell into which they have sunk. But in order for this task to be accomplished and in order to assist our people to establish themselves in the Land, it is mandatory and necessary for us to learn to adjust to the special conditions typifying this country.

We must not ignore the facts that there are in our country [Arab] neighbors with whom destiny placed us together and that the country is also surrounded by Arab countries. It is consequently unacceptable that we continue to live in this country without increasing economic, cultural, and social interactions with neighboring Arabs. We [in *The East*] are not to be counted among those [Jewish political] circles that have already "discovered" the road to peace and understanding with our neighbors. We admit to not knowing which precise way would lead us to peace and full understanding, nor, for that matter, how to arrive at these ends. We have nevertheless known one thing for a long while—and our [Sephardic] elders never ceased warning the [Euro-Zionist] leaders about it: we must examine the question thoroughly and carefully.

This question must be on the mind of every Jew in our country and in the Diaspora. Because the more we think about this question and try to identify a dignified way to resolve it for both ourselves and our neighbors and the more we study the lives, language, and culture of those living next to, and among us, the closer we will get to achieving our goal. From the podium [of this new publication *The East*] we will explore every seed for Arab-Jewish rapprochement and strive toward any attempt for understanding with our neighbors—an understanding founded on mutual respect.

that the rising Yishuv in Zion must live not only with Palestine's Arabs but also interact with the millions of Arabs in the surrounding, neighboring countries, all by and large united by virtue of culture, economy, language, and religion.

In the past, as today, the leadership of the Yishuv and the Zionist trade union [The Histadrut] neglected to draft a clear outline for political action for itself and for us; a basic, clear plan for immediate action and for determining our policy and relationship with the Arabs in our country and in the neighboring countries. We have linked our entire destiny exclusively with the West—and this is notwithstanding the fact that the Jewish people originate in the East. From the moment we began returning to our land this fact alone should have obliged both our leadership and each and every one of us to reacquire those [Eastern] qualities that reacquaint us with our spiritual backbone and our surroundings generally. From the outset of our project in the Land, we locked ourselves into a parochial working framework embodying unjustified and pointless arrogance.

Intoxicated by the [Balfour] Declaration, we immersed ourselves wholeheart-edly in building our material and spiritual home with love and dedication. But our lack of settling experience—coupled with our enthusiastic ambition to turn a promise into reality—blinded us from seeing all the obstacles, that is, the land's special conditions and the customs and manners of those already living in it. Furthermore, those who recently arrived in the Land brought with them a European lifestyle altogether different from the one prevailing in the Land. It was a fundamental error—indeed an unpardonable one—that we failed from the outset to establish contacts with our neighbors, to get to know them and to form cultural and economic relations with them. This state of affairs has led to the emergence of a deepening and fear-ridden alienation between our neighbors and us.

All of the earlier warnings expressed by the best members of the Land's older [Sephardic] community—those who right from the outset cautioned our lead-ers—were in vain. These warnings, incidentally, did no harm to our fundamen-tal national aspirations; the exclusive purpose of those [Sephardic old-timers] who advised caution was to insist on propriety when forming relations with those [non-Jewish Arabs] who were already living in the Land. The great burden carried by the Zionist leadership inside and outside the Land was known to us. The task of rescuing millions of tortured Jews in Europe provided no rest for our leaders. It is nonetheless hard to comprehend how these leaders failed to grasp the situation and did not search for a more realistic course of action that takes into account the Land's existing reality.

One cannot ignore the fact that the pace of Zionist activity in the last two decades facilitated the development of national feelings among our neighbors, strengthened their insistence on their culture, and facilitated distinct and comprehensive action in the political, public, economic, and spiritual realms. We therefore face the consolidation of an Arab national movement in the Land—a movement forming a parallel force to our own actions. This force—which is seeking help from the surrounding [Arab] nations who enjoy political independence within recognized borders—could not have remained idle and inactive once we appeared in the Land and ignored their [Arabs'] existence and presence there. These are not the only factors inflaming relations between the two peoples. There were, and remain, external forces greatly influencing the current reality in the Land. One must not overlook the poison of Axis agents who persistently poured oil on the fire of hate and separation between Jews and Arabs.

We [the Sephardic Jews associated with *The East*] do not follow the same ways and methods that certain [Jewish political] circles among us have sometimes devised in the past, and are still using today. These are the same circles who rushed to offer solutions to the acute situation we all face with no preparation and without a shred of psychological understanding that can only be acquired via everyday [Arab-Jewish] contact, intimate knowledge, and mutual interests. Those [non-Sephardic Jewish circles] who took it on themselves to offer all sorts of half-baked solutions should believe me when I say that members of the Old [pre-Zionist] Yishuv—whether Ashkenazic or Sephardic—cannot and do not ignore the fact that the problem pertaining to our relations with our neighbors becomes considerably more complicated each day. It is unacceptable that [newly arrived Ashkenazi] people—who have neither adjusted yet to the local environment, nor become familiar with the nature of the question—have nevertheless the audacity to discuss its solution.

From everywhere and every corner, people come to offer unreasonable solutions to the Arab-Jewish question in the same extremist ways in which we [Jews in Palestine] tend now to deal with every question as well as with the same intolerance that has become part of our individual and public character. Such [Jewish] individuals cause irreparable damage to our future in the Land and have only confounded the problem further.

There is, on the one hand, the [members of the] new Union—and similar bodies that preceded it—who stand up and announce concessions that they are prepared to make at our expense before studying the problem and before teaching the Yishuv and the Hebrew masses the essence and nature of the problem. These bodies also declare amendments to our fundamental principles, amendments that empty the living spirit from our very being in the Land. And on the other hand—when we finally see the Left starting to study and explore the question [of Arab-Jewish relationships]—it turns "quixotically" to uproot any possibility of creating a spirit of understanding with the analogous social class among our neighbors, which now constitutes the only social stratum on which we can depend if the aim is the creation of a mode of understanding based on *mutual Arab-Jewish respect*.

It is for these reasons that I am unable to extend help to this new body called the Union. I do not think that before the preparatory groundwork for Arab-Jewish understanding has been completed, and before we do everything we possibly can to create *an atmosphere of understanding and acknowledgment among ourselves and with our neighbors*, one can truly devise solutions while it remains doubtful whether it is possible to find a partner among the Palestinian Arabs who would be willing to sit and talk to us.

It is precisely at this juncture that I wish to urge members of the old Yishuv in the Land—as well as the Jewish communities in the Near East—to cease being self-effacing and indifferent concerning this painful question, that is, the question of cultivating relationships and contacts between us and our [Arab] neighbors. It is incumbent on members of the old Yishuv and the [Jewish] communities in the neighboring countries to take the initiative and prepare the ground for mutual understanding.

I confess that I still do not have a solution to this thorny question. [. . .] All that I therefore ask right now is this: *a more serious approach to studying the problem of getting to know our neighbors—to form with them economic, social, educational, and spiritual bonds*. That is the only way that can one day lead us down the path culminating in an honorable solution—one that will not only be accepted by the Yishuv and the various strata of the Hebrew people, but will also be acceptable to both our Arab neighbors in Palestine and the neighboring countries.

Further Readings

Brit Shalom Society. *The Statutes of Brit Shalom*. Jewish-Arab Affairs. Occasional Papers Published by the "Brit Shalom" Society. June 1931. 1931.

Buber, Martin, and Paul R. Mendes-Flohr. *A Land of Two Peoples: Martin Buber on Jews and Arabs*. New York: Oxford University Press, 1983.

Eliachar, Elie. *Hovah 'alenu Limno'a Giz'anut Yehudit Bi-Medinat Ha-Yehudim* (We must prevent Jewish racism in the state of the Jews). Jerusalem: Va'ad 'edat ha-sefaradim, 1967.

———. *Israeli Jews and Palestinian Arabs: Key to Arab-Jewish Coexistence.* Jerusalem: Council of the Sephardi Community, 1970.

———. *A Jew of Palestine before the Royal Commission.* Jerusalem, 1936.

———. *Living with Jews.* Translated by Peretz Kidron and Marzell Kay. London: Weidenfeld and Nicolson, 1983.

———. *The Sephardim in Israel: Problems and Achievements.* Jerusalem: Council of the Sephardi Community, 1971.

Gillon, Philip, and Elie Eliachar. *Israelis & Palestinians, Co-Existence or . . .: The Credo of Elie Eliachar.* London: Collings, 1978.

Ratsabi, Shalom. *Between Zionism and Judaism: The Radical Circle in Brith Shalom, 1925–1933.* Leiden, Netherlands: Brill, 2002.

Ibrahim al-Kabir

Also known as A. S. Elkabir (following a different transliteration), Ibrahim al-Kabir (d. after 1964), born to a distinguished Iraqi Jewish family, was one of the leaders of the Jewish community in Baghdad. An economist, he served as director-general of the Iraqi Treasury between 1934 and 1948. He was also a director of the National Iraqi Bank and represented Iraq at meetings of the World Bank. Together with his brothers Heskel and Yusuf, a noted lawyer, Ibrahim al-Kabir was an outspoken representative of the so-called Iraqi Orientation, a strand of thought among Iraqi Jewry that strove for full integration of Jews into the country's public life. Toward the end of his life, al-Kabir wrote two memoirs: *My Communal Life* and *My Ideological Life: Illusions and Positions*.

23

Evidence Given to Palestine's Anglo-American Committee of Inquiry, Which Visited Baghdad

Ibrahim al-Kabir, "Testimony before Anglo-American Committee of Inquiry," Public Record Office, London, 371/52514.

Al-Kabir delivered this testimony on March 16, 1946, to Sir John Singleton, Frank Buxton, and Reginald Manningham-Buller, members of the Anglo-American Committee of Inquiry that visited Baghdad and Riyadh, March 16–21. The committee, created in 1946 in order to agree on a policy regarding the admission of Jews to Palestine as part of the solution to Jewish refugee problem in the wake of World War II, published its report in Lausanne, Switzerland, on April 20, 1946. The committee reported that Palestine alone couldn't be the only solution to the Jewish refugee problem and recommended that, among other things, only 100,000 Jewish refugees from Europe be admitted to Palestine.

I have been invited to testify before the honorable committee. I must in the first place stress that I will speak in a personal capacity. I hold no mandate, formal or implied, to speak on behalf of the Jewish community, who, as far as I know, have no political leaders.

The Jews in Iraq claim residence in this country for over twenty-five centuries. They have participated in the commercial, financial, scientific, and even the literary and political activities of the country. They had their places of worship, schools, etc. Islam acknowledges the Jewish faith, and its adepts are not persecuted. All of this gave to the Jews a feeling of citizenship on a reasonable, if not equal, footing that has been maintained for centuries. It must be remembered that Iraq during this period was ruled by foreign rulers, nationalism and minority problems were unknown, and the Jews enjoyed life just like other citizens.

The laws of the country do not make any discrimination against the Jews. Their rights and privileges are protected by the constitution like the other racial and religious minorities. The constitution provides for the free exercise of cults, the use of languages, the opening of schools, and the establishment of religious courts and other institutions. Their [the Jews'] representation on the legislative and other representative bodies is secured by law. It can hardly be believed that, unless the political system of this country is basically changed, the Jews can be singled out for oppressive legislation.

The Jews participate in the economic life of the country; they have access to all professions. They have served their country commercially and financially by establishing contact with commercial firms abroad. Among them there are lawyers, doctors, poets, government officials, etc. Some of the services like the army, police, and others are closed to them, which creates a certain resentment and sense of inequality for which they find no justification, even though this inequality is compensated for by a higher ratio of activity in the commercial and other fields.

The Jews do not feel any social disability. They are admitted on an equal footing in the clubs, schools, societies, etc. In recent years, their admission to public schools has to a certain extent been curtailed, and it is believed that this is due to the government's desire to maintain a certain equilibrium between the various elements of the population.

The government's attitude toward the Jews as regards [to] protection, application of the laws, etc. has not always been uniform. It must be admitted that the adoption of antisemitism as a dogma by many countries, the systematic policy of persecuting the Jews, [and] the Palestine crisis, particularly when it reached an acute form, had their repercussion in governmental, educational, social, and other circles in this country. Some casual outbursts have created among the Jews a sense of bitterness, of resentment that is rendered more intense by twenty-five centuries of peaceful life, common language, customs, and ideals and the belief that they contributed neither directly nor indirectly to the Palestine troubles.

The systematic propaganda campaign conducted from abroad and particularly Germany has created among sections of the [Iraqi] population a sense of hostility toward the Jews, which must be a source of concern and difficulties for both the government and Jews. It is felt that, but for Palestine and the worldwide antisemitic dogma, the position of the Jews abroad would not be less favorable than [the position of] other communities.

The Jews in Iraq do not feel that they have a problem to be solved with outside help. Their domestic troubles—if any—must be settled by mutual understanding and cooperation [with the Arabs in Iraq]. They do not feel the necessity of emigrating to Palestine, America, or any other country, and if there are some exceptions, they must be due to commercial, religious, and perhaps other sentimental reasons.

The Jews in Iraq have no political organizations; they are not politically minded. The masses know very little about Palestine except what they read about it in the Bible and other religious texts. There may be some extremists on both sides, but their influence must be negligible. The masses have great sympathy with the Jews of Europe in their great ordeal, and those of them who are politically minded—and they are very few—believe that the Jewish troubles cannot be solved by immigration to Palestine, if emigration is the only solution. (The ideal solution would be to revert to the principle of liberalism, which few people thought would end in a horrible tragedy.)

Further Readings

Elkabir, A. S. *My Communal Life.* 1964.

———. *My Ideological Life: Illusions and Positions.* 1964.

Kazzaz, Nissim. *Ha-Yehudim be-'Irak ba-Me'ah ha-'Esrim* (The Jews in Iraq during the twentieth century). Jerusalem: Hebrew University Press, 1991.

———. *Sofa Shel Gola: ha-Yehudim be-Irak aharei ha-Aliyah ha-Hamonit 1951–2000* (The end of a diaspora: The Jews in Iraq after the mass immigration: 1951–2000). Or Yehouda, Israel: Babylonian Jewry Heritage Center, 2002.

Meir-Glitzenstein, Esther. *Zionism in an Arab Country: Jews in Iraq in the 1940s.* London: Routledge, 2004.

Rejwan, Nissim. *The Last Jews in Baghdad: Remembering a Lost Homeland.* Austin: University of Texas Press, 2004.

Shiblak, Abbas, *The Lure of Zion: The Case of the Iraqi Jews.* London: Al Saqi, 1986.

Yusuf Harun Zilkha and Sasson Shalom Dallal

Yusuf Zilkha (b. 1921) and Sasson Dallal (1929–49) were both born in Baghdad. Zilkha was a railway clerk, journalist, author, and Communist activist, who was elected leader of the League for the Struggle against Zionism ('Usbat Mukafahat al-Sahyuniyya) at the age of twenty-five. Dallal was a clerk in the Ministry of Supply, a member of the League, and, briefly in 1949, acting head of the Iraqi Communist Party.

In the aftermath of World War II, a group of leftist secular Jews—most of whom later helped form the League for the Struggle against Zionism—convened in Baghdad to reflect on the sociopolitical direction that Iraqi Jews should follow amid the global triumph of anti-Nazi Communism, the continuation of British colonialism, and the concurrent consolidations of Zionism and Arab nationalism. They also discussed whether emigration to Palestine was an appropriate response to these developments and to the horrible massacre of Iraqi Jews in June 1941, called the *Farhud* (violent dispossession). In addition to Zilkha and Dallal, the League's two dozen participants included Salim Menashe, Nissim Yehezkel Yehuda, Masrour Saleh Kattan, Ibrahim Naji, Ya'cob Masri, Dr. Meir Ya'cob Cohen, Ya'cob Sehayik, Moshe Ya'cob, Naim Salah Tweig, and Aharon Makmal. The members of the group concluded that the (possible) establishment of a Jewish-Zionist state in the heart of the Arab world was likely to serve the interests of imperialism and the Jewish bourgeoisie. They submitted the League's manifesto, which expressed these ideas, to the Iraqi Ministry of the Interior in the hope of obtaining the permission needed to organize legally. On June 16, 1946, the director of the Special Political Department of Criminal Investigations reported that the applicants "have no leg to stand on in society, and do not have the skills to lead such an important association, not to mention the fact that most hold Communist views; the activities of these people appear to be nothing but Communist activities under the guise of a struggle against Zionism." Yet Iraqi authorities still permitted the group to organize because they hoped its members would articulate a Jewish anti-Zionist perspective to members of Palestine's Anglo-American Committee of Inquiry, who were visiting Iraq. In addition to political advocacy, the

League conducted cultural, dramatic, and sports activities, yet its permission to operate was revoked within months because as it turned out, its members were not prominent enough to testify in front of the Committee of Inquiry, unlike Ibrahim al-Kabir (featured above).

During the 1940s many Jews worked on Iraqi periodicals and newspapers, and on two occasions, where their involvement was deemed too noticeable, the authorities arrested the journalists. One such case involved the League's publication, *al-'Usba*, which had a daily circulation of 4,000–6,000 copies. The authorities banned the publication and imprisoned its editors, Zilkha and Kattan. Compared to Zionists, anti-Zionist Marxist Jews—whether supportive of or opposed to the UN General Assembly Resolution 181, which decided on the creation of two states, one Jewish and the other Arab, in Mandatory Palestine—faced greater hostility and harassment from both government authorities and conservative Iraqis linked to the Istiqlal Party, which was both rabidly anti-Communist and Arab nationalist. On February 13, 1949, the Jewish Communist leader Yehuda Salman Saddiq was executed—together with three of his leading comrades, whom the repressive authorities ensured were of Christian, Sunni, and Shiite origins. It was then that the brilliant Dallal was made acting head of the Community Party. Yet four months later, he too was executed. In Iraq during the 1940s, both Zionist and anti-Zionist Jews met with suspicion and treatment. That is probably why Zilkha, who ironically moved to Israel in the early 1950s, expressed little interest in discussing with researchers his Iraqi Communist past.

24

Zionism against Arabs and Jews

Excerpt from Yusuf Harun Zilkha, *al-Sahyūnīyah 'adūwat al-'arab wa al-yahūd*
(Zionism against Arabs and Jews), in *'Usbat Mukāfahat al-Sahyoniyya fī al-'Iraq
1945-1946* (The League for the Struggle against Zionism in Iraq 1945-1946),
ed. 'Abd al-Latīf al-Rawī (Damascus: Dar al-Jalīl, 1986), 99-185.

This was one of the first pamphlets published and circulated when Iraqi authorities
permitted the League for the Struggle against Zionism to organize in Iraq. The
pamphlet was originally published in Baghdad in 1946 by Matba' Dar al-Hikmah.

1. THE JEWISH QUESTION AS AN
INTEGRAL PART OF COMMUNITY ISSUES

The Jewish Question is not a stand-alone problem but is, rather, closely
related to general community issues. It is part and parcel of these issues, arising in the context of a societal drive toward development and progress. Many
historians attribute the rise of the Jewish Question to the presence of Jews in
the Diaspora since the Babylonian captivity. Examining this historic era to
date, no Jewish Question can be detected in countries enjoying prosperity and
progress. The question normally persists in countries where ruling regimes historically weaken and where newly developing progressive classes strive to come
to power.

Put differently, the main reason for the emergence of the Jewish Question
does not lie in the exodus of Jews; it is instead rooted in developmental processes
that societies undergo, as well as in the struggle of the disadvantaged against
ruling elites seeking to maintain privileges. Every ruling regime commonly
covets power and practices exploitation, with no intention of surrendering, irrespective of the ordeals and scourges that might befall the people it rules over,
or the tragedies and pains these subjects are certain to experience as a direct
result. In practice, such ruling regimes often have recourse to the most virulent
means and despicable methods that manifest themselves in such forms as terrorism, persecution, torture, murder, and destruction—to say nothing of the
transmission of misleading venomous ideas and opinions with a view toward
perpetuating them.

When Jews were led astray in most parts of the world due to their fragmentation and dispersal among powerful warring empires—and later due to the nature of their professions and crafts—it could already be foreseen that ruling classes would regard them as scapegoats, and sacrifice their lives as innocent offerings on the altar of their rule. This has been visible in both recent and distant history.

Take the case of tsarist Russia. Led by the working classes and enlightened populations who were subject to the tsar's tyranny, the Russian people became aware of the real causes of their misery and distress and undertook a formidable fight for freedom to rid themselves of bondage, whips, and persecution, notwithstanding the ensuing hunger, misfortune, poverty, and deprivation brought to the people by the decadent regime. Against this backdrop, the tsarist rulers perpetrated appalling massacres against Jews, incited ethnic nationalism, ignited disputes, and wrought havoc with the aim of diverting popular rage away from the regime and toward the Jews (or any other national, racial, or religious minority) and of trying to persuade the masses that their problems were exclusively associated with the presence of Jews. The White Army commanders committed genocide against Jews with a view to diverting attention among the masses from fighting against the tsar.

Yet persecution of Jews was not enough to prevent the collapse of the empire [in 1917], and the same applies to other regimes that resorted to this technique—for the popular masses, having been devotedly and justly determined to become free from oppression, could not be led astray so easily. Therefore, once they felt that they had been misled, they became cognizant of their true enemy: the actual source of their problems, that is, the ruling elites. They thus began working for the deposition of their rulers, the overturn of their corrupt regime, and its replacement by a new regime [that would be] more progressive and enlightened. History has shown how ruling feudal systems were brought down in Europe and many other countries, notwithstanding their attempts to stay in power, their persecution of Jews and non-Jews, and their atrocities and acts of intimidation and killing of liberals and intellectuals.

I reiterate that, notwithstanding their attempts, these regimes failed to survive (and this will be the case for any other ruling class that attempts to derail the passage of history) because their historic role had been fulfilled, and society was ready to embark on a new era. For a society to shift from one system to a better one, it is logical that the struggle of the people will primarily be led by its most organized, tenacious, and progressive elements. In other words, any development will remain out of reach unless preceded by "spontaneous" struggle, as some may prefer to put it![1]

What is argued here about tsarist Russia applies to Nazi Germany as well. When as a consequence of the dissemination of the socialist trend, Germany was threatened with demise, the German capitalist class delivered its own "solution" of persecuting Jews. All the evils of the capitalist system were ascribed to Jews—allegedly responsible for causing the war [World War I] to erupt, Germany to be defeated, and various crises and unemployment to emerge. It was through these and other Nazi practices that capitalist rulers were able to deceive the German people and redirect their opposition. To this effect, world capitalism—attending to its own interest in keeping the capitalist system safe in Germany (and everywhere else)—offered extensive assistance to the Nazis in suppressing and subduing the German popular movement, especially with the working class in such a state of discord.

The same things that happened in tsarist Russia, Nazi Germany, Italy, and Japan took place in Britain, with colonialists encouraging [Sir Oswald] Mosley's [1896–1980] fascist movement—and other fascist movements in colonized or quasicolonized countries—by supplying and supporting them with money and gold, as is happening nowadays in Egypt, Iraq, Syria, and Lebanon, and their remaining areas of influence. It can thus be concluded that the history of the Jewish Question revolves around sacrificing Jews to the interests of the ruling classes. The Jewish Question exists only for reasons of self-preservation in countries where the regimes are prone to collapse, the community is in a state of roiling turmoil, and the masses are enraged. [. . .] This leads us to conclude that the Jewish Question is part and parcel of larger community problems, making it impossible to bring about its settlement independently from the circumstances and conditions of society as a whole.

2. ZIONISM AND JUDAISM

It is critically important for anti-Zionist advocates to differentiate between Zionism and Judaism. The former is a racist movement designed to dominate

1. [Although this terminology may echo the thoughts of Antonio Gramsci (1891–1937), it is unlikely that Zilkha knew much, if anything, about Gramsci's work. Gramsci's writings emerged several years after World War II, when the Italian Communist Party began to publish sections of his *Prison Notebooks* as well as some of the 500 letters he wrote from prison.]

Arab Palestine, evacuate its indigenous population, and form a Zionist government. Judaism, on the other hand, is a divine religion that has nothing to do with political Zionism. However, the latter is often well disposed to agitate in the name of the Jewish faith, with the tendency to manipulate it to serve colonialist ends, similar to any other reactionary exploitative movement.

Nazism, for example, capitalized on its characteristic inclination to lobby for racism, hostile nationalism, and the superiority of the Germanic race. The Japanese fascist military also took advantage of religious rituals and habits to enhance its influence and solidify its position to wage a treacherous colonial war. The two movements yielded nothing but ruin and plight for the German and Japanese peoples. If we were to warn against Zionist manipulation of the principles of the Jewish religion, we would also be warning the sons of our [Iraqi] people against religious abuse by [Iraqi] elements known for their fascist tendencies in our country, as well as against the spread of dissonance and discord. [. . .]

The fact that Jewish populations in many countries of the world are concerned with fighting against Zionism and revealing its negative intentions is sufficient proof of the truth of our analysis. Jews in the Soviet Union, for example—who number only a few million—do not support Zionism but rather are antagonistic toward it. [. . .] Jews in Arab countries also denounced Zionism, with 1,000 Jewish youths forming an anti-Zionist group, and spiritual and pious Jewish leaders in Damascus and Aleppo participated in demonstrations protesting against Zionism. It was good for Arab national liberation movements that the Arab League and national institutions in different Arab countries differentiated between Zionism and Judaism. Zionism is forcefully poised to confound itself with Judaism. It falsely claims to "represent world Jews." It should thus be expressly declared that whoever confuses Zionism for Judaism—no matter what his religion, denomination, or ideology—is, in fact, serving, willingly or unwillingly, Zionism and its master, that is, colonialism.

3. THE EMERGENCE AND HISTORY OF ZIONISM

In the wake of the grand French Revolution proclaiming the principles of freedom, fraternity, and equality, a then-looming wave of freedom in Europe was reflected in popular opinions about the Jews, who struggled side by side with other citizens, to erect the pillars of freedom whose existence was put at risk by reactionary movements [. . .]. Attacks on individual freedoms were accompanied by racist persecutions against Jews, which history taught us were but a recipe for arbitrary repressive practices against all popular movements as well as reactionary actions directed at the elimination of the freedoms and rights of all citizens. Antisemitic propaganda today is aimed at dividing national liberation movements and, in particular, striking at working classes—the social category chiefly fighting to access broader rights and freedoms and [for] a better regime for all. [. . .] At this juncture Jews are obliged to integrate themselves into national liberation movements and to fight against Zionism as much as they resist antisemitism—which was actually what they did vis-à-vis liberation movements in Europe before the rise of Zionism, and its bid to exclude and isolate Jews from the interests and objectives of their homelands.

The political Zionist movement, which calls for the creation of a national home in Palestine, was founded by an Austrian Jewish journalist named Dr. Theodore Herzl in 1895. The first Zionist Conference, held in Basel in 1897, declared that the aim of Zionism was "the creation of a national home for Jews in Palestine." Since its foundation, the Zionist movement has aimed at keeping Jewish communities away from the general struggle for freedom and justice, hand in hand with other citizens, under the pretext that the solution to the Jewish Question should be dealt with independently from the resolution of other problems in the countries in which they live. That is why Zionism has failed to win a considerable number of Jewish supporters—especially from among the working classes—even in tsarist Russia, where terrible massacres were perpetrated against Jews on a much larger scale than in other countries. [. . .]

Like any weak, exploitative reactionary movement, Zionism can survive only by marketing itself to colonialists, as an agent friendly to any and all of them. British colonialism purchased it as a newborn—although the possibility of Zionism trying to sell itself to the highest colonial bidder cannot be discounted. In this manner Dr. Herzl, founder of the Zionist movement, did not hesitate to court the favor of Sultan Abdul Hamid II, an incredibly tyrannical ruler who tightened his grip on the freedoms and rights of his people, and [was] one of the most reckless rulers with regard to the life of his nation and sons of his homeland. Yet Herzl's attempt failed. He then sought another tyrant—the kaiser of Germany—an autocrat who held human freedom and dignity in contempt. Having also failed to win him over, the founder of Zionism headed for British Minister of Colonies Joseph Chamberlain—or the so-called messenger of the empire—to satisfy his power craving.

Dr. Herzl later showed no reluctance in proceeding to the minister of the interior of the Russian tsarist government—the number one mastermind of atrocious massacres against Jews—to ask for his assistance with the Zionist movement, which he readily gave, as it offered a way of excluding the Jewish masses from the country's ongoing revolutionary struggle and curbing the "increased" number of Jews in Russia. [. . .] This demonstrates that Zionism is constantly at the service of colonialists and reactionaries, enemies of humans and humanity. As for the British minister of colonies, he had offered Zionists the Uganda region in Africa as a national home for Jews, but they rejected the offer during their 1905 Congress, insisting on having Palestine as their "National Home." The reason for this refusal was the Zionists' realization that their acceptance of the offer was likely to strip them of the power of manipulation and sorcery in the name of faith (with due consideration of the difference between Palestine and Uganda from the point of view of location, significance, and natural resources).

If what really mattered was the creation of a national home for Jews, then why refuse Uganda? This verifies the fact that the Zionist movement is deceiving the Jewish people with false hopes, and manipulating them to the advantage of a handful of capitalist stakeholders whose interests are closely related to colonialism in its various forms, and so they [Zionist leaders] seek to serve it [colonialism]. Nevertheless, a group of Zionists did agree to the Ugandan offer and broke away from the mainstream Zionist movement, declaring their willingness to take any country other than Palestine for the creation of the Jewish State. Headed by the English writer Israel Zangwill [1864–1926], this group was short-lived with no lasting impact.[2] [. . .]

5. ZIONISM'S RELATIONSHIP WITH BRITISH COLONIALISM

[. . .] British colonialism has been trying since the last century to intervene in the internal affairs of Palestine and the Arab countries, mindful of the significant geographic and strategic location of these countries, especially Palestine. Colonial powers at the time—notably tsarist Russia, France, and Germany—were intervening in the affairs of Palestine through "minority protection": Russia particularly did so allegedly for "Orthodox [Russian Orthodox Christians] pro-

---

2. [It is critical to note that section 4 of this text—which is not included here due to space constraints—is entitled, partly metaphorically and partly figuratively, "Zionism and Nazism: Twins."]

tection" and France for "Catholic protection," while the politically and militarily ruling Ottoman Empire claimed to be the protector of Arabs and Muslims.

When British colonialists were bent on intervening, they found it necessary to look for a group whom they could "take on the trouble" of protecting (as British colonialism has developed the habit of "going through hell" to do "good," as it is currently doing by "sacrificing" and "paying high costs" in money, weapons, and troops for the sake of "preserving security and independence" in Indonesia!). This explains how British colonialism—having wearily searched Palestine for a group to protect—singled out "the Jews" and so declared "its protection" of them, using them as a pretext to intervene in the affairs of Palestine. On this basis, the British government had established a British Commission in Jerusalem in 1838, which announced "the protection of Jews in general" as one of its underlying objectives.

Lord Shaftesbury [1801–85], whom Zionists regarded as a humanist and idealist, backed Palestine's colonization by "the progeny of Abraham" while simultaneously strongly opposing for "religious" reasons the liberation of Jews in Britain. Furthermore, many British Tories were supportive of the idea of colonizing Palestine as a bridge to enable them to extend their colonization to the Near East and Arab countries. [. . .] That is how the relationship between Zionism and British colonialism developed.

6. ZIONISM AND THE BALFOUR DECLARATION

Since its very inception, the Zionist movement has been lurking and seizing opportunities to make its services available to colonial powers. It was most inclined to become an agent of British colonialism, an effort that was well received. When World War I broke out, these conflicting colonial powers were in dire need of help and desperate for the "purchase" of an agent. Time was then opportune for the movement to promote itself on the "colonial market." [. . .] Mr. [David] Lloyd George and Mr. Arthur Balfour (later Lord Balfour) maintained the view that Britain could avail itself, during times of war, of Zionist advocacy and support, which prompted them to promise the Zionists Palestine as a "national home for Jews," failing to recognize that by so doing, they were generously giving others "money from a purse that is not his own," and also failing to remember the promise given previously to Sharif Hussein, guaranteeing the independence of Palestine and the rest of the Arab countries. Furthermore, Mr. [Ernest] Bevin (then British Labour Minister) said: "We have to fulfil our promises." If a government is concerned with honoring its pledges, how can it simultaneously give two contradictory promises?

Let us read the Balfour Declaration and see the capitalist colonial spirit inherent in every word:

Foreign Office
November 2nd 1917

Dear Lord Rothschild,

I have much pleasure in conveying to you on behalf of his Majesty's government the following declaration of sympathy with Jewish Zionist aspirations, which has been submitted to, and approved by, the Cabinet.

His Majesty's government view with favour the establishment in Palestine of a national home for the Jewish people, and will use its best endeavours to facilitate the achievement of this object, it being clearly understood that nothing shall be done which may prejudice the civil and religious rights of non-Jewish communities in Palestine, or the rights and political status enjoyed by Jews in any other country.

I should be grateful if you would bring this declaration to the knowledge of the Zionist Federation.

Yours sincerely,
Arthur James Balfour

[...] The British government says it "will use its best endeavours to facilitate achievement of this object" (the Jewish national home) and that "nothing shall be done which may prejudice the civil and religious rights of non-Jewish communities in Palestine." If this were the case, then prejudicing the rights of the Arabs of Palestine was not intentional. How, then, can this be imagined to "benefit" their country? [...] The purpose of the Balfour Declaration was (i) to win the support of the Zionist movement during World War I; (ii) to take this declaration as a pretext for colonizing Palestine; and—as articulated in the statement of the Anti-Zionist Group in Baghdad on the anniversary of this declaration—(iii) to divert the Arab struggle for liberation and emancipation from colonialism to the Jewish population in Arab countries. This was how Britain conspired to implement—in cooperation with its agents—its well-known "divide and rule" colonial policy.

Neither Zionists nor British colonialists are in denial of their intimate relationship. Lord Millgate [1831–89], a prominent British and Zionist monopolist, wrote: "Colonial objects and interests of the British Empire may be fulfilled in the most peaceful manner by providing a habitat for a number of Jews in Palestine and placing it under British rule." He further wrote: "Bringing in three million Jews will once and for all depress the prospect of any successful armed uprising that may contest the outcomes of the Mandate policy." The famous Zionist leader Menachem Ussishkin [1863–1941] was also quoted as saying: "An all-Arab Palestine means that, sooner or later, Great Britain will be forced to quit [Palestine] as it is gradually doing today in Egypt. But once the majority of its population becomes Jewish, this means putting in place a close, alliance-based relationship between the Jewish and English peoples." The famous Zionist writer Louis Golding [1895–1958] wrote: "Great Britain is interested in the first place in having its presence maintained in Palestine and its only way to be there rests with the promise it gave to the Jews" (*The Jewish Question*, 1938, p. 186). He added: "The British will also have a colony of faithful, obedient subjects who will guard the Empire's most vital transport routes" (ibid., p. 198). [. . .]

This is the relationship between the Zionist movement and British colonialism—a linkage undeniable by both parties. We cannot comprehend how the Zionist movement is not ashamed to boast of its relationship with colonialism—viewing it as the way to "save" the Jews and "solve their problem." Regardless of its form or origin, colonialism is an incarnation of the worst type of selfishness and egoism and—most harmful of all—creates exploitation and profit depletion in any group that carries it out. Colonialism does not care about the destiny of its own people, plunging them into warfare, pillage, and plunder that incur nothing but catastrophe and death. Colonialism thus combines many vile traits, a conclusion that accepts no argument and is not likely to be questioned. Yet Zionism is joined in close association with colonialism, and pursues and regards it as "the rescuer and salvation" of the Jews!

It is a truism that the Zionist movement is aware of what colonialism really is and is well informed of its ways and means. [. . .] Zionism does not represent the interests of Jews, and neither does colonialism. Neither ideology pays heed to the interests of the majority of the people. Instead, Zionism accounts for the interests of a handful of Jewish capitalists and key colonial monopolists who—like their counterparts worldwide—would sacrifice anything for the aim of gaining profit. This was how Zionism bound itself irreversibly to world colonialism: by getting involved in a Zionist-colonial capital-based relationship.

7. THE ZIONIST–COLONIAL CAPITAL RELATIONSHIP

The Zionist movement had opted for Palestine as the site of its "national home" because Palestine's land is fertile and rich in minerals and natural resources. Palestine was chosen for its geographic and strategic location, in which the British Empire had developed an interest. Zionists felt the temptation and accordingly headed for cooperation with the British colonial power to enter Palestine and avail themselves of its treasures. Therefore, it is now conceded that world Zionist figureheads are similarly the representatives of the two major capitalist powers, Great Britain and the United States. The United States' total capital assets invested in Palestine up until 1936 have been put at £10 million, whereas aggregate British capital had reached £20 million. Capital from both countries is still flowing extensively into Palestine.

Examples of this relationship:

The board of directors of the Palestine Electricity Company—which is British—was made up of Lord [Hugo] Hirst [1863–1943], director of the General Electricity Company in Britain and manager of several electric power projects within the [British] Empire; the Zionist Lord Melchett [1868–1930], chairman of the Imperial Chemical Industries; [. . .] and Viscount Herbert Samuel [1870–1963], member of the British government and Britain's High Commissioner in Palestine (and supporter of the "Jewish National Home"); Mr. Harry Sacher [1881–1971], a Zionist leader and director of Marks and Spencer Company and Palestine Potash Company (also British), which had vested interests with the Imperial Chemical Industries; and also Mr. Simon Marks [1888–1964], head of Marks and Spencer Company, and its deputy director, Mr. [Israel] Seiff [1889–1972], both of whom are eminent Zionists, while the spouse of the latter is a well-known Zionist leader.

There were also American Jewish capitalists acting as liaisons between the Zionist movement and American colonialism. For example, a number of guarantee companies invested gross capital in building and construction projects amounting to £1.75 million in late 1935, while Lloyds and Barclays Banks processed substantial loans to Zionist organizations that deal with issues of land. This was all run by Zionists who were also American capitalists. The social status of Palestine and the nature of its lands—which are notably fertile and rich in mineral wealth—encouraged both Jewish and non-Jewish capitalists in the United States and Britain to export their operational capital to Palestine, in deals worth a total of £30 million. In the July 9, 1940, issue of the *Jewish Chronicle*, it was noted that the total Jewish capital invested over the twenty-two-year period of the British Mandate in Palestine had reached £105 million, only £19.8 million of which had been contributed by national corporations.

These figures clearly show that Zionism is a movement of opportune capitalists who are profit driven, and not a "national" movement for "rescuing Jews," as claimed. Proof of this can be found in the fact that four-fifths of the capital invested in Palestine belongs to purely capitalist companies, so that if we were to assert the Zionists' view that "the capital of national corporations" invested on a "national home" basis is the property of "all Jews in Palestine," as is also claimed with respect to Zionist colonies (kibbutzim), for example, we would come to the conclusion that more than four-fifths of Zionist operational capital in Palestine is personal and not provided by purely capitalist companies! It should be noted in this context that profit accrued from capital pooled by national corporations is again siphoned off into the pockets of a small group of capitalists, either directly or by mediation. [...]

9. ZIONISM AND COLONIALISM AS ENEMIES OF THE JEWISH QUESTION

Zionism is therefore closely associated with colonialism, [...] without whose presence Zionism's survival is impossible. The question is whether colonialism has ever been in favor of the people's interests? Colonialism has always been the opponent of all peoples destined to suffer the deleterious consequences of colonial policies—as conspicuously demonstrated in the promise for Palestine that was simultaneously given to the Jews, in the Balfour Declaration, and to Sharif Hussein [in 1915–16]. Colonialism was principally designed to divide the Arab peoples and mute their struggle, with the aim of reversing its direction from colonialism to a struggle toward the [Arab] Jewish community. The British colonial power wanted meanwhile to leverage its position and further promote its influence by bringing in massive forces "in protection of minorities" against whom Britain itself was concocting plots and hatching intrigues.

T. E. Lawrence ["of Arabia"—1888–1935] was the empire's main spy. A self-described "friend of the Arabs," he was actually a proponent of Zionism. Why was he playing the dual role of combining Arab "friendship" and Jewish-Zionist "advocacy"? He wanted to draw a wedge within Arab ranks, strike at national movements, and enforce the famous "divide and rule" policy. Perhaps General [later Major-General and Sir] Edward Spears [1886–1974]—also known as "a friend of Arab oil"—would today like to play Lawrence's role. We hear now about British and American colonialists lamenting the miserable conditions of Jews and the injuries inflicted on them and the rest of European peoples by criminal Nazis. If they are truly sympathetic to Jews, why, then, do they allow anti-Jewish movements to be formed in their own countries?

In the United States, Henry Ford [1893–1947], the owner of the Ford Motor Company, helped by Father [Charles] Coughlin [1891–1979][3] under the cover of piety—the same role that fundamentalists perform today in the name of religion in Arab countries—was awarded a decoration by Hitler in 1937 in recognition of Ford's help to Hitler's antisemitic efforts. In Britain, the Fascist Party is now promoting anti-Jewish propaganda. Until war was declared, this party was not subject to any governmental pressure. On the outbreak of the war [World War II], its leader, Mosley, was detained and the party's activity was suspended only formally. But the British government released the fascist leader from detention while the war was ferociously raging, with Nazism then threatening peoples with slavery and destruction. His release was allegedly on health grounds—after which he continued with his antisemitic calls, which were antidemocratic and in opposition to human freedom in general. Now that the war is over, he has announced his continuing adherence to his fascist line of thinking and stated that he will not budge from this position nor stop launching campaigns against Jews and popular democratic movements.

[. . .] Mosley continued with his criminal actions in the heart of the City of London and under the eyes of the "socialist" Labour government—with even members of the Labour Party finding excuses for his exercise of these detrimental activities. Even Professor Harold Laski [1890–1950] went so far as to say that freedom allows Mosley to operate and that closing down his party "is a breach of this freedom." But Mr. [Herbert Stanley] Morrison [1888–1965]—a top Labour Party leader and interior minister in [Sir Winston] Churchill's coalition government—has failed to recognize that this same freedom should stop him from suspending the *Daily Worker* newspaper for over eighteen months, while its supporters have vigorously struggled for its recovery throughout this period. This was the kind of propaganda taking place in Britain and the United States, by those who strongly regretted the Jews' condition.

As for other countries subject to British influence, all the organizations that

3. [Coughlin was an antisemitic American Catholic priest whose mass radio broadcasts in the 1930s rightfully earned him the modern nickname of "the father of hate radio."]

previously sold themselves to German fascists have resurfaced, with colonial powers now supplying them with money and directing them according to their [colonial] wishes. Thus they have resumed their acts of sabotage, yet now under a new name and serving a new master! Riots that erupted in connection with Jews in Egypt and Tripoli provide further evidence of criminal actions and underground plots by colonial hired agents against Jews and Arab liberation movements alike.[4] [...]

Colonialists' tears for Jews are mere crocodile tears. Colonialism does not want the Jewish Question resolved but rather tends to create, in each country and in every piece of land, the impossibility of peace; colonialism resembles malignant microbes able to live only in troubled water. It is also taken for granted that colonialism creates problems of a Jewish nature in countries where they do not exist. A case in point is Palestine, where there was no clash between Arabs and Jews before the advent of British colonialism, along with its agent, Zionism. [...] Both have one concern in common: to sacrifice everything as offerings on the altar of their selfishness and greed. As far as both were concerned, the most cherished of human ideals and values can be ground to dust. Both are inimical to peoples, to Arabs and Jews as well as to the sound settlement of the Jewish Question, as happened in the Soviet Union, for example. Colonialism and Zionism, then, are hostile to Jews. On this basis, every Jew who feels for his people and desires their equal treatment like other peoples—and struggles for the dignity and rights of Jews—shall be obligated to spell out his hatred for colonialism and Zionism, and engage in a struggle against both because the presence of colonialism and Zionism is the corrupt environment in which antisemitic microbes are nurtured.

10. THE SOLE FINAL SOLUTION
TO THE JEWISH QUESTION

As indicated above, Jews became part of human society 3,500 years ago and, accordingly, their question cannot be disassociated from general social-

4. [Zilkha is referring here to, first, the political mobilization in Egypt on November 2, 1945 (the twenty-third anniversary of the Balfour Declaration), which acquired an anti-Jewish character as a consequence of collective action by activists linked to the Muslim Brothers and Young Egypt, and to, second, anti-Jewish acts in fascist-ruled Libya during the same week. Henri Curiel also mentions these events in his 1949 and 1953 texts (see below in this book).]

community problems. Persecution of Jews occurred when the ruling class became decadent to the extent that its downfall was foreseeable. Given that each
ruling class is set to remain in power as a "parasite" living on the drudgery of
the masses, it normally tries to retain its prestigious status, which prompts it
to resort to whatever evil is necessary to safeguard its possessions and to try
to transform people's struggle against it into a struggle against minority Jews.
Cases in point include tsarist Russia and Nazi Germany. The main reason for
the Jews' exodus was their domestication of commerce and industry as a vo-
cation and craft—by virtue of the geographic location of [historic] Palestine
[Eretz Yisrael]—which was a meeting point of commercial roads when the
Jewish State was first created. This led Jews to head for the world's commercial
and industrial centers. Again, the Jewish Question did not arise from the idea of
their exodus but from the fact that the new communities in which they found
themselves were undergoing development: Jews were persecuted in societies
whose ruling classes were threatened with being overthrown in the face of the
people's struggle for their rights.

Evidence has shown that vocations and industries that Jews had domesti-
cated subsequent to their settlement in old Palestine—coupled with historic
developments that followed the decay of their state—had resulted in the wide-
scale Jewish exodus. That also explains why Jews were also spread out in some
regions—for instance, the city of Najaf—as they were among tribes in rural
areas and villages. Were they forced to go to these areas and preferred to settle
there rather than in such major cities as Baghdad, for example? The answer is
no: they were scattered as a consequence of their search for a living. This by no
means implies that either all or most Jews were merchants or industry owners;
the fact is that society in the postindustrial revolution world placed Jews in the
same general classes by which society is typically divided, that is, workers and
capitalists (with the exception of farmers—because very few Jews worked in
agriculture in capitalist countries). The pressures exercised by capitalist societies
and the cessation of many vocations and industries—as was the case in some
European countries—partly forced Jews to continue working as craftsmen.[5]

Jews, then, are part of human society, and their problems are part of soci-

5. [Zilkha echoes here elements included in the thesis written inside Auschwitz by his
contemporary Abraham Leon (1918–44) in his work *The Jewish Question: A Marxist Interpretation*. Nonetheless, Zilkha obviously neither knew about this work nor had read it when
he wrote this text.]

ety's larger issues. After the lapse of thousands of years since their dispersion to virtually every place in the world, do they today form a nation? Perhaps the best consistent definition of a "nation" is a "fixed group of people, historically linked with a common language, common land, common economic life and common psychological composition, with expression in a common culture."[6] If any of the above-mentioned components are missing, there shall be no nation. It is conceded that the nation—like any historic phenomenon—is subject to the law of evolution; it has its history, beginning and end. [. . .] Do these prerequisites apply to the Jews at present?

The answer is no; not a single constituent component can be applied to the situation of the Jews. They do not form a fixed group of people, they are not historically linked (but rather dispersed), and they have no common history (the history of Arab Jews is different from that of Russian or English Jews; similarly, the history of German Jews is unlike that of Turkish or American Jews, etc.). English Jews are part of the English nation, and Arab Jews are part of the Arab nation. Likewise, Jews have no common land or language (German Jews speak German, English Jews speak English, and Arab Jews speak Arabic). They have no shared psychological makeup that manifests itself in a common culture due to the presence of Jews for thousands of years in various societies, with each Jewish community becoming part of the larger society where they live. Jews also do not have a common economic system. [. . .] The idea of Jewish unification is therefore quite fantastic, for Jews have become an indivisible unit of the communities into which they are integrated.

As for the religious bond, nowadays it does not constitute a factor in terms of a common interest or the general struggle for rights and freedoms and, accordingly, does not constitute a factor in the composition of a nation. This is explained, for example, by the fact that there are different national populations who are believers of the same religion; a fact that may be a reason for the lack of harmony felt by Jews living today in Palestine, where German Jews look down on Eastern Jews, and so on.[7] [. . .]

6. [In this definition, as well as the discussion that follows, Zilkha largely applies the classic work on nationalism developed for the Communist Party by Joseph Stalin in *Marxism and the National Question* (1913).]

7. [Although Zilkha is a lucid early observer of intra-Jewish ethnic rivalries that would gradually deepen, it is also clear that his observations seriously underestimate the power and persistent work that the Zionists carried out in relation to the general critical issue of national consolidation.]

Zionists in no way believe in serving the interests of the overwhelming majority of Jews. They claim that they "do not want to assemble all the Jews in Palestine because this is impossible. Russian Jews categorically refuse to migrate to Palestine and so is the case in relation to British and American Jews, but we [Zionists] still want the one or two million Zionists to populate our national home." Although this is the unsurprising opinion of many Zionists, it is shameful that this is also the opinion of Professor Laski, chairman of the British Labour Party's Executive Committee, who claims to be a socialist and whose students confirm this claim. The key quality of a true socialist is that his examination is markedly realistic and scientifically based; that he is free of empire-based considerations; that he struggles solidly and forcefully for principles of freedom—all these are fundamental principles of socialism. As is the case since 1914, it seems obvious today that "moderate" socialists—who sought to "mitigate" teachings of socialism as a science by their distortion—are mostly serving the opponents of socialism and national liberation movements. Some "moderate" socialists are often hostile to true socialists even in relation to the Soviet Union—the only socialist country—including Laski, whose activity to merge into the Western bloc provides the strongest evidence of this trend.

In an article titled "Allegiance to Chaim Weizmann," Professor Laski—who claims to be a socialist and thus is supposed to be supportive of the Arab liberation movement—writes: "I believe there is no solution to endless [Jewish] tragedies other than the institution of a Jewish government in Palestine—and it must be Jewish and in Palestine." He adds: "all of this provided that (i) it should by no means have a bearing on the allegiance of the Jew wishing to maintain his British, American, or even German nationality and fully participate in a Germany rehabilitated from barbarism to civilization and provided that (ii) the formation of a Jewish government in Palestine does not impact on the life and prosperity of Arabs."[8] Laski then writes: "It is normal that the Jewish government in Palestine means the creation of a society comprised of two to three million Jews."

We now wish to ask Zionists and/or Professor Laski: How could a state whose population is no more than two million ensure protection to more than thirteen million Jews scattered all over the world? Before the outbreak of World War II and given the then historic stage and circumstances, the Soviet Union—with a population of 200 million and governed by a formidable regime—failed to pro-

8. [These observations obviously correspond to the two principal conditions in the Balfour Declaration.]

tect the Ukrainian minority (unjustly uprooted in the aftermath of World War I from Soviet Ukraine) against persecution and suppression by Poland's fascist reactionary government. How would "the Jewish state" with a population of just one or two million possibly be able to protect Jews dispersed all over the world if a hostile anti-Jewish fascist regime were to emerge in a colonial country?

Whoever fairly and honestly seeks a proper solution to the Jewish Question will have to struggle to stamp out any traces of anti-Jewish fascist reactionary movements in some parts of the world—an action that would probably result in the resurgence of these hostile movements. This struggle involves fighting against all reactionary movements intended to hobble and impede the progress of humanity toward freedom, independence, and happiness and that attempt to tear mankind apart into denominations, doctrines, and racist responses—including the reactionary Zionist movement itself—especially now that the world has become dramatically interrelated. We can touch on the deception in which such Zionist propaganda is enveloped. We cannot comprehend how Professor Laski envisions "a Jewish government in Palestine with two or three million Jews with no intention of impacting on the Arabs' situation and prosperity." We hold that a simple study would confirm that Palestine is not in a position to absorb such a number, let alone without affecting negatively the general well-being of the Arabs.

We arrive now at the most critical issue, namely, the fact that Palestine is the property of its Arab people. It has been Arab for many centuries and cannot be ceded by its legitimate owners. How can Palestine be usurped from the Arabs? Would that not cause a plunge into a bloody struggle between Arabs and the usurpers of their Palestine? Is that not an explicit suggestion that Zionists and their colonial masters intend to use Jews as a tool to hide their abhorrent ends and greedy ambitions and to take advantage of Arabs and Jews alike? Arabs will not give up their land. Our Arab liberation movements have proven that it is not only their Palestine that will not be relinquished—but also not one inch of Arab land will be given up, notwithstanding any initial failure of struggle or jihad (which is not to say that any Arab struggle or jihad will always be a failure).

History bears witness that, sooner or later, every free progressive struggle is inevitably successful. Arabs' struggle [jihad] for their independence, freedom, and happiness is sure to succeed. Neither Zionists nor their colonial lords can usurp Palestine or any other Arab territory as long as the Arabs are Arab. This brings us to the conclusion that the idea of creating a "national home" in Palestine as a solution to the Jewish Question is far-fetched and harmful to the Jews for a number of reasons. To begin with, Jews are part and parcel of the societies in which they live, so it is quite impossible for them to huddle together in Palestine. Secondly, Zionism is an exploitative movement that proved its infidelity to the Jewish population and deliberately attempted to isolate them from popular struggles for freedom and happiness. Thirdly, Zionism is the agent of colonialism, on which it depends. It is also subject to colonial manipulation—as such colonialism sacrifices all humanity along with its Jews for the sake of satisfying greed. Lastly and most importantly, Palestine is Arab. Arabs—in all their different homelands—will never surrender it.

An academic study of the Jewish Question that is free of personal interest and purpose is bound to reach the conclusion that the idea of a "national home" in Palestine is a fantasy, and that Zionism is a movement detrimental to Jews. [. . .]

[We agree with Professor Laski that] that the way a given society treats its Jews reflects the way it treats its individuals and that if Jews were fully emancipated in a society of which they are a part, then this would generally lead to the emancipation of the entire population. Jews, then, would come to enjoy freedom as part of this society. This was the case in the Soviet Union and is now the case in southeast Europe, for example. Yet the Zionist attempt to detach the Jewish masses from the general struggle, as supported by Laski, will not serve the community, but will instead harm it because it undermines the unity of the struggle by disassociating Jews from it. That is where Laski's fallacy lies, namely, by deeming Zionism a "fighter for the whole world." [. . .]

Jews constitute part of the society where they live, and their Question cannot be separated from the issues of that society. As current community problems have been engendered by the presence of colonialism, the Jews' problem can be resolved only in connection with the settlement of the national issues of the country they are in. In Palestine, the Jewish Question would be resolved through the elimination of colonialism and the establishment of an independent democratic Arab state. It is thus the duty of every Jew to partake in the general struggle of his people toward freedom, happiness, and prosperity. This is where the only final solution of the Jewish Question lies. Jews accordingly need to cooperate with emerging liberal powers in today's societies by helping—with all their strength—national powers denouncing Nazism and antisemitism as well as racist movements (including Zionism). They must struggle for the welfare of the people, no matter what their religion, race, or nationality, and by fighting for freedom for people of every class: workers, farmers, and intellectuals.

The struggle of Jews—side by side with conscious liberal forces—is the recipe for their salvation. We can see how a major Peoples' Party in Palestine is now approaching the Jewish Question rationally and correctly. We refer here to the National Liberation Group Party, fighting whoever tends to direct the Arab national movement along the track of racism, standing up in defense of the rights of Jewish workers in the same way it does for Arab workers. This party is anxious to institute an on-the-ground solution to the Palestinian issue on the basis of halting Jewish migration and establishing an independent democratic state with no trace of colonial intervention and that secures the rights of Arabs and Jews alike.

With regard to the problem of Jewish detainees in German prisons, we hold that the management of these miserable Jewish groups should be handed over to Jewish democratic institutions that will have to duly understand that Poland, for example, is no longer like hell to Jews, but now has in place a popular democratic government that resists all antisemitic and racist propaganda. We likewise think that the United Nations and relief agencies should duly provide the necessary assistance to those afflicted. Yet the present colonial administration of these detention camps is doing the precise opposite by treating prisoners inhumanely and by distributing to them unfair Zionist circulars inciting them to migrate to Palestine, not for their own rescue but in order to use them as scapegoats for colonial rule there.

We appeal to every Jew to understand these facts; to apprehend thoroughly the meaning of Zionism and colonialism and their unequivocal wrongdoings in connection with the Jewish Question; to know that the Jewish Question can be resolved only by cooperation and struggle hand in hand with liberal progressive forces that are both intrinsically and resolutely against all manifestations of abuse, racist propaganda, and antisemitism; forces that are struggling for the realization of people's prosperity, freedom, and good irrespective of race, religion, or nationality; forces that struggle against colonialism and its agents.

25 | Last Letter

Sasson Shalom Dallal, "Last Letter," in Yūsuf Rizq-Allāh Ghanīmah, *A Nostalgic Trip into the History of the Jews of Iraq*, trans. Reading A. Dallal (Lanham, MD: University Press of America, 1998), 175–76.

The night before his execution by the Iraqi government, Sasson Dallal wrote this letter to his brother David (1898–1988). The letter was translated from Arabic by Reading Dallal, David's son (with Sheila Dallal's editing), and the translation was included in Reading Dallal's translation of Ghanīmah's 1924 *Nuzhat al-mushtāq fī tārīkh Yahūd al-'Irāq.*

Dear Brother:

It is an enchanting evening. The wind has been blowing steadily the whole day. It suddenly dropped at nightfall. All is still. There is no stir in the air. The world seems fast asleep. I cannot sleep. It is hard to sleep knowing that tomorrow at dawn I will die. Ever since I was arrested, I wanted to write to you. I was not sure of what to say. I was confused and afraid. I was not sure that you would sympathize with my activity and ideas, ideas that could only prove valid where our lives most need them. I was not sure that your academic life in America would make you see objectively the justice and validity of our cause. Tonight, knowing that the coming dawn will start my eternal night, I venture to write to you the thoughts and ideas which are teeming in my brain now.

A wave of terror has taken the country; thousands of people are being arrested, tortured, and executed. I am not the only one to die tomorrow. There are ten others with me. The people as a whole are persecuted. Life in our country recalls the days when the forces of fascism were marching on, murdering thousands of innocent people. I have not lived long enough to enjoy and know what life is. I opened my eyes fighting for a free life and tomorrow at dawn I am dying for the life I never knew.

I pray to God that my fight has not been in vain. The forces of reaction cannot rule forever. They have been defeated before by the will of the people and by the same will, they will be defeated in the near future. I am dying tomorrow because I have faith in mankind to master their destiny, which is democracy, peace, and the perfect life. The forces of reaction that are still murdering people to lengthen the time of their criminal rule are afraid of the future. In the future, they see the shadow of their end. This shadow is perverting their minds. They are insane. They have exhausted their ideas. They are bankrupt in their policies, lies, propaganda, and promises. They are terribly afraid of the wrath of the people. They can rob me of my life, but they cannot change my thinking, which is that of all Mankind. I am free because I know the truth and neither prison nor execution can take away that freedom from me.

Tomorrow at dawn I shall die. Yes, they can end my life and stop me from exposing and fighting them, but with my death, thousands of others will rise against them. We are [the] many, they are the few. Do not grieve for me, dear brother, instead carry my memory with you and perpetuate the fight, which will glorify the future of all humanity. And always remember that I am not sorry to die. In fact, if I am given once again the chance to live, I would follow the same path.

Goodbye to all, and my love to you.

Further Readings

Al-Latīf al-Rawī, ʿAbd, ed. ʿUsbat Mukāfahat al-Sahyoniyya fī al-ʿIraq 1945–1946 (The League for the Struggle against Zionism in Iraq 1945–1946). Damascus: Dar al-Jalīl, 1986.

Al-Maʿādīdī, ʿIsām Jumʿa Ahmad al-Sihāfa al-Yahūdiyya fī al-ʿIrāq (Jewish journalism in Iraq). Cairo: Dār al-Dawliyya li-al-Ithtithmārāt al-Thaqāfiyya, 2001.

Batatu, Hanna. The Old Social Classes and the Revolutionary Movement in Iraq. Princeton: Princeton University Press, 1978.

Giladi, Naeim. Ben-Gurion's Scandals. Flushing, NY: Glilit, 1992.

Rejwan, Nissim. The Last Jews in Baghdad: Remembering a Lost Homeland. Austin: University of Texas Press, 2004.

Snir, Reuven. "Arabic in the Service of Regeneration of Jews: The Participation of Jews in Arabic Press and Journalism in the 19th and 20th Centuries." Acta Orientalia 59, no. 3 (2005): 283–323.

———. "Arabic Journalism as a Vehicle for Enlightenment." Journal of Modern Jewish Studies 6, no. 3 (2007): 219–37.

Somekh, Sasson. Baghdad Yesterday. Jerusalem: IBIS, 2007.

Usuki, Akira. "The Anti-Zionist Movement among the Iraqi Jews: Zionism, Arab Nationalism, and Communism in Iraq Immediately after the Second World War." Journal of the Faculty of Liberal Arts (Saga University, Japan) 21 (March 1989): 1–26.

Marsil Shirizi

A leading Marxist activist and the author of many works in Arabic, French, and Italian, Marsil Shirizi (b. 1913)—also known as Marcel Israel and Marcel Ceresi—was born in Cairo's Mit Ghamr neighborhood to a Jewish-Italian family. At twenty-one, he joined the antifascist International Peace Movement, and in 1939 he cofounded—with Henri Curiel and Hillel Schwartz—the Marxist movement al-Itihad al-Dimuqrati (The democratic union). Personal, tactical, and ideological differences among the cofounders, whose political orientations varied, led Shirizi to form Jama'at Tahrir al-Sh'ab (People's liberation group). Of Egypt's many Marxist Jews, Shirizi was probably the most militant believer in the need to Egyptianize the communist movement, while also believing that "native" Egyptians alone should hold leadership roles.

In 1939, while he was in charge of the warehouses of a Ma'sara company that made pipes, Shirizi researched and wrote *Explaining Reality: Dialectic and Historical*. The first part of a two-part work, the book was 300 pages long and written in French. With the help of two comrades, Shirizi translated the text into Arabic. In October 1941 the police attacked Jama'at Tahrir al-Sh'ab and incarcerated many of its members, including Shirizi. While in prison, he wrote in Arabic the second part of his study, titled *Changing Reality: Theories and the Egyptian Revolution*. After Nazi troops led by Field Marshal Erwin Rommel attacked Egypt in July 1942, the Italian antifascist movement approached Egypt's secret police to facilitate Shirizi's escape from prison to Palestine, where he would be safer. His comrade Bakr Seif el-Nasr, who was the son of Egypt's minister of war, played a crucial role in this rescue.

Shirizi returned to Egypt in 1944, reorganized Jama'at Tahrir al-Sh'ab, and resumed communist activism within the Egyptian national movement. For the next three years, he was in charge of the group's cadre school and conducted research projects that the board of Jama'at Tahrir al-Sh'ab assigned him. In 1947 Shirizi joined the efforts to unify Egypt's communist factions into the Movement for National Liberation Organization (*al-Haraka al-Dimuqratiyya li'l Tahrir al-Watani*, known as HADETU). Uninterested in joining HADETU's central committee, Shirizi continued his activities in the Jewish League to Combat Zionism (*al-Rabita al-Israiliyya Lil Mukafahat al-Sahyuniyya*), which he founded in 1946 as part of HADETU. But in 1947 the group was dissolved by Prime Minister Fahmi al-Nuqrashi. In July 1948 a group within HADETU formed al-'Umaliyya al-Thawriyya (Revolutionary workers) with the help of Shirizi. In March 1949—while Shirizi was a member of the preparatory committee involved in the formation of the Egyptian Communist Party—he was arrested again. When the Wafd Party—Egypt's most influential national party—formed a government in January 1950, he was released with many other detainees. Shirizi resumed his activism, only to be deported to Italy in 1953. Joining the Italian Communist Party, his first contribution was a report on the state of Egyptian communism.

26 | Anti-Zionism for the Sake of Jews and the Sake of Egypt

Marsil Shirizi, *Awrāq munādil Ītālī fīī Misr* (Papers of an Italian fighter in Egypt)
(al-Qahirah, Egypt: Dar al-'Alam al-Thalith, 2002), 52–56.

> The Jewish League to Combat Zionism was formed under the leadership of Shi-
> rizi. The following statement was written in 1947 in both Arabic and French and
> published by the league for HADETU's Foreigners' Department as part of the overall
> efforts to unify the Egyptian Communist movement. It is translated here from the
> Arabic version included in Shirizi's autobiography from 2002.

The Jewish League to Combat Zionism was formed to counteract the impend-
ing danger of Zionism with regard to the settlement of the old and painful Jewish
Question. The League founders are well acquainted with the manifold difficulties
and obstacles that will doubtless appear in their way while [they are] carrying on
with their struggle, not only for the sake of the Egyptian Jewish community, but
also for the benefit of world Jews. The League founders are best informed of the
precarious and crafty means used by Zionist politicians and those who manipulate Zionism as a tool to serve their colonial policies in the Middle East. They
do not underestimate the deep infiltration of the perilous dreams transmitted
by Zionist promotional material into the minds of Jews. Since the inception of
their struggle against Zionism in Egypt, the League's distinguished founders are
poised between, on the one hand, betrayed victims who were misled by Zionist
publicity and, on the other hand, this group of politicians and hacks that take
advantage of the Jewish Question to achieve their objectives and satisfy their
selfish ambitions. Our struggle against Zionism is part and parcel of the general
struggle toward the resolution of the Jewish problem.

1. THE JEWISH QUESTION

The ashes of the six million Jews who were sacrificed by brutal fascists during the Nazi era in Europe attest to the presence of a Jewish problem—rather
than an anti-Jewish movement, as claimed by Zionists—being a phenomenon
correlated with Jews' specificities; a phenomenon, similar to economic crises

and wars, originating from the depths of our social structure, which likewise provides evidence of the imbalances in our society. Given the shortcomings and grievances in our community, and because there are people who are persecuted and exploited, those responsible for such exploitation and persecution attempt—and unfortunately often succeed—to reverse the struggle of their victims, which is increasingly becoming a threat to their status, to whom history has long assigned the role of the scapegoat, that is, the Jews. Anti-Judaism is a favorite weapon of reactionary movements. It is directed not only at Jews but also at the Jewish population, against whom the fascists tend to divert their struggle and [whom they tend to] keep in the shackles of slavery.

The Jewish problem is relevant not only to Jews, whose adversaries hold them responsible for all our community's imperfections; it also concerns peoples victimized by these disadvantages. This simply accounts for democratic drives all over the world in repulsion of anti-Jewish movements, which are used as a weapon in the hands of enemies of progress and freedom. Therefore, the best guarantee for ensuring a final, decisive solution to this old Jewish problem is the community of interests and a realistic alliance between the Jewish population and world democratic forces.

Unlike Zionists, who regard antisemitism as an inevitable and everlasting phenomenon, we fully trust humanitarian approaches and the forces of progress and have high hopes for a better future. We believe in the imminence of a world free of misery, war, and hostility as far as Jews are concerned, and where all the shameful atrocities of the present will become the history of an abhorrent past. The Jewish problem has developed into a peculiar threefold issue. First, there is the problem of Jewish minorities spreading into most parts of the world. This is the main side of the Jewish story, as it relates directly to the overwhelming majority of Jews. Second, there is the problem of the Jews in Palestine, whom Zionists depict as the embodiment of the entire Jewish Question. Third and last, there is the problem of [refugee] Jews in Western Europe, who have no home but the camps for displaced persons. These three issues comprise the present manifestation of the historic Jewish Question.

2. THE JEWISH MINORITY PROBLEM

In historical terms, Jews have lived in the Diaspora for centuries on all continents and in most parts of the world. They were also destined to live as minorities side by side with the majority of the population, to share their actions, pains, and aspirations. Hence was the inception of the Jewish problem. Antidemocratic elements in society took advantage of the presence of a number of Jews among those responsible for the misery of the people to ignite the masses' agitation against the entire Jewish minority, thus wreaking havoc and rolling back the national social struggle of the people in favor of a meaningless struggle against the "Jewish race."

Zionists claim that the only solution to the Jewish problem is to gather Jews in Palestine and create a Jewish state similar to other states. We declare that we are not opposed, in principle, to the idea of forming a Jewish nation somewhere in the world. However, from a scientific point of view—and mindful of the current world circumstances—we find it fantastic and impossible to compose a nationalism embracing all or the majority of Jews, or even a significant section of them. We likewise oppose the notion of Palestine being chosen as the country in which a number of Jews are expected to be assembled to make it possible to work out a solution to the Jewish Question. What we have against Zionists is that they want to attract Jews to Palestine despite the opposition of Palestine's Arab population and with the help of oppressive colonial forces. Instead of settling the Jewish Question, Zionism leads—on the contrary—to its further complication and heightened severity. There is no such country on earth where Jews live, flanked as they are by antagonism and an unfair colonial regime, as they do in Palestine.

Zionism is now helping turn the Arab world, well known for its traditional friendship with Jews, into a fertile soil for anti-Jewish movements. Clear evidence of the failure of Zionism in resolving the Jewish Question is that six million Jews were massacred after half a century of world Zionist activity and a quarter of a century of Zionist activity in Palestine. Born in old Jewish districts as an inspiring movement for hope, Zionism has developed into nothing but a tool in the hands of world colonial powers bent on using Jews to cement their hegemony on the Middle East. We regard Zionism as an anti-Jewish movement because it ultimately serves foreign interests that are, meanwhile, malevolent toward Jews. We declare that the sole direction Jews need to take rests with dedicated open engagement in the national life of the country in which they live. We are neither requesting full integration, nor assimilatory fusion, of Jews into the surrounding majority. Anecdotal evidence has shown that this has not been applicable everywhere. But we are sure that the de facto participation of Jews in the movement is the only foreseeable way to cripple the action of their enemies and to draw us all nearer to the day when the anti-Jewish experience becomes history.

Anti-Jewish movements are only in progress when democracy is in recession.

Fascism is the chief enemy of Jews. It is therefore our duty to fight against it with all our strength, to eliminate its remnants and face up to the trials of its resuscitation. We are not only accusing Zionist politicians of turning Jews away from struggle against their number one enemy—fascism—but we also press against them the charge of increased cooperation with fascist-minded elements, which involves an unforgivable treason to Judaism. This issue is inseparable from the general issue of the people. Peace for Jewish minorities can be guaranteed only through alliance with democratic forces, which, by ensuring freedom and well-being for all peoples, will ensure freedom and well-being for Jews as well.

3. THE QUESTION OF PALESTINE

Our opposition to Zionism, which claims the solution to the Jewish problem is to gather Jews in Palestine, does not signify our disinterest in the Palestinian issue in relation to the fate of Jews in Palestine—who now account for one-third of this country's total population. Our opposition to Zionism does not prevent us from invalidating all attempts at expelling Jews from Palestine and failing to recognize their right to full citizenship. We are proud of the achievements of our brothers in Palestine in the cooperative and physical sphere. We want to keep these achievements safe and secure in their growth. This is our way of exposing Zionism and fighting against it. Zionism puts Jewish survival in Palestine at stake by dangerously collaborating with colonial powers in control of Palestine and using its best endeavors to do so, as well as through discrimination between the Jewish and Arab populations. In so doing, Zionism intends to make Jews a flexible machine in the hands of colonialists to be at the forefront versus Arab liberation movements and to separate them from their natural allies—that is, world democratic forces.

The awareness of the Jewish population in Palestine is steadily gaining steam. Their sensitivity to the risks involved in Zionist criminal policies is also growing. The authoritarian police regime fettering Palestine today—having transformed it into a military fortress—clearly unmasks selfish purposes nurtured by colonialism, to which Palestine is no more than a base for keeping the Middle East under control and defending monopolistic oil interests. The question of Palestine is typically one of emancipation from persecution and colonialism. This means that Palestine's Jews are left with only one option, which is to maintain understanding and work together with the Arabs to liberate Palestine from colonialism. Palestine, as [an] independent and democratic [state], is the only entity that can secure for its Jewish residents a prosperous, free, and productive life. As for the constitutional forms the independent democratic Palestinian state could take, we are of the opinion that it is up to Palestinians themselves, Arabs and Jews, to handle this issue as appropriate.

Zionist politicians are panicking in their opposition to the independence of Palestine. In their view the question of Palestine is the equivalent of the Jewish migration problem—and that is merely it. This view serves no party but colonialism because it covers up its [colonialism's] military, political, and economic domination and empowers it to play the role of the "arbitrator" by further fanning the fire of disagreement between Arabs and Jews. We refuse to support a migration policy that is opposed by the majority of Palestine's population and that is in direct contravention to its alleged humanitarian purposes. We are not in need of migration that plunges our Jewish brothers in civil war–like atmosphere in Palestine, which could end up with them behind barbed wires in British detention camps in Cyprus. However, we are all the more certain that a free, independent Palestine will engage willingly with other democratic states in sheltering displaced Jews.

We see that Jewish terrorism in Palestine is fascist-oriented, basically targeting Jewish people, and in reality serves only colonialists—who found in terrorist movements under the guise of security maintenance an apparent legal justification to turn Palestine into an armed camp servicing their aggression, as well as an apparent moral argument to subdue residents by a regime of perpetual persecution and forced submission. We hold Zionists responsible for the fascist ideas and means inculcated into Jews, since terrorist movements are the logical consequence of the adventurous Zionist policy. To form a unified front along with the Arab liberation movement for the sake of a free independent [and] democratic Palestine is the way of salvation for the Jewish population in Palestine.

4. DISPLACED PERSONS

We are positive that every human, no matter what his religion or nationality, who values his humanity is likely to experience this feeling of appalling disgust vis-à-vis the heinous crimes perpetrated by fascist criminals in the death camps [in Europe]. It is, therefore, conceded that the anniversary of those miserable people whose lives were taken away due to Hitler-style barbarism should be duly commemorated. Hundreds of thousands of refugee souls who were rescued from these camps only after a lapse of two years following the end of the war were still locked up in migrants' prisons in Western Europe. We condemn Zionists for their disinterest in displaced Jews unless related to their selfish and bigoted interests. They decline to think of any solution to those afflicted other than to go to Palestine, prolonging their agony for the sake of forwarding Zionist policy.

We consider the problem of our brothers in displaced person camps as a humanitarian issue of concern to world consciousness. We thus address our call to all world liberals to find a solution to this painful problem. We deem it obligatory to ensure the possibility of immediate repatriation of displaced Jews in German and Austrian camps to the countries they were expelled from by the fascists. This solution is much easier to apply today, given that most of the displaced used to live in the now liberal Eastern European countries that now sentence to death those convicted of committing anti-Jewish crimes. Concerning those who wish for psychological reasons to make a new start away from distressing memories, we look to all countries—especially those with massive territories—to receive them and help them relocate there.

5. THE JEWISH COMMUNITY IN EGYPT

The Egyptian Arab Jewish community has lived for long centuries side by side in amicability and fraternity with the rest of the population in Egypt. Suffice it to recall such names as Philun of Alexandria, Sa'ad [Sa'id] bin Yūsuf al-Fayyūmi, and Mūsā Bin [ibn] Maymūn as a proof of free Jewish thought in Egypt.[1] A few years ago, Egyptian Jews themselves were under pressure from, and much influenced by, the widespread concerted Zionist propaganda trying to instill in them the chauvinistic and racist ideas that overwhelmingly direct their approach to creating the so-called Jewish state in Palestine. The ongoing economic crisis was increasingly affecting Jews (as most of them belong to the middle class). How often owners of Jewish crafts, small merchants, and workers, who share the hardships of life, fell prey to Zionist publicity that made them dream of escaping their abject life to settle in Palestine as farmers in the open air, without having to worry about their means of subsistence. Besides the lies of Zionist propaganda, some Zionist businessmen also brought pressure to bear on them.

1. [Shirizi is referring to three well-known Jewish thinkers who were born or lived in Egypt: Philo of Alexandria (20 BCE–50 CE); Rabbi Sa'adia Gaon (882/892–940); and Moses Maimonides (1135–1204).]

We expressly criticize Zionist propaganda in Egypt aimed at the drastic ostracizing of the Jewish community by the Egyptian people. We are determined with all our strength to fight against agents of Zionism in Egypt who betray the real interests of Egyptian Jews to serve interests absolutely at variance with those of Jews and even of the entire Egyptian people. We believe it is the sacred duty of Egyptian Jews to declare unabated and merciless war on Zionist ideas and their promoters. We have to rid Jewish youth in Egypt of the poisons of Zionism.

We also declare that the only way forward for Egyptian Jews is to demonstrate full solidarity with the Egyptian national movement for the realization of all its objects. Jewish community interests are in no way different from the general interests of the Egyptian people. Egyptian Jews cannot live as equals on fraternal basis with the entire population unless Egypt is independent, free, and democratic. The Jewish League to Combat Zionism is aware that—to the credit of its struggle against the scathing Zionist influence—it is serving the interests of the Jewish community as much as it respects the interests of the Egyptian nation.

6. PURPOSES OF THE LEAGUE

The League develops objectives in concert with its sound plan to solve the Jewish problem in its different aspects. Zionism, meanwhile, is designed to throw the entire world's Jewish population into confusion and place them in a tight spot. It also endangers the fate of the Jews in Palestine and for selfish reasons capitalizes on the misery experienced by migrants. Zionism finally endeavors to seriously isolate the Egyptian Jewish community from the total Egyptian population. Therefore, the League can safely assert that Zionism represents the most dangerous movement that has ever surfaced in Jewish history and is a hindrance to the settlement of the Jewish problem.

Struggle against Zionism is a sacred obligation for every male and female Jew to discharge, especially given that the advance of world democratic forces opens new avenues for us toward a prospective solution of the old Jewish Question. While the League is struggling against Zionism, it is fighting for positive elements that will render it easier to settle the Jewish problem. The purposes of the Jewish League to Combat Zionism can be defined as follows:

- Struggle against Zionist propaganda that is in conflict with the interests of both Jews and Arabs.

- Close links between Egyptian Jews and the Egyptian people in the course of struggle toward independence and democracy.
- Bringing together Jews and Arabs in Palestine.
- Action to resolve the problem of displaced persons.

The Jewish League to Combat Zionism has limited its active membership to Jews because it considers itself a Jewish movement chiefly operating in connection with the Jewish community. Based on its opposition to Zionism, it is inclined to serve the real interests of the Egyptian Jewish community. Despite its independence from all political parties, the League announces its readiness to cooperate with all parties sincerely in support of its struggle in a bid to achieve its aims. Credited for its success in the anti-Zionist struggle and in attracting Jewish masses toward the Egyptian popular national movement, the League declares that it is in the service of Egypt and its interests, [and] that it is proud of this and assured of the justice of its call, as well as of the outcome of the struggle it is staging and the support of democratic public opinion. It [the league] is getting on board in its fight against Zionism, tool of colonialism and enemy of the Jews. It acts under the slogan of "Anti-Zionism! For the sake of Jews! For the sake of Egypt!"

The Jewish League to Combat Zionism
Cairo, June 1947

Further Readings

Beinin, Joel. *The Dispersion of Egyptian Jewry: Culture, Politics, and the Formation of a Modern Diaspora*. Berkeley: University of California Press, 1998.

Botman, Selma. *The Rise of Egyptian Communism, 1939–1970*. Syracuse, NY: Syracuse University Press, 1988.

Ismael, Tareq Y., and Rifa'at El-Said. *The Communist Movement in Egypt: 1920–1988*. Syracuse, NY: Syracuse University Press, 1990.

Shirizi, Marsil. *Awrāq munādil Ītālī fī Misr* (Papers of an Italian fighter in Egypt). Al-Qahirah, Egypt: Dar al-'Alam al-Thalith, 2002.

Henri Curiel

A cofounder of several communist groups in Egypt and a leading Marxist organizer during the 1940s, Henri Curiel (1914–78) was born in Cairo to a well-off Jewish family. Although his family had lived in Egypt for three generations and also possessed Italian citizenship, its members adopted a Francophone identity in linguistic, cultural, and educational terms. At the age of twenty-one, Curiel chose to take Egyptian nationality—relinquishing his right to his father's Italian passport. His charismatic and controversial political life began in the early 1930s, when he joined the antifascist International Peace Movement. In 1939 he and his older brother, Raoul, attempted and failed to enlist in the French army. Subsequently Henri Curiel cofounded, with Hillel Schwartz and Marsil Shirizi, the Marxist movement al-Itihad al-Dimuqrati (The democratic union). One of the group's aims was to further the Allied cause in Egypt. To this end, Curiel also cofounded Amitiés Françaises—responding to Charles de Gaulle's call to generate worldwide resistance to Nazi Germany. Personal and ideological differences among al-Itihad al-Dimuqrati's founders led to a parting of the ways. Curiel established the al-Midan (The square) bookstore and arranged rigorous translations of Marxist studies into Arabic to deepen Egyptians' political consciousness.

In 1942 Egypt was on the verge of falling into the hands of German Field Marshal Erwin Rommel. Unlike many Jews, Curiel chose to stay in Cairo to engage in anti-Nazi resistance. He was taken into the al-Zeitoun detention camp by the Egyptian police, some of whose members were openly sympathetic to Britain's German enemies. In that year Curiel witnessed demonstrators chanting Rommel's name—supporting Hitler against Churchill—and thus following the precept that "my enemy's enemy is my friend." Throughout his subsequent Marxist activism with Jews and non-Jews alike, Curiel worked to popularize the notion that Nazism represented the highest form of European colonialism. In 1943 he founded both al-Haraka al-Misriyah lil Tahrir al-Watani (The Egyptian movement for national liberation, or EMNL) and the Sudanese Communist Party. Using money his father left him, he formed a school for cadres where Egyptian intellectuals taught workers and peasants about Egyptian history, Marxism, and political economy. In 1948 Curiel was detained for eighteen months in Huckstep (see below). The authorities freed his friends in exchange for their permanent departure from Egypt. Although Curiel was determined to remain in Egypt, the authorities stripped him of his nationality, clearing the way for his deportation.

On August 26, 1950, Curiel was secretly transported to Port Said and placed on a ship that took him to exile in Genoa. From there he found his way to France, where he resided as a noncitizen. Until 1957 Curiel continued to immerse himself in Egyptian affairs and the Arab-Israeli conflict. But in that year he joined a French network that, during the Algerian War (1954–62), supported the Algerian National Liberation Front. When French security services rounded up the organization's leaders, Curiel was asked by the Algerians to take over the reins. However, on October 20, 1960, he was imprisoned by the French police, who detained him for eighteen months and issued papers for his deportation. At the time the French-Algerian Peace Accords were signed, Curiel was able to escape deportation because of his antifascist activism in Egypt during the 1940s. His former involvement in Amitiés Françaises linked him to members of the Free French Resistance, some of whom in the 1960s were now ministers in de Gaulle's cabinet. They ensured that he would not be deported. Curiel gave his parents' Cairo villa to the new Algerian government, to serve as its embassy.

Curiel then formed Solidarité, an organization whose mandate was to train political activists in such areas as first aid; reading maps; interpreting terrains; shaking off people shadowing them; and using codes, portable presses, and invisible ink. Although mainly helping third-world militants—including African National Congress members—Solidarité also supported antifascist groups in Spain under Franco, Portugal under Salazar and Caetano, Greece under the colonels, and Chile under Pinochet. Solidarité's work earned Curiel enemies worldwide. In the late 1960s and early 1970s, he was also responsible for arranging secret meetings between Israeli doves and members of the Palestine Liberation Organization. On May 4, 1978, Curiel was assassinated by two gunmen in the elevator of his Parisian apartment building. The French police failed to discover the assassins' identities and affiliations, and thus it remains unclear whether they were agents of South Africa's apartheid government, Palestinian militants, hawks within Israel's security services, or someone else.

27 | Egyptian Communists and the Jewish Question

Henri Curiel, "Les Communistes égyptiens et le problème juif," 1949, in
"Inventory of the Papers of the Egyptian Communists in Exile [The Rome
Group]," International Institute of Social History, Amsterdam, No. 317.

This item is a typescript of Curiel's testimony given in Huckstep, a British Army
camp in Cairo south of Heliopolis, that was made into an internment camp for
various political activists including Marxists, Islamists, and Zionists. Curiel spent
eighteen months there. The translation produced is of almost the entire testimony.

I. FROM NOVEMBER 1945 TO DECEMBER 1947

On November 2, 1945—on the occasion of the twenty-eighth anniversary of
the Balfour Declaration—British imperialism, fearing the growing strength of
the Egyptian national movement, attempted to create a diversionary maneuver
by setting up, through their profascist [local] movements, an antisemitic dem-
onstration in Cairo. To this end, a wide-ranging press campaign was undertaken,
and imperialism was counting on their plan's successful execution. But they did
not consider the Communists, and above all the Egyptian Movement for National Liberation [EMNL], which published and distributed tens of thousands
of clandestine pamphlets. By denouncing antisemitism unequivocally, these
pamphlets put the Egyptian populace on their guard against the imperialist maneuver. Militant Egyptian Communists, at the risk of their lives, participated in
the demonstrations and managed to alter their course. In the final reckoning that
day, British imperialism suffered an overall defeat (notwithstanding their few
small successes on the local scale—for example, the destruction of a synagogue).

From that day and right up to 1948, all attempts to implant antisemitism in
Egypt were to suffer a resounding defeat. During the days of 2nd November
1946 and xxxx 1947[1] the initiative passed completely into the hands of the Communists, supported and guided by Egyptian public opinion, which did not
allow the fascist organizations—tools of imperialism—to register even partial
successes in their aims of imposing antisemitism. For their part, the Egyptian

1. [The 1947 date is replaced by "xxxx" in the original.]

Communists—in this instance the EMNL—published many illegal publications denouncing antisemitism as a weapon in the hands of the imperialists to divert national movements away from their principal national struggle.

II. FROM THE [1947] PALESTINE PARTITION PLAN TO THE [1948] WAR

Ever since Gromyko presented his thesis on the Palestinian question,[2] the EMNL—now the Democratic Movement for National Liberation [DMNL]—has taken a position in support of the partition of Palestine in all of its clandestine publications. When [on November 29, 1947] the UN General Assembly voted to approve the Palestine partition plan [UNGA Resolution 181]—the DMNL supported it as the only just solution *given the current circumstances.*

It is worth mentioning that the DMNL was the first organization in the Middle East to take this position—whilst unmasking imperialist maneuvers that were intended to divide the [Egyptian] national movement around the Palestinian question. This advocacy was accomplished through the DMNL's legal publication, *al-Jamahir* [The masses], as well as the January 1948 tract following the banning of *al-Jamahir* by the Egyptian authorities. This activity [in support of UNGA Resolution 181] was carried out notwithstanding many instances of police harassment, the frequent arrest of *al-Jamahir*'s editors, the banning of the publication, attacks by fascist gangs on *al-Jamahir*'s offices [and the throwing of hand grenades at the office], as well as armed assaults in the streets of Cairo against *al-Jamahir*'s personnel.

On the occasion of [Egypt's] declaration of war [against Israel], the DMNL published in its clandestine publications—and particularly in its illegal news-

---

2. [Andrei Gromyko (1909–89) was the Soviet Union's representative to the United Nations from 1946 to 1952. The Soviet Union traditionally supported the establishment of a unitary secular and socialist state in Mandatory Palestine. However, by the period May-November 1947, when the Palestine question was discusssed in the United Nations, the Soviets opted for a more pragmatic position, leading them to support the partition of Mandatory Palestine into two states (one Arab and the other Jewish), each with a democratic internal structure but also institutionally joined together through an economic union. Soviet leaders believed that this solution would provide the quickest way to terminate the British colonial presence in, and long domination over, Palestine while leading to the eventual involvement of military and administrative Soviet contingents within the international force whose aim was to guarantee and implement this transition.]

paper *Mukawama* (Resistance)—declarations that condemned the war as unjust while also highlighting to the Egyptian masses that the only way to solve their problems was to struggle against imperialism and for national liberation. [The slogan was] "Our front is not in Palestine but in the Canal Zone and Sudan." Communist militants distributed these pamphlets and publications despite the great risks they faced, including detention camps or imprisonment for up to fifteen years.

On Falujah Day in Cairo,[3] around thirty Communists were imprisoned after they distributed pamphlets condemning the war as well as the farce of Falujah Day. The Egyptian Air Force's military engineers voted (in March 1948) not to undertake any extra work in preparation for the Palestine War. Thirty of them were deported to desert oases—from where about fifteen were sent to the detention camps. Other Egyptian Communists infiltrated a Sudanese battalion returning from the [Palestinian] front and convinced the Sudanese conscripts to refuse to fight and return to Sudan; in fact, the battalion was sent back to Sudan.

Within the detention camps—[including Huckstep, where the present 1949 text was written—the Editors]—the Egyptian Communists, living side by side with Jews, refused to allow any discriminatory measures to pass unchecked and acted in solidarity with the Jews in the defense of their common interests (that is, self-defense against fascist attacks, action to improve the quality of food, hunger strikes for freedom, etc.). In addition, the Manifesto of the Seventeen Activists, published inside the camp and sent to the authorities despite the fact that Egypt was under martial law, is a document attesting to the indefatigability of the Egyptian Communists in defending the rights of oppressed minorities, in this instance the [Egyptian] Jewish minority.

III. CURRENT [1949] POSITION

In the face of the aggravation of the situation in Egypt, police repression, and above all the affirmation of *state antisemitism*—Egyptian Communists are in sup-

3. [Located northwest of Gaza city, al-Faluja was a Palestinian village in the territory that UNGA Resolution 181 had allocated to the Arab state in November 1947. On March 14, 1948, a battle between armed Jewish forces and residents of the village left thirty-eight Palestinians and seven Jews dead, as well as dozens wounded. Between November 1948 and February 1949, the Israeli army managed to capture some four thousand Egyptian soldiers there. Curiel's text was written around this time, and it is unlikely that he knew as many details of this episode as are known today.]

port of Egyptian Jewish immigration to Israel—while making clear to these Jews who can no longer live in Egypt that, if Israel is a sizable bourgeois democracy, it is still far from being a popular democracy and that, although some of their problems will be solved, many will remain unsolved. The DMNL additionally recommends to Jewish militants, whether Egyptian nationals or stateless persons—for whom circumstances such as detention and incomplete assimilation have diminished their ability to continue the struggle in Egypt—to relocate to Israel in order to be able to increase their revolutionary potential under [changing and] new conditions. If they do immigrate to Israel, such Egyptian Jewish militants will have the task of bringing the Communist movements within Egypt and Israel closer together for democratic collaboration in their respective struggles and—above all—for the rapprochement of the Israeli and Egyptian peoples in the defense of their common interests.

28

What Ought to Be the First Official Message from the DMNL to the Israeli Communist Party?

Excerpt from Henri Curiel, "Note sur les relations entre Israel et les Pays Arabes," August 1953, in "Inventory of the Papers of the Egyptian Communists in Exile [The Rome Group]," International Institute of Social History, Amsterdam, No. 338.

This document is an internal memo that Curiel wrote when the DMNL was deliberating what should be its first official message to the Communist Party of Israel. The memo is an analysis of the issue in eight parts. It is written exclusively from the Arab viewpoint—particularly from the Egyptian point of view—as the Israeli viewpoint on the matters discussed can be easily understood. Readers should bear in mind that this analysis was written for internal party purposes and exclusively for DMNL members who knew Curiel and his positions well. Consequently, Curiel did not feel the need to fully elaborate on some themes. The translation produced is of almost the entire item, with only minor omissions, indicated by ellipses.

A. THE IMPORTANCE OF THE QUESTION

The issue of relations between Israel and the Arab states in general—and Egypt in particular—is of vital importance for the following four reasons: (i) current relations between the Arab states and Israel constitute a grave danger to peace in the Middle East (We deem this thesis [to be] self-evident and see no need to elaborate on it here.); (ii) current Arab-Israeli relations are a major obstacle to the Arab peoples' national liberation. [. . .]; (iii) current Arab-Israeli relations effectively allow the imperialists and their agents in the Arab countries to organize acts of provocation designed to direct the Arab peoples away from their struggle for freedom. The campaign of 1948—which had this as one of its principal objectives—could be repeated at any moment. Moreover, the Israeli army—with a strength of around 100,000 fighters and equipped by the Americans—does not figure in the imperialist plans merely to act against democratic countries; Israel is additionally destined to play the role of "policeman" in the Middle East against movements for democratic liberation; and (iv) finally, current relations between Israel and Arab states are a major obstacle to the struggle of the people in Arab countries for democratic regimes. Every time their democratic demands make themselves felt too keenly, it is effectively child's play for the reactionary Arab governments in power to provoke incidents that distract the attention of the masses or—if necessary—proclaim martial law, for example. In brief, these are the main dangers in the current situation.

There is, however, a long list of other dangers that are worth mentioning even if [only] in passing: (i) current Arab-Israeli relations facilitate a politics of armament with all the corresponding dangers to democracy—that is, the army is destined to crush any popular movement; (ii) this rearmament carries financial costs and economic difficulties such as those arising from "blockades," from the cessation in trade with neighboring countries, the costs of occupation, etc.; and (iii) the reinforcement of national chauvinism and the existence of foreign territories occupied by Egyptian forces are also a source of danger.[4]

But it is not fear alone—or the dangers to our people—that ought to make us find a solution to the problem of Arab-Israeli relations. We must first and foremost play the role that has been given to us to save the Arab nation of Palestine, threatened by total destruction. We must then play the role that has been given to us to establish between the Arab peoples, on the one hand, and the Jewish and Arab peoples of Israel, on the other hand, those links of fraternity that should exist between all peoples. The result of all of the above is that the problem of Arab-Israeli relations is vital to us. It will soon surpass the problem of our relations with Sudan. That is why the DMNL's message to the Israeli Communist Party should have marked both the end of our unpardonable passivity and an important step toward accomplishing our tasks in this area.

B. THE FAILURE AND THE TREACHERY OF THE ARAB RULING CLASSES

Our obligations are all the more imperative since in this area the ruling strata have failed so resoundingly and have shamefully betrayed the interests of Palestine's Arabs that they otherwise claimed to be defending. Moreover, the ruling powers utilize the current antagonism between the Arab states and Israel for

4. Without including the need to reinforce the internal unity of our people by struggling against antisemitism, on the one hand, and against Zionism, on the other. [In this paragraph, Curiel is referring to Egypt's control of the Gaza Strip (made part of the Arab state in UNGA Resolution 181) following the 1948 Arab-Israeli War and the 1949 Arab-Israeli Armistice Agreements.]

the most selfish of class aims—aims that it is up to us [the DMNL] to unmask. By denouncing this failure—and by unmasking the ruling strata once more by presenting the foundations for a real solution—the representatives of the working classes play the role of ultimate defenders of the national interest.

The Arab ruling classes—and especially the Egyptian ruling classes—have betrayed the Arab nation of Palestine in at least four ways. First, by rejecting the partition plan that would have led to the establishment of an Arab state in Palestine: they feared the construction of a democratic Arab state like the plague. Second, by triggering a military campaign that ended in disaster: not only for the armies of the [various] Arab states but, above all, for Palestine's Arabs. It is those Arab rulers who bear the greatest responsibility for creating the refugee problem. By triggering this war at the instigation of the imperialists, the Arab ruling classes—who claimed to be coming to the rescue of the Arabs of Palestine—were pursuing other goals. They wanted to distract the Arab masses in their countries from their own problems and utilize the state of war in order to liquidate popular movements which, after World War II, have grown to such an extent that they put in peril the outrageous privileges that the ruling powers enjoy.

Third, the treason of the Arab ruling classes became self-evident when Arab governments accepted the formation of [the Hashemite-ruled kingdom of] Jordan. This dealt a cruel blow to the evolving Palestinian Arab nation and placed it once more under the yoke of the English imperialists—Jordan's real masters. Last, the Egyptian ruling classes—who fully take on the inglorious role of "*leaders*" [in English in the original] in all their successive acts of betrayal—have one particular additional responsibility. They have colonized the Gaza Strip, maintaining there a reign of terror; have taken away all the Arab region's democratic and national rights; and have transformed the Arabs of Gaza into their subjects in all senses of the word. They have made Gaza a true Egyptian possession that they did not hesitate to "offer" as a sweetener to the English imperialists so they would evacuate the Suez Canal Zone.

Arab ruling classes wish to maintain the current state of Arab-Israeli affairs in order to defend their selfish class interests.

The current situation can be summarized in two main points: the existence of [Arab-Israeli] tension and the existence of an economic blockade [against Israel]. The [Arab] ruling classes benefit from maintaining this state of affairs. We have already seen how a state of tension allows the ruling classes to distract the attention of the masses. The blockade itself in no way helps the [Palestinian]

Arab refugees. The blockade represents the fear of both useless and corrupt local capitalists vis-à-vis Israeli competition. The blockade allows capitalists—above all, Egyptian capitalists—to keep Arab markets to themselves. The blockade likewise represents the fear of coming into contact with a legal Communist Party [in Israel]—which includes Arab leaders and militants while also possessing an Arabic-language press and a Parliamentary Tribunal. The Arab governments fear this more than anything else, lest this example become a threat to them. They fear that the publicity given to the activities of Arab Communist deputies—to their interventions—may reveal to the masses the true face of Communism.

Regarding the [Palestinian] Arab refugees, the Arab rulers treat them not as brothers but as enemies: they are forbidden to move into Egypt, establish themselves there, or work there. No efforts are made to alleviate their terrible suffering. It is because Arab rulers want to keep the refugees in this lamentable state, where they found themselves, so that they might use them as elements of agitation at the moment when they have to distract the attention of the masses. Cognizant of the spirit of fraternity that exists between the Arab peoples, they try to use it for their own sinister designs.

C. THE CURRENT POWER IN EGYPT IS FOLLOWING THE SAME POLICY AS THE ONE THAT PRECEDED IT

Egypt's current ruling power[5]—which established itself on the basis of popular support—promised a change of policy. Yet by the logic of its antipopular attitude, it has ended up following the same policy as its predecessors, to an even more extreme degree.

(1) One of the first acts of the new ruling power was to liquidate the "Palestinian government" that was ratified by the Arab League. Although this Palestinian government was deeply reactionary, its liquidation signified the definitive recognition of the annexing of one part of Arab Palestine to Transjordan and, above all, the destruction of the last vestiges of the autonomous representation of Arab Palestine. It pursues a policy of provocation to distract the attention of the masses. Unspeakably, this is what has been used during these few weeks. Wishing to come to agreement with imperialism—and in so doing willing to break

5. [Curiel refers here to the Free Officers' Movement that ended the monarchy in 1952.]

the popular opposition—it uses not only the traditional "conspiracy theory" but it also plays the "threat of Israel" card.

(2) The overwhelming desire of the new ruling power is to please the capitalists by maintaining and reinforcing the blockade. It rides roughshod over the rights of Gaza's Arabs and sends captured democratic elements to be tried in military courts. (Note: This was written before the regime changed its direction. Its position on the Palestinian question has often varied, and this should be the subject of a separate report.)

D. IN THE FACE OF THE RULING CLASSES' FAILURE AND TREACHERY, THE DMNL, REPRESENTING THE WORKING CLASS, ASSERTS THE REAL NATIONAL INTERESTS

OUR MOVEMENT'S TRADITIONS: One of the glories of our movement is that it is the champion of proletarian internationalism in Egypt. Its position vis-à-vis the relations between Egypt and Sudan was one manifestation of this internationalism. Its position concerning the leading role of the Soviet Union has been another. Finally, its position on the Palestinian question has been one of the finest chapters in its history. [. . .] We reentered the Egyptian political arena in October 1945. From November 2nd [of] that year—on the occasion of the so-called Palestine Day (organized by the Muslim Brotherhood at the instigation of English imperialists)—the Movement [the DMNL] took a stance on this important issue. To mark the occasion we distributed a pamphlet. At the same time as it revealed Zionism in its true colors as an instrument of imperialism, it also unmasked "Palestine Day" as an attempt to divert attention from the rising current of the national struggle. [. . .]

But naturally, the most glorious episode concerns the DMNL's position following the United Nations' November 1947 decision in support of partition in Palestine. We ought to shout out loud that our ability to take this position was due to the fact that the Soviet Union and the democratic countries had given it their support. In recognition of the Soviet Union's leading role—that is, understanding that the positions taken by the Soviet Union coincide completely with the peoples' interests—we have supported the partition from the beginning. It did not take long to realize how this solution was profoundly advantageous—not only for the Jews, but also for the Arabs—[and] how much its application and in particular the formation of a democratic Arab state in Palestine served the cause of liberation, democracy, and peace throughout the whole Middle East.

We take pride in having been the only ones to defend this position publicly. The other Communists did not dare to take this position overtly, or criticize it. They held that the Soviet Union was far away and was ignorant of the reality in the Middle East! As regards the DMNL vis-à-vis the rising tide of chauvinism, it bitterly defended its position in the interest of the national movement, in the interest of the Egyptian people, and in the interest of the Arab and Jewish peoples in Palestine. We have never flinched from the insults, calumnies, threats, blows, and even terrorist attacks (a bomb [was] left at the offices of our journal). We struggled both before and under martial law; we struggled in the prison camps (as shown at the time of the hunger strike in July 1948, reported by *Pravda*), and outside them (a pamphlet was issued on the day of the Falujah combatants' parade). The struggle was taken to the heart of the army and right onto the battlefields. All the other nationalist parties without exception left themselves to be won over by chauvinism and participated enthusiastically in the ill-advised campaign. [...]

There is no doubt that the courageous stance taken by the DMNL in its pamphlets, proclamations, and press helped the other parties to rethink their position. It is true that we were thrown in the detention camps and that the military tribunals filled the prisons with Communists. But there have also been those in other Arab countries suffering the same—even where the attitude of the local Communist Party was most violently opposed to the partition plan. It is likewise true that we did not at first see—and thus unmask—the American imperialist plans to make Israel a base against the Soviet Union and against Arab national and democratic movements. However, we did accomplish our own essential task, that is, to struggle against our own reaction and against chauvinism at home. Moreover, we must note that in spite of all the difficulties that this position brought with it, it was enthusiastically adopted by the DMNL in its entirety, with the exception of one or two intellectuals, which demonstrates the extent to which the Movement [the DMNL] was fundamentally sane.

Finally, it is true that we did not succeed in thwarting the plans of the imperialists and reactionaries, nor in stemming the unnamed suffering caused to the Arab peoples—and above all to the Arabs of Palestine—by the disastrous Palestinian campaign. But the Communists did not hold back from reaping the fruits of their just, courageous stance. The Egyptian people understood that the Communists alone saw correctly: they understood from their own experience that the war into which they had been dragged—ostensibly to save the Arabs of Palestine—was in fact fomented by the imperialists and reactionaries to distract them from their own national struggle. This position—taken by the Communists alone against all the traditional parties—constituted a turning point in the Communists' authority and prestige in the political arena on a national scale. All alliances formed after 1950—those with the nationalists, the Socialists, and the Muslim Brotherhood (which led to the repeal of the treaty of 1936 and the accords of 1899[6]), those with the Free Officers (that led to the fall of the Farouk regime)[7] [...]—had their foundations in the correct position taken by the DMNL pertaining to the Palestinian question.

As far as we have been able to judge from attending various democratic congresses, the position of DMNL comrades certainly differs from the one generally taken by Communists in other Arab countries. DMNL comrades have confidence in the Israeli CP [Communist Party] and in the Jewish and Arab peoples in Israel. [. . .] In 1948, even if they did not approve of it, the Egyptian population was aware of the Egyptian Communists' position regarding the problem. Is this the case today? It is clear now that if we do not struggle to propagate and to defend our positions, we allow the dominant classes once again to impose theirs. This would mean passing the initiative—and thus the direction in this domain—to the dominant classes; it would mean abandoning the independent position of the proletariat; it would mean leaving the proletariat to be dragged along by the bourgeoisie.

We are certainly talking about an arduous problem, and the various positions are confused. We cannot take a stance as easily as we could in 1948, when the Soviet Union showed the correct way in the most desirable fashion. We must exercise our brains somewhat, something we must confess to not enjoying. We cannot follow the example of other Arab Communist parties. As for the other Egyptian Communist organizations, they also "shy away" from the issue. But all this means only one thing: that it is the DMNL that must talk when the oth-

6. [Curiel refers here to the Anglo-Egyptian Treaty of 1936—also known as the Treaty of Alliance between His Majesty, in Respect of the United Kingdom, and His Majesty, the King of Egypt—which stipulated that the United Kindom should withdraw all its troops from Egypt except for those necessary to protect the Suez Canal. The accords of 1899 restored Egyptian rule over Sudan, but jointly with Britain—which effectively provided a legal basis for the continuation of British rule in Sudan.]

7. [King Farouk (1920–65) was ruler of Egypt from 1936 until he was removed by the Free Officers in 1952.]

ers hold their tongues; that it comes down once more to the DMNL to be at the vanguard in this field.

E. A POWERFUL ALLY: THE ISRAELI COMMUNIST PARTY AT THE HEAD OF DEMOCRATIC FORCES IN ISRAEL

Amid these difficulties—yet unlike in 1948—we now have prospects for a powerful ally: the Israeli Communist Party (ICP), experienced vanguard of the working class in Israel, leading both Arab and Jewish democratic forces. These forces are powerful and have recently achieved some important victories. Let us refer to one dimension that will allow us to evaluate their power and to understand the manner in which they might assist us. In the schemes of the American imperialists and Israeli reactionaries, Israel should be a base for aggression against the Soviet Union and other democratic countries. What is more, Israel is led by a government that is counted among the most servile to the Americans. Now, on the foundations of the Soviet Union's correct policies—and in spite of the gravest provocations fomented by imperialist agents inside Israel (the terrorist attack on the Soviet Legation in Tel Aviv, etc.)—the ICP's action at the head of nationalist and democratic forces obliged the Israeli minister for foreign affairs, Mr. Moshe Sharett [1884–1965], to solemnly swear to never participate in any pact of aggression directed against the Soviet Union or democratic countries.

We have said that in the imperialists' schemes, Israel should play the role of "policeman" in the Middle East. But if the Israeli people convinced themselves that the Arab peoples did not hold a grudge against its [Israel's] existence—that the national and democratic movements took a stance and struggled for an equitable solution to the conflict—the imperialists' schemes would once more be frustrated. And just as the Israeli Army cannot be used against the Soviet Union, it could not be used against democratic and national Arab movements. What do we have to do to get these forces to work in our favor? We need two things.

The first is that all national and democratic movements in the Arab countries need to take a stand and take action—and as far as we are concerned, we foremost mean those in Egypt. It must be said that they are still very weak at the moment. Second, these stands and this action must be brought to the awareness of the Israeli masses. We can be certain that the Israeli Communist Party will acquit itself handsomely of its duties in this plan. Yet the democratic forces inside Israel and the action of the Israeli Communist Party at their head can aid us powerfully in another sense. They exist and are struggling for the same goals as we are: not only with regards to the general issues [...] of peace and democracy but also with regard to the issue of the relationship between Israel and the Arab countries. The Israeli Communist Party, together with the Left Socialist Party, is restlessly leading the principled struggle against Zionism and Zionist ideology.[8]

If only the Arab peoples, and the Egyptians in particular, knew of the existence and actions of these forces, it would be a decisive blow against chauvinism's toxic influence, which the ruling classes are developing with all their strength in their own interests and against the national interest. We must recognize that also in this field we have taken neither serious nor systematic action to make the Israeli Communist Party's heartfelt struggle well known: for the defense of Arab interests inside Israel, the defense of refugees' interests against the bourgeoisie's plans for expansion, [and] against the policy of provocation [led] by the Israeli government that will not abandon it in the face of the Arab governments' policy of provocation.

The Israeli government's policy has become much more aggressive than that of the Arab governments. Although there certainly are many reasons for this, one does still concern us: the absence of a clear stance and of action on the part of those democratic forces in favor of peace and against reenforcing an army of aggression. We must remedy this anemic response at the first possible opportunity and widely publicize the actions of the Israeli Communist Party—our powerful allies at the head of the Arab and Jewish democratic forces within Israel.

F. FOR A SHARED POSITION AMONG DEMOCRATS IN ARAB STATES

With regard to other Arab countries, appreciable, relatively powerful democratic forces can be found in Syria and Lebanon. It must be said that their Communist Parties' reserve means that they take neither a vigorous, nor clear enough, position on the issue of relations with Israel. This results in the domination of chauvinist ideology. This ideology was used against the DMNL in 1948 and is cer-

---

8. For example, you have the definition of Zionism given by the Israeli Communist Party's General Secretary Shmuel Mikonis [1903–82] published in *La Voie* [*Ha-Derech*; The way], the party's theoretical organ, no.7, June 1953: "According to Marxism-Leninism, Zionisme [*sic*] was and remains a reactionary national bourgeois trend, connected during all the years of its existence with Imperialism, allied with it and loyally serving it ..." [The quotation is in English in the original.]

tain to be used against us again. That is why we must do our best to bring about, on a regional scale among the Arab countries, a shared position pertaining to the question of Arab-Israeli relationships as a means to enable a shared struggle and reciprocal support to bring about a solution to contemporary problems. One of the most efficient ways to start this is to boldly take a stance ourselves and struggle against our own chauvinism.

G. FOR FRATERNAL AID TO THE ARAB REFUGEES OF PALESTINE

The lines that join the Palestinian Arab refugees to us are not just the standard lines of solidarity between all people and especially between the Arab peoples. We have a particular dual responsibility to the refugees: (i) in general we bear a large part of the responsibility for the sad exodus that has become their lot—be this in Israel or Jordan or as refugees in other countries; and (ii) for a large number of the refugees we bear a direct responsibility inasmuch as they are suffering under the martial law imposed by Egyptian reactionaries [over Egypt and the Gaza Strip]. We must tear from the faces of the reactionaries the hypocrite's mask of defender of Arab Palestine and the Palestinian refugees. We must show how they are the chief assassins of the Palestinian Arab nation.

We must simultaneously struggle in defense of the rights of the Palestinian nation. We should give aid unsparingly not only to the courageous Palestinian Communists—who, risking their own lives, lead the struggle for the rebirth of the Palestinian Arab nation—but to all national forces, in the widest sense, who long for this rebirth and the formation of a democratic Arab state while recognizing Israel's sacred right to exist as an independent state. This action will also help us against the accusations that the reactionaries are bound to make, that is, that we would like to "betray" Arab interests in Palestine. It is through asking these questions on the practical front that we will be able to respond best, as well as through allying ourselves with the Palestinian Arab national forces, foremost those of the refugees in the Gaza Strip.

H. OUR POSITIONS

Consequently, the following recommended positions emerge:
We struggle for the resurrection of the Arab nation of Palestine, destroyed in the main by the adventurism and selfish policies of the ruling classes in the

Arab countries. We demand that the part of Palestine colonized by Transjordan be returned to the Arabs of Palestine and administered democratically and in full sovereignty by them. Being Egyptians, we demand above all that the part of Palestine colonized by Egypt be returned to the Arabs of Palestine and administered democratically and in full sovereignty by them.

While we wait for this, we demand: the dissolution of martial law in Egypt, the abolition of all antidemocratic measures, and a general amnesty in Gazan territory. We likewise demand: that the refugees administer themselves democratically, that all measures of discrimination against them are dropped, and that a true fraternal aid effort be made on the material and moral fronts. That is how we will be able to obtain the legitimate removal of reactionary and feudal governments that do not have the right to negotiate in the name of the Arab nation of Palestine. They are the principal cause for the state to which this nation has been reduced.

It is the democratically elected representatives of the Arabs of Palestine who alone have the right to discuss their problems with Israel. The refugee problem and the problem of the borders of the democratic Arab state of Palestine are, it seems, the main problems. In all discussions and whatever results from them, the Arabs of Palestine would have our total support and the support of the other Arab peoples, and of the democratic camp as a whole. It is in this fashion that the Arab nation will be reborn after a period of enormous hardships and will become stronger and more glorious than ever.

We struggle for a peaceful solution to the conflict between Israel and the Arab countries, particularly Egypt, and for the establishment of friendly relations with the Jewish and Arab peoples of Israel. Chauvinist Arab reactionaries will once again try to stir up the masses against us and will accuse us of betrayal, when they are the real traitors and we are the true defenders of the national interest. But we must demonstrate that there is no other way out. If we manage to clarify the dangers of the current situation, then the only remaining solution is peace negotiations. If, on the other hand, only *agents provocateurs* are able to speak of finding a way out by a new war, then it is for us to demonstrate which reactionary and imperialist interests are defended by those who want to maintain the current state of war. While they claim that their "blockade" will bring about the end of Israel, we will demonstrate how it is folly to try to make the people believe in it through the help of brainwashing, buttressed by iron censorship and repression. It is with these lures that they fool the people in order to perpetuate a situation replete with dangers to the nation from which they themselves draw considerable benefits. [...]

Our struggle to establish friendly relations between the Jewish and Arab peoples of Israel does not imply a lessening—but instead a strengthening—of our struggle against Zionism. Only this struggle will stop any confusion between the right of the Jewish nation in Israel to constitute an independent state and Zionism. Zionism wishes to make Israel the homeland of all Jews. This is not only dim-witted utopianism that goes against the interest of all the world's Jews who are nationals of their home countries; it also constitutes—with all the expansionist implications that come with it—an ideology of aggression against the Arab countries. And we must equally put into relief the unbreakable links between Zionism and global imperialism.

In our struggle for these positions, we must defend the theses expounded above:

The seriousness of the problem and the importance of arriving at a solution are as much in the interest of the other Arab peoples as in the interest of the Arab nation of Palestine, condemned to destruction if a solution is not found quickly.

The feudal and reactionary ruling classes, instruments of imperialism, have committed a total betrayal regarding the Palestinian problem while simultaneously betraying national interests and those of the Arab nation of Palestine.

Egyptian Communists, particularly the DMNL, representing the working classes and the masses, have always defended the national interest and the interests of Palestine's Arabs.

We must struggle against chauvinism and show how the most legitimate representatives of the Jewish and Arab peoples of Palestine—and above all the Israeli Communist Party, the vanguard of Israel's working class—are our allies who are struggling for the same aims as we are.

We must demonstrate that, across the whole Arab Middle East, representatives of the working class and democrats defend positions similar to our own.

We must demonstrate that it is the democratically elected representatives of the Palestinian Arabs who should talk about their lot, rather than reactionary governments of other Arab countries that have demonstrated their incapability and that have betrayed their interests manifold times.

I. FOR A SYSTEMATIC ACTION BY THE DMNL

We therefore propose the following six-point plan of action:

1. To debate the report and to make, with the shortest possible delay—but on the scale of an enlarged Central Committee including those comrades

who are detained or in exile—the resulting alterations which will allow it to be adopted [as policy].

2. To disseminate and debate the ultimate modified report across the whole DMNL.

3. To present it for discussion in view of adopting a common position shared by all Egyptian Communist organizations while being prepared to take account of their observations.

4. To organize the struggle to defend our position on the national scale and to take on the task of getting other organizations to join us in our struggle.

5. To stand up for our positions in the arena of the Democratic Front.

6. To stand up for our positions in the arena of progressive Arab groups and the world's democratic camp, following proceedings concerning which we shall be making suggestions separately.

29

Some Clarifications on "Social Democracy"

Henri Curiel, "La social démocratie du point de vue théorique,"
December 1957, in "Inventory of the Papers of the Egyptian Communists
in Exile [The Rome Group]," International Institute of Social History,
Amsterdam, No. 371.

In this essay, Curiel addresses the question of social democracy from a Marxist
point of view that draws heavily on both Egyptian and Israeli experiences.

SOCIAL DEMOCRACY FROM A
THEORETICAL STANDPOINT

Social democracy is essentially the ideology favored by the workers' aristocracy. It was spawned in the imperialist era at the moment when the bourgeoisie—thanks to the high profits elicited by colonial exploitation—accorded a privileged status to certain elements and occasionally to certain strata of the working classes. Nevertheless, this stratum of the working class—particularly powerful in capitalist states possessing colonies—exists to a varying extent in all states. The primary content of this ideology is Reformism [Marxist revisionism]. This consists of claiming that reforms granted by the capitalists are the class struggle's essential objective. It places the struggle for reform first and considers regime change as the automatic result of these reforms. In actual fact, reformism consists of accepting [the idea] that the working class will remain in a subordinate position. It consists of searching for partial and limited solutions and avoids confronting the issue of changing the proletariat's conditions. Reformism is always paternalist and more often than not oppressive.

This ideology is defended by those whose position under the current regime is relatively good: they do not want to risk losing it through revolutionary action, and they do not really want regime change. Yet the influence of this ideology does not extend merely to the stratum of privileged workers; it has a tendency to penetrate other levels of the proletariat and may be adopted by quite sizable proportions of the masses. This ideology is represented in different capitalist countries by the "Socialist," "Social Democratic," or "Labor" parties, etc. . . . The majority of these parties are grouped under a "Socialist International."[9] At the heart of this organization is the British Labor Party, which plays the dominant role. It is effectively the strongest party and the most traditionally linked to the existence of a workers' aristocracy—constituting the most powerful and best-organized party in the world. Asia's socialist parties—while being closely linked to the [Socialist] International—differ in certain aspects from the European socialist parties and constitute an autonomous group. Israel's Mapai Party—which is also a member of the International—belongs to this group, too. This group has its center in Burma—the only Asian country where a socialist party has exercised power for an appreciable length of time.

On the trade-unionist front, social-democratic ideology dominates within reformist unions. In many states, central unions are dominated by reformist ideologies. Internationally, they are grouped under the International Confederation of Free Trade Unions (ICFTU). The specific content of this ideology varies according to the situation and the general conditions. For example, contemporary rightist socialist parties usually maintain links with American imperialism. That is also the case with regard to certain Asian socialist parties, being anti-Soviet and anti-Communist. Social-democratic ideology is also reflected in the different political positions taken up according to circumstances and conditions. Finally, the ideology of social democracy often exists within the majority of Communist parties. In effect, these are permeable to the ideas that surround them and especially [those concerning] certain "Labor"-oriented forms of bourgeois ideology.

THE SITUATION IN EGYPT

In Egypt, there is no party or [other] organization that adheres officially to social democratic ideology. This is due to a long list of specific circumstances, some of which are worth mentioning. To begin with, in our country the stratum of privileged workers is extremely narrow. Second, the Egyptian bourgeoisie is so reactionary that it is opposed to the most basic of reforms. The class struggle has not yet reached the stage where the bourgeoisie—fearing regime change—is prepared to pay the necessary price to corrupt a stratum of the workers and to struggle against the revolutionary movement by opposing it with a reformist

9. [Formed in 1951, the Socialist International is an organization of democratic socialist, social democratic, and labor parties that are not communist.]

movement. Finally, Egypt's backward social and economic situation does not provide the possibility of noticeably improving living conditions through the granting of reforms—as effectively practiced in advanced capitalist states.

But there exist in Egypt a number of trade unionist elements linked to, and heavily dependent on, the bourgeoisie. The ideas prompted and defended by the bourgeoisie's spokespersons *within* the workers' movement are so reactionary that they simply fall on unfavorable ground and thus rarely succeed in resisting proto-Communist activities. To clarify this point, one only needs to compare this phenomenon with a country like France, where reformists both hold great influence and boast deep roots inside the working class. Even in so far as there is not a concrete social-democratic current, the influence of social-democratic ideology is felt more completely in the ranks of the Egyptian Communist movement. That is not in the form of a particular ideology, but in the form of a discernible tendency. This ideology is reinforced by the fact that we are in a period of national struggle and in alliance with the bourgeoisie. This ideology, as we have seen, is reflected in the complex positions taken, which differ according to the period.

As far as we can tell, in the past al-Tali'a[10] expressed in its own fashion what is called "economism," that is, support by the stratum of backward workers rather than by the workers' aristocracy. In more general terms, social-democratic ideology represents the influence of the bourgeoisie in the workers' movement. It is expressed by waiting games, the separation of theory from practice, etc. [...] In Egypt its principal supporters are the numerous elements of bourgeois origin who did not know how to liberate themselves from the influence of their class. In our opinion, this ideology represents a dominant tendency foremost in Iskra[11]

10. [Tali'a al-'Ummal (The workers' vanguard) was a movement founded in 1945–46 by the three prominent Egyptian Jewish Marxists, Ahmed Sadiq Sa'd, Ramond Douek, and Yusuf Darwish. Alone and together, the three wrote many texts. Because of space constraints, we were unfortunately unable to include any of them in this book.]

11. [Curiel's words mirror the chronic state of sectarianism that typified Egyptian Communism in the 1940s and 1950s. Iskra al-Sharara (The spark) was a party founded by Hillel Schwartz—another Egyptian Jewish Marxist and theoretician of the Egyptian Left at the time—in 1942–43. It was largely similar in outlook to Curiel's EMNL, but Sharif Hatata has noted that "there was a difference in social constitution and in the degree of fusion with the [Egyptian] national movement—to which the EMNL was closer. There was a difference, therefore, in the way all problems were looked at. The words were the same but what was put inside by each group was different" (quoted in Botman, *The Rise of Egyptian Communism*, 53).]

and second in the Egyptian Communist Movement.[12] It is present in the UEPC[13]—the party of those bourgeois intellectuals with closest ties to the current regime.

PERSPECTIVES

First, it is possible to foresee the formation of a social-democratic political organization linked to the development of Egyptian capitalism and the formation of a stratum of privileged workers. The existence of workers' deputies and of a unionist bureaucracy has traditionally constituted the leadership of social-democratic parties. These elements are presently linked closely to the regime [of the Free Officers]. Contradictions may arise, and an independent political current could come into being with a social-democratic ideology. On the trade-unionist front, this tendency is already more advanced, and its development is strongly helped on the international front by the ICFTU. Second, within the Egyptian Communist movement, it is possible to predict that social-democratic tendencies will continue to develop, given the class origins of a large number of leading groups and the incarceration of the more revolutionary elements.

Two tasks follow from these observations: (1) the necessity to struggle against the influence of social-democratic ideology at the heart of the working classes; the Egyptian Communist movement must define it in a precise fashion, unmask and fight against those political positions that reflect this ideology at each particular stage; and (2) the necessity to struggle against the influence of social-democratic ideology at the heart of the Egyptian Communist movement. It is up to revolutionary elements to define this in a precise manner, unmask and fight against those political positions that reflect this ideology at each particular stage.

Further Readings

Amitai, Yossi, *Egypt and Israel: A View from the Left, 1947–78* [in Hebrew]. Haifa: Haifa University Press, 1999.

Avnery, Uri. *My Friend, the Enemy*. London: Zed, 1986.

12. [Founded by Fu'ad Mursi and inspired by European Communist movements (in particular, the French Communist Party)—the Egyptian Communist Party was set up in opposition to the DMNL.]

13. ["In November 1957 the DMNL, and factions which had temporarily split from it, joined with the ECP to form the Unified Egyptian Communist Party. When the Workers' Vanguard entered the party on January 8, 1958, it was renamed the United Communist Party of Egypt" (Botman, *The Rise of Egyptian Communism*, 141).]

Ballas, Shimon. *Horef Aharon* (Last winter). Jerusalem: Keter, 1984.

Beinin, Joel. *Was the Red Flag Flying There? Marxist Politics and the Arab-Israeli Conflict in Eqypt and Israel, 1948–1965*. Berkeley: University of California Press, 1990.

——— and Zachary Lockman. *Workers on the Nile: Nationalism, Communism, Islam and the Egyptian Working Class, 1882–1954*. Princeton: Princeton University Press, 1988.

Botman, Selma. *The Rise of Egyptian Communism, 1939–1970*. Syracuse, NY: Syracuse University Press, 1988.

Curiel, Henri. *Al Mizbach haShalom* (On peace's altar). Jerusalem: Mifras, 1980.

Ismael, Tareq Y., and Rifa'at El-Said. *The Communist Movement in Egypt: 1920–1988*. Syracuse, NY: Syracuse University Press, 1990.

Perrault, Gilles. "Henri Curiel, Citizen of the Third World." *Le Monde Diplomatique English Edition*, April 1998, http://mondediplo.com/1998/04/13curiel, accessed June 2, 2012.

———. *A Man Apart: The Life of Henri Curiel*. Translated by Bob Cumming. London: Zed, 1987.

Sami Michael

Born Salah Menashe in Baghdad in 1926, Sami Michael is today one of Israel's best-known Mizrahi authors. His literary, intellectual, and political career stretches over decades both in Iraq and later in Israel. Often using the Arabic-sounding nom de plume Samir Murad, Michael began writing for Iraqi newspapers when he was seventeen. At that time he also joined the Communist Party of Iraq. In 1948 he escaped from Iraq and moved to Iran, where he joined the Iranian Communist Party and ultimately prepared to return to Iraq. A year later, having been sentenced in absentia to death in Iraq, Michael moved to Israel and settled in Haifa's remaining predominantly Arab neighborhood, Wadi Nisnas. At that time he joined the Israeli Communist Party. Shortly thereafter, at the invitation of the Palestinian Israeli author and Communist leader Emile Habibi, Michael began writing in Arabic for the party's Arabic newspapers *al-Ittihad* and *al Jadid*. In 1955, disillusioned with Soviet domination, Michael left the Israeli Communist Party.

Michael is one of the few Arabic-speaking writers who migrated from writing in Arabic to writing in Hebrew, a complex experience he discussed on various occasions. He is also the most successful author to have made this switch. His first novel in Hebrew, *Shavim ve-Shavim Yoter* (All men are equal, but some are more), published in 1974, is centered on the hardships of Mizrahi Jews in the transit camps (*ma'abarot*) and slums of Israel after emigrating to Israel from their Arab countries of origin. Several of his other novels—*Victoria, Storm among the Palms, A Handful of Fog,* and *Aida*—are set in Iraq and discuss the social and political life of Jews in Iraq before and after the founding of the State of Israel. Arguably his most important novel is *Hasut* (Refuge), which is set in Israel during the 1973 Yom Kippur War and discusses the life of an Iraqi communist Jew in Iraq and Israel. Altogether Michael published eleven novels, three nonfiction works on Israeli society and culture, and several plays. He also translated Naguib Mahfouz's magnum opus *Cairo Trilogy* into Hebrew (the first translation of this work into any language). In addition, he translated the works of some of the great Arab poets. Very active politically, Michael has written numerous essays on issues such as equality and social problems in Israel, the Mizrahim, Arab-Jewish relations, religion, and human and civil rights. Since 2001 he has been president of the Association for Civil Rights in Israel.

The Newly Arrived Men of Letters

Samir Murad [Sami Michael], "al-'Udaba' al-Qādimuna al-judud un,"
al-Jadid 1, no. 9 (1954).

This essay in Arabic was written under Michael's nom de plume in 1954. We translate it here in full, with the original editorial note that was attached to it. The Arabic monthly *al-Jadid* was first published in November 1953 as a supplement to the Arabic weekly *al-Ittihad*, a publication of the Israeli Communist Party (commonly known in English by its Hebrew acronym, MAKI). *Al-Jadid*'s editors included leading Palestinian intellectuals and activists such as Emil Habibi, Jabra Nicola, Emil Toma, Hana abu-Hana, and Taufik Ziad. Arabic-speaking Jews were involved in *al-Jadid*'s editorial and writing work, including Sami Michael, Abraham Hayyat, Shimon Ballas, David Semach, and Sasson Somekh—most of whom were members and founders of the Nawdat al-asdiqa' al-adab al-'arabi al-taqqaddumi (Club of the friends of progressive Arabic literature). During the early 1950s, the club was mainly a group of Communist-oriented Jews who were interested in literature and native speakers of Arabic. They held meetings in Tel Aviv to discuss issues of literature, politics, culture, and society. One of the themes that the group debated was whether, as politically conscious men of letters, they should continue to publish in their native Arabic or make the effort to publish in their newly acquired Hebrew in order to increase their impact among Hebrew-speaking members of the Israel working class. This essay by Michael was the first published installment in this debate.

[*Al-Jadid's taftih* (opening editorial note).] *With this article our magazine opens a discussion among men of letters—and those concerned with literature—about the crucial issue of literary production. The theme has preoccupied the minds of many in the field of literature among those [Arabic-speaking Jews] who have recently arrived in the country [from Arab states]. Al-Jadid is open to publishing whatever its readers write on this topic, since discussion and clarification will surely help the intellectuals among the new arrivals find their literary way in Israel.*

It is possible for an engineer to leave his country and emigrate to another country and continue to practice his profession without much difficulty. But the engineer of the human soul—the man of letters—who leaves behind his homeland quickly feels like a fish out of water. He confronts serious hardships that cannot be overcome without strenuous efforts. At once, such a man loses that lively connection with the people, his audience, the connection that gave him inspiration and nurtured his soul—where he drank, murmured, chanted, and heard and wrote in his native [Arabic] language, which he fully loved and tasted. He loses that dear atmosphere anchored in the heart; all of a sudden he lands in a strange atmosphere—alien to his understanding, taste, language, and history.

The man of letters who cares about his links with the people—who is of the opinion that there is no backbone to his literary production except when his social source is present, typified by the dynamics of the people and their pursuit of the future—has to write in a style that the people among whom he lives understand. He has to stay true to the social content of his literature, while innovating and recreating his national form in a new garb that the nation where he lives can taste. For the true realist man of letters does not only write *about* the social masses, he also writes *for* them. He does not merely write to express feelings and emotions deep in his soul that leave him restless until he writes them down; instead he also writes because he yearns to find similar ideas, feelings, and emotions in the hearts of the people whom he knows and understands, and whose happiness he considers as his life's highest objective.

Although I think that there is no disagreement about this description, there still remains a point of contention regarding the way that the new men of letters who have come to Israel should pursue.

A POINT OF DIFFERENCE (DISAGREEMENT)

There is a group of people who claim that it is not possible for the man of letters to change his literary form or style as a chameleon changes its color. The man of letters who has a particular national understanding, who is skilled in its language and influenced by its traditions, who has learned how to address this understanding and dwelled in its conventions and convictions cannot simply shed all of this and inhabit a new nationality [that is] alien to him.

This group of people likewise says that the impossibility of such a transformation for the man of letters seems particularly obvious in Israel. Jewish nationalism in Israel is still nascent, made up of new arrivals coming from diverse places. This nationalism was formed after it was wrenched from different nationalities that still have their influence; there is no indication that the people of Israel will abandon these backgrounds that have been neither fully nor absolutely absorbed into the new nationalism. Therefore, the newly arrived man of letters not only faces new understandings, beliefs and traditions, language and customs; in addition he needs to acquire each element of which Israeli Jewish nationalism is made up. That is difficult for an individual to accomplish, even over the course of decades.

To support its view, this group refers to the phenomenon of Arab émigré men of letters, those who remained Arabs in their literary output despite the change in their "nationalist atmosphere." Though some of them wrote in English, this did not negate their Arab identity. This group then reaches the odd conclusion, which their reasoning concerning the issue in question inevitably leads to—that is, that newly arrived men of letters "will always remain on the shore, without being able to jump in the water and swim in it."

CAPITULATION BEFORE THE BITTER REALITY

We do not deny the serious difficulties that the man of letters newly arriving in Israel faces. The harsh life, the bitter struggle for the sake of a better life, the ugly settlement conditions in tents susceptible to being blown apart by gusts of winds, and the grinding depression that those new arrivals face make focusing on reading and writing one of the ideals of which it is difficult even to dream. This economic situation—in addition to the cultural policy of the government—makes it impossible for those new arrivals to be intellectually accommodated in this new country. Above all, this regressive black current, forcefully imposed on Israeli culture, which they are proud of calling "Western culture," creates a suffocating atmosphere for every living artistic talent and dims the light of sound thinking.

We do not deny the difficulty of embarking on the study of the characteristics of Israel's nascent Jewish nationalism so as to understand it accurately and abandon any sectarian, degraded, and rotten elements, while taking what is positive and vital in it. However, at the same time I think that one of the most dangerous attitudes is precisely that view taken by the group that completely brushes off the entire issue with the stroke of a pen under the pretext that it is impossible "to jump into the water." First and foremost, the position of this group is to capitulate before this bitter reality. This leads to the denial of any advantage from the attempts that some new arrivals from the men of letters undertake to understand the new atmosphere and adapt to it. This adaptation does not imply by any means that under any condition there should be an accommodation or absorption of negative aspects within this new reality. There should be, however, an initial stage of attempting to understand the new reality, before negative aspects can be erased and replaced with a better reality.

At the end of the day, it is clear that the view of this group paves the way for regressive bourgeois writing so that it can spread its poison with no competition standing in its way. It is likewise clear that some of the new arrivals among the men of letters make no attempt to comprehend the new reality. Writing for them is a way to get the crumbs from the table of the elite bourgeoisie. Literary production for them is a secure means of income. They adapt quickly to the new stringent situation, and they start contributing to the doubling of regressive writing and understanding and throw it on the people. They claim that they are very welcomed, while people stand on the shores without daring to jump into the water. They see no benefit in challenging the tumultuous waves and imagine that they would be swamped the moment they touch them.

The men of letters among the new arrivals live mostly at the crossroads. The pretext through which the current regime uncovers its unashamed face is shown clearly. There are people who seek bread from the rubbish, and there are children afflicted with disease and poverty. The governing elites try to create a distorted generation. The army of jobless is stranded between the tent and the workplace, unable to find a means of income. The entire philosophy of the governing class and its lies and opinions get mired in the winter's mud. Therefore, there should be a lesson from those jobless in the tents to the governing class, which fears their progress; the appearance of somebody from among those slim and malnourished bodies who accuses them. What could file the charge and correct the wrongs except these daring hands of the men of letters who bear in mind the interests of the tortured masses? How happy and grateful would the governing class be if the men of letters from the new arrivals imposed silence on themselves by their own free will?!

THE ONLY WAY

It is true that the Jewish nation in Israel is a nascent nation. But we cannot deny that this nation has acquired traits and characteristics particular to it. These features are for the sake of development, progress, and clarity. But there are secondary features still peculiar to the new arrivals that clash with the basic characteristics—like different languages, customs, and unique traditions. If we want to be realistic, we have to direct the new arrivals to the study of these basic nationalist Jewish characteristics and toward a positive integration into this nationality, toward increasing likability; development of all that is humane, progressive, and scientific; and the fighting of all that is regressive, nonmaterial, and fractured.

This is what our inner feelings oblige us to do, to follow the popular will in all circumstances. People do not know how to stand for long on the shore. People constantly undergo changing dynamics. If we have decided to stop, this means we have subjected ourselves to isolation and unity and have retreated back to dreams of "the happy past." We would lock ourselves in ivory towers, away from difficulties and hardships. This means that people will give way to new men of letters who are worthy of them. They will be born as they walk, will learn to speak as they firmly put their feet on the ground.

This situation was well understood by [some] men of letters and poets who were once new arrivals, such as Alexander Ben Mordechai, Avi Shaul, and others. It is incumbent on the new arrivals among the men of letters to follow in their footsteps, since there is no other way. The admission of inability, dwelling on memories from the past; the indulgence in wishful dreams and the disgust at reality without engaging in changing it; the incomprehension of the direction and aspirations of the people; the negligence of the future, and blindness to what exists—all of these are not characteristics of the sincere man of letters who is devoted to his people and their wishes. These are the trademarks of the man of letters who has been humiliated by reality, ruined by despair, depression, hesitation, and lack of confidence in himself.

Realism in literature makes it incumbent on the men of letters of the new arrivals to treat the issues that preoccupy people's minds and among which they live as being at the center of life, not at its periphery. This is done in order to contribute to the creation of a humane, progressive Hebrew culture, entrusted with the interests of the Israeli people and respect for other peoples. There is no other way before the men of letters except the choice of either being both Jewish and internationalist men of letters or sliding down the path of cosmopolitanism.[1]

---

1. [During the early 1950s the notion of "cosmopolitanism" among Arabic-speaking Communists carried negative connotations of American liberalism, in contrast to the notion of (socialist) internationalism—which was viewed as favorable and desirable. Contrast this tendency with Jacqueline Kahanoff's writings, below in this volume.]

Further Readings

Ballas, Shimon. *First Person Singular* [in Hebrew]. Tel Aviv: Ha-Kibutz Ha-Meuchad, 2009.

Berg, Nancy E. *More and More Equal: The Literary Works of Sami Michael*. Lanham, MD: Lexington, 2005.

Kabha, Mustafa. "Eastern Jews in the Arabic Press in Israel, 1948–1967" [in Hebrew]. *Iyunim Bitkumat Yisrael* 16 (2006): 445–63.

Michael, Sami. *Memories*. Jerusalem: Center for Programming, Department of Development and Community Services, W.Z.O., 1986.

———. *Refuge*. Translated by Edward Grossman. Philadelphia: Jewish Publication Society, 1988.

———. *Victoria*. Translated by Dalya Bilu. London: Macmillan, 1995.

Nassar, Maha. "The Marginal as Central: *Al-Jadid* and the Development of a Palestinian Public Sphere, 1953–1970." *Middle Eastern Journal of Culture and Communication* 3, no. 3 (2010): 333–51.

Schwartz, Stephanie Tara. "The Concept of Double Diaspora in Sami Michael's *Refuge* and Naim Kattan's *Farewell, Babylon*." *Comparative Studies of South Asia, Africa and the Middle East* 30, no. 1 (2010): 92–100.

Somekh, Sasson. *Call it Dreaming: Memories 1951–2000* [in Hebrew]. Tel Aviv: HaKibutz HaMeuchad, 2008.

Jacqueline Shohet Kahanoff

Born in Cairo to an Iraqi father and a Tunisian mother, Jacqueline Kahanoff (1917–79) was undeniably the leading proponent of the notion of Levantinism, which she developed after moving to Israel during the 1950s as a holistic, eclectic, and multicultural alternative to Israel's newly formed society. Like many children of affluent Egyptian families, she was educated in the French Mission School in Cairo. At the age of twenty-three, Kahanoff left Egypt for America; in 1945 she graduated from Columbia University's school of journalism. A young divorcée, she supported herself with various menial jobs and began to write prose and nonfiction in English. In 1946 Kahanoff won the *Atlantic Monthly* award for best short story for her feminist story "Such Is Rachel," and soon afterward she was awarded a Houghton Mifflin Fellowship to write her novel *Jacob's Ladder*. The novel, which was published in 1951 under her maiden name of Shohet, depicted life in Egypt between the two world wars. Kahanoff returned to Egypt and then lived in Paris for two years before moving to Israel in 1954. With her second husband, she settled in Be'er Sheva and worked as a foreign correspondent for US publications.

Although she was then still on the margins of Israel's Eurocentric literary and cultural scene, she had already formulated her unique vision for Israeli society as an integral part of the Mediterranean and Levantine world. Her vision reflected her own cosmopolitan upbringing between East and West. As Ammiel Alcalay puts it, "from growing up in the privileged class in colonial Egypt to sweeping floors in America to support herself; from having the revolutionary and future president of Algeria, Ahmed Ben Bella, sheltered as a house guest by her parents [in Egypt] to her increasing isolation in Beersheba — the range of Kahanoff's experience presented an almost unfathomable paradigm to the assumptions reigning within Israeli society of the time [1950s]" (Alcalay, *Keys to the Garden*, 18). In 1959 Kahanoff published the first installment of her influential cycle of four essays, "A Generation of Levantines." It was chiefly through the prolific Iraqi-Israeli author Nissim Rejwan (b. 1925) that Kahanoff was introduced to Aharon Amir (1923–2008), editor of the vanguard Hebrew journal *Keshet* (Rainbow). Her essays then began to appear in print regularly. They were subsequently gathered in her much celebrated, pioneering book *From the East the Sun* (1978). Although Kahanoff passed away less than a year later, her writings had a profound impact on many Israeli authors.

31

Bridge to the Oriental Immigrants

Excerpt from Jacqueline Kahanoff, "Gesher el 'Ole Ha-Mizrah," *Al Ha-Mishmar*, May 11, 1956.

Kahanoff wrote this essay as part of a series of reports she did on the conditions of Mizrahi immigrants in the transit camps and the cities of Israel. The essay also included some lengthy interviews. We present here the first part of the essay, without the interviews.

[…]

THEY NEED AN ATTENTIVE EAR

The most striking feature in the life of the immigrants from the Orient is their physical and cultural isolation. People mingle with each other in the streets, in clubs, kibbutzim, factories, and this daily interaction [and] this intense negotiation are decisive factors in creating the sense that all belong to one country and all share an interest in its fate and proper conduct. It is easy to overcome the divide between those of Polish and South African descent, between the New World of European origin and the Older World of this country.

This is not the case with the immigrants from the countries of the Orient. When it comes to them there is hardly any interaction. Rosh Ha'Ayin is populated almost entirely with Yemenies; Patish, Maslul, and Mivtachim[1] are settlements of Persians and Kurds; one finds North Africans in Lachish and other settlements, and in the transit camp near Be'er Sheva. Interaction between these groups and the "European race" in Israel is rare, formal, limited to the teachers, social workers, agricultural experts, and the like. Moreover, the Oriental groups do not have much interaction among themselves; each group adheres to its language and customs or is isolated because of transportation difficulties.

Even when people from two different ethnic groups [Ashkenazim and Mizrahim] live near each other, and their economic level is more or less the same, there is a boundary between them. I know an Iraqi who used to be a high-ranking

---

1. [These three locations were all *moshavim* (cooperative agricultural communities).]

official in the government in Baghdad. He told me that when he moved with his wife and seven children to their new home, their Polish neighbors wanted to move after hearing the news that a "tribe of Cushites"[2] was about to move in next to them. When the Iraqi family arrived, the Poles were standing outside, staring cantankerously at the new residents. They did not care to exchange a word with their neighbors for two years. But one day the Polish family heard one of the Iraqis, a high-school student, uttering a Yiddish proverb. Since then the situation has changed dramatically. The Poles now call the Iraqi boy "Motel'e" and greet his parents with "Shalom."

My Iraqi acquaintance related this tale to me in order to show that two groups can merge. But his wife, after describing her Polish neighbors as "ignoramuses who have to move up," narrated her own pedigree, so as to teach me how old and respected her heritage is. Some of the kids in this family have a "Mizrahi complex" that brings to mind the "Jewish complex." Much of this complex is based on a sense of systematic discrimination. When one of them fails in school, he either thinks that this is because the Ashkenazi teacher does not love him, or that "they" do not want the "Sephardim" to acquire education and develop.

Note with what kind of "graciousness" the "white" lady moves aside in order to make room for the Kurd coming to sit next to her; and when he gets out of the car and politely says "goodbye," no one even nods back silently. As if the Kurd is not eligible even for this measure of equality—the exchange of greetings—and the only way to relate to him is to ignore his very presence.[3]

Of course, we cannot compare these instances of social discrimination with the persecutions of Jews in Central and Eastern Europe. But it is this statement that Oriental immigrants find irritating. They naively thought that "people who suffered so much from prejudice in Europe will not cultivate similar attitudes." The tragedy of the Oriental immigrants is that when they came to Israel they expected their brethren to welcome them entirely differently. But the gap between the ideals of Zionism and Israeli reality, between what they imagined and what actually happened, caused traumatic shock. The thought that they are "second-

2. [Kahanoff uses the term "Chushyyim," which is borrowed from the biblical reference to black Africans or Ethiopians (Amos 8:8; Jeremiah 13:23). Standard translations render this word "Cushites." However, in this context it should be understood as "Negroes" or worse.]

3. [Compare this to the discussion about the question of greetings between members of varying religious groups in Egypt, in Murād Farag's selection in this volume.]

class citizens" bothers and depresses them. It seems that many among them do not talk about anything but the discrimination they ostensibly experience. When they want "to prove themselves," they develop a certain aggression in speech and action that is entirely different from the tradition of manners [and] propriety of the Orient. It seems to them that this is the suitable way to "assert their own rights."

Because of this discrimination and because of the fact that the Oriental immigrant was uprooted and transplanted into a new and strange culture, there are times that he feels in exile in Israel. And like exiles, he seeks comfort in idealizing his previous life. Indeed, his physical suffering back there was often severe (but not as severe as many Israelis think), but he had a sense of wholeness—wholeness in his hopes, his ways of life, beliefs, personality, and self-respect.

We must realize that the Oriental [Mizrahi] immigrant is disconnected from his previous "self" much more completely than any European immigrant. After all, Jews from Europe built Israel, and the new European immigrant meets here familiar elements of life and manner. He can speak Yiddish; he eats his usual food, without being criticized for that. Often he uses his technical skills to find a suitable job. The terms "labor union" and "nationalism" are familiar to him, and he knows the mechanisms of the modern industrial society thoroughly.

This is not the case with the immigrant coming from the Orient, who needs to adapt quickly to a totally strange culture.[4] Despite the true yearning for Zion, the ideal of modern Zionism is not sufficiently clear to him, because he often still considers Judaism religion and not nationality. The national idea emerged in the lands of Islam only with the impact of the West, and it is still not entirely detached from the religious perceptions of Islam. This condition also characterizes Oriental Jewish perceptions of nationalism, even though they were more amenable and more open than Muslims to Western influence. Yet Europeanization went hand in hand with assimilation [in Israel], and the cultural elites became distant from Judaism as well from the Jewish environment within which it emerged. As a result, more often than not, Oriental Jews who come to Israel do not have natural leaders, people who can serve as a connecting link between cultures and help their brethren adapt to modern society. Thus, the responsibility for guiding new immigrants from the Orient and for their transfer from

4. [Kahanoff seems to reproduce here too uncritically the prevailing stereotypes of her time about the total lack of modernity among Middle Eastern Jewish communities before 1950.]

one cultural realm to another is placed on the shoulders of Israelis who never experienced the hardships that such transformations entail.

The Jews of the Orient face a conflict that they cannot contend with on their terms because in Israel they find themselves in a reality that does not fit them at all. They feel discriminated against, neglected, and sometimes they feel despair. Therefore, Oriental Jews tend to interact with the state of Israel in a manner somewhat similar to the way in which the Jews of the ghetto used to react to their hostile environment, a manner that brings to mind the attitude of colonized peoples toward the white rulers. Oppression, even when it is only imagined, always produces the same results. Oriental Jews tend to isolate themselves, not only because of external circumstances but also voluntarily. They tend to live in their own world, the way European Jews lived before: closed lives dictated by the hostility of the peoples within which they lived. Much like the Jews in exile, Oriental Jews express their self, their true self, only when they are among their own people. Thus many Mizrahi Jews boast that the "Sephardim" are the aristocracy of the Jewish people, the "true" Jews, and that the Ashkenazim are descendants of Northern Tribes that converted to Judaism.[5]

Often they are submissive when they interact with officials, managers, and so on, because "otherwise they do not give jobs." But among themselves they criticize all "the authorities" and call them "small tyrants" and even "little Hitlers" who "push us around and treat us like trash." Oriental Jews particularly resent the newcomers from Eastern Europe, perhaps because these become grocers or low-ranking state officials "on their backs," and with whom they mostly interact on a daily basis.

A Moroccan Jew once entered a grocery store in Be'er Sheva and asked for white bread.[6] The grocer told him that there were no loaves of white bread left.

5. [Kahanoff refers here to the notion that Ashkenazi Jews are not "true" Jews but instead descendants of the Khazars, a seminomadic Turkic people from southern Russia that converted to Judaism between the eighth and tenth centuries CE. There is no doubt that the Khazar elite did convert to Judaism, and that this had some impact on the demographic and cultural history of European Jewry. Some Mizrahi references to the Khazar episode, both in the past and the present, include a sense of hostility toward Ashkaenazic Jews. On the Khazars and Judaism, see Arthur Koestler, *The Thirteenth Tribe* (New York: Random House, 1976).]

6. [Until the 1990s Israel had only two kinds of bread, both of them European. What was called "white bread" was made of refined flour and was much lighter than what was called "black bread." However, this "black bread" was not true black bread, which would become available in Israel many years later.]

When the Moroccan left with black bread, the grocer took a white loaf from under the counter and handed it to a "white" customer. "He can satisfy himself also with black bread," he [the grocer] said. The Moroccan, who was stalling at the door (perhaps he suspected he was being harassed) and heard the grocer, shrugged, "Nazi!" A journalist who visited a new factory to do a report for a Jewish-American magazine wanted to interview two workers, a Tunisian and an Indian. Both refused because "we do not want American Jews to think that we are treated nicely in Israel."

Indeed, it seems that even the old solidarity of "all Israelis are guarantors for each other" has been lost here. External obedience that hides rage, rebellious-ness, and bitterness is a dangerous state of mind. The loyalty and solidarity of the Oriental Jews, once they exceed the boundaries of the family and the clan, are perceived as "Sephardic" loyalty and solidarity, a sort of a new nationalism: emotional, extreme, quick to feel offended.

Not only the elderly, the "desert generation," feel and speak this way. A physi-cian working in a Yemeni transit camp told me that on Fridays, when the chil-dren accompany the teachers and the welfare workers to the bus station, they sing: Shabbat Shalom teachers, Shabbat Shalom asses, Ashkenazi bastards . . ."[7] And this they do to the people most devoted to them! It is therefore clear that this educational devotion did not produce more positive interactions with the ethnic group to whose service these people are committed.

Nonetheless, many Mizrahim view themselves with Ashkenazi eyes and expose acute aspects of the old, familiar Jewish self-hate. A woman who heard praises of her son's good looks said "he is not handsome, he is black." An Orien-tal boy said he wanted to learn Yiddish so that if he reminisced with his friends about their places of origin, no one would interrupt and order him to speak Hebrew and not Arabic, which is a "bad language."

I heard a saddening story about a youth who said he wanted "to be Ashkenazi" when asked what he wanted to be when he grew up. There are youths who block their ears and refuse to hear about the history of the first [Zionist] pioneers. They want war and follow Herut[8] because they hardly have heroes of their own.

Those who came from the Orient needed to adapt to a society that they did

7. [In Hebrew this song rhymes nicely: "Shabbat Shalom Ha-Morim, Shabbat Shalom Ha-hamorim, Ashkenazim mamzerim."]

8. [Herut was the main right-wing party in Israel during the 1950s. The precursor of the later Likud Party, Herut was led by Menachem Begin.]

not help design, a society that often considered them a "raw material in need of molding," in need of education, in need of Zionist training. It is possible that they are not Zionist, but they are loyal to Jewish tradition and ideals, just like European Jews at the time, before the rise of nationalism, and the penetration of secularist ideas into their societies. When the Oriental Jews immigrated to Israel they hoped to leave their mark on the world around them, to make history instead of becoming its objects, its mute witnesses or victims. They hoped to continue to weave their traditions but to renew them as well, just as the Jews of Europe realized their ideals in Israel, albeit in a way much different than what they imagined when they yearned for Zion in Poland or Russia.

The Oriental Jews in Israel wish both to modernize and Europeanize, as well as to rediscover, or reinterpret, their Judaism as "equals among equals and brothers among brothers." But their inferiority complex, inhibitions, prejudices, and lack of understanding often deny them the sense of being at home in Israel and a willingness to make their contribution to her. It seems that an untapped source of energy was wasted. The Jews of the Orient never imagined that absorption and adaption is a unidirectional road; they thought that this would be a process of negotiation and mutual impact whose one goal is the unity of the Jewish people.

If the Jews of the Orient need help, one must not view them as raw material waiting to be molded. They must be *encouraged to discover and liberate themselves*, just as the psychoanalyst treats his patient by helping him expose and examine the things he hides from himself. This way the patient is able to reconcile the conflict with which he contends and make a choice that suits his personality. But one must remember, the patient is the one who makes the choice, not the psychoanalyst.

The Oriental Jew needs to express what he has in his heart more than he needs to be talked to. Above all, he needs an attentive ear in order to break the wall of silence and isolation that encircles the neurotic who, whenever he speaks, always tiptoes around things, exposes a bit and hides twice as much. The Oriental Jews suffer from a kind of collective neurosis, and the strict "missionary" manner with which many well-intending Israelis approach them cannot replace the unmediated, humane, sympathetic one they need. All in all, the Oriental Jew, like the patient in the psychoanalyst's clinic, can be reconciled with himself, make peace with his self, and maintain a friendly relationship with the outside world. What is needed for this is a bridge, a bidirectional bridge of negotiation; a bridge built on a river whose two banks are in the same country and not in two different lands.

In our Jewish heritage there are many common elements (and above all is the sense of loyalty to each other) that make the building of this bridge possible. The task is on us all, all the time. It requires both sides to unpack the burden of prejudices, self-deceptions, empty pride, and fears that encircle us and prevent us from seeing each other. [. . .]

Further Readings

Alcalay, Ammiel. *After Jews and Arabs: Remaking Levantine Culture.* Minneapolis: University of Minnesota Press, 1993.

Alcalay, Ammiel, ed. *Keys to the Garden: New Israeli Writing.* San Francisco: City Lights, 1996.

Benhabib, Doli. "Women's Skirts Are Shorter Now: Levantine, Female Identity as Elitist Disguise in Jacqueline Kahanov's Writings." *Women's Studies International Forum* 20, nos. 5–6 (1997): 689–96.

Nocke, Alexandra. "Israel and the Emergence of Mediterranean Identity: Expressions of Locality in Music and Literature." *Israel Studies* 11, no. 1 (2006): 143–73.

Ohana, David. "The Mediterranean Option in Israel: An Introduction to the Thought of Jacqueline Kahanoff." *Mediterranean Historical Review* 21, no. 2 (2006): 239–63.

Rejwan, Nissim. *Outsider in the Promised Land: an Iraqi Jew in Israel.* Austin: University of Texas Press, 2006.

Starr, Deborah A., and Sasson Somekh, eds. *Mongrels or Marvels: The Levantine Writings of Jacqueline Shohet Kahanoff.* Stanford: Stanford University Press, 2011.

David Sitton

David Sitton (1909–89), born in Jerusalem to a Sephardic family, was a writer and an activist intellectual for many years, both before and after 1948. He was a younger associate of leading figures in the Sephardic community of Jerusalem, including Elie Eliachar, with whom he later founded the World Sephardic Federation. During the time of the British Mandate, Sitton was arrested for underground activity and spent time in prison. After the founding of Israel, he became very active in the Sephardi Council in Jerusalem (Va'ad 'adat ha-Sefaradim bi-Yerushalayim), and founded and edited its main publications *Ba-Ma'arakha* (The struggle) and *Shevet ve-'Am* (A tribe and a people). From the outset, both journals were the main publications representing not only the Sephardim, but also the Mizrahim. Both focused on social, political, and cultural issues of the day. *Ba-Ma'arakha*'s official title was *Bit'on ha-tsibur ha-Sefaradi u-vene 'adot ha-Mizrah* (Journal of the Sephardic public and the eastern communities), and *Shevet va-'Am* was subtitled "The Forum for Discussing the Problems of the Sephardic Public in Israel and the Diaspora." With Sitton as editor, both journals were, for many years, effectively the only arena in which social, political, and cultural issues pertaining to the Mizrahi experience in Israel were discussed critically. Most significantly, one of the first articulations of the link between "backwardness, equality, and [Ashkenazic] hegemony"—the three keywords in post-1970 Mizrahi political and academic discourse in Israel—was published by Sitton in an essay of that title in *Shevet ve-'Am* in 1958. In addition to being an editor, Sitton wrote numerous works on Sephardic and Mizrahi culture, folklore, and ethnography, as well as works of fiction.

32

A Call for Deepening "The Mizrahi Consciousness" among Us

Excerpt from David Sitton, "Le-Ha'amakat Ha-Toda'a Ha-Mizrahit Be-Kirbenu," *Shevet ve-'Am*, November 1958, 7–14.

Sitton published this essay at a time when there was a growing consciousness of the social and cultural bitterness experienced by many educated Mizrahim. These Mizrahim were unable to find jobs that suited their skills because the cultural orientation of Israel was moving further away from the Arab Middle East. At the same time, it was becoming clear to many in Israel that the country's Western orientation was hurting its relations with countries in the third world.

A

We do not intend to opine here about the question of Israel's [international] political "orientation"—that is, whether Israelis should turn their eyes to the Western world or strive to integrate within the Asian world. This very important question should be discussed calmly and without a fit of temper. We should analyze Israel's situation thoroughly and view our situation from every angle. When we reach a negative or positive conclusion concerning each option, we must not despair even then. Again, this is a serious question that we need to contend with thoroughly and completely. One day we will also be able to clarify some concepts and issues that are currently vague.

There are those who argue that Israeli society must not integrate within the Arab-Oriental world surrounding us in any way because Jews comprise a minority community [there]. Even if we become four to five millions Jews living in Israel we might still be, God forbid, culturally assimilated within the forty to fifty million Arabs in the region and disappear from the global stage forever. After two millennia of exile, our whole existence and presence in the world came into being only because we enclosed ourselves in ghettos and removed ourselves from the gentiles. Indeed, once we broke down the ghetto walls and began mingling with the gentiles, assimilation commenced, devouring us, and a major part of our society and body politic was lost. Jewish individuals with superb talents left us to live in foreign lands, took up leading positions in powerful nations, [and] achieved the highest places in the fields of science, policy, government, and finance. But not only did they not help their own people, they became obstacles to our own development.

Zionism arose to redeem us from both the seclusion inside the ghetto and the danger of assimilation. Thanks to the concentration of the [Jewish] nation in Israel, we are able to develop our own values and use what is good and admirable in the people of Israel's character at the time when we return to our homeland. We have come to restore values that were in deep sleep; we are returning to normal life like any other nation. Settling in this land provides us with what is good and vital for man; we are developing new and diverse economic sources. Most important, we are creating new forms of social life that are quite far from the social life we had, even in the exemplary free countries of Western Europe and the United States. All of this gives us spirit and confidence that we are marching toward a brighter and better future.

It is therefore nonsense to think that the Jewish people—while becoming rooted in this land and while developing sublime values in their spiritual and material lives—might still become assimilated in the Oriental environment. Even if our surrounding environment makes giant steps forward culturally and otherwise, the people around us would still remain incapable of leaving their mark on us, or become culturally superior to us. The very opposite should be the case: we must strive by all means and ways to break down the Great Wall of China that the leaders of Arab nationalism have erected around Israel. We must do this in order to give generously from our culture and spirit to the neighboring countries and establish cooperation and contact with them in all spheres of life—spirit and action, cultural and material. This way, we can put an end to the mutual suspicion that wears down ourselves and our neighbors equally.

It is well known that the Great Wall that the leaders of Arab nationalism built and fortified around us was built only because of the fear that, with its dynamism, the Jewish state might encourage the millions of wretched and poor who live a life of slavery in the surrounding countries to rid themselves of the yoke of their rulers and tyrannies that anesthetize them with slogans and distract their minds by increasing hatred toward us. Any contact between Israel and the neighboring countries—in the cultural, financial, and commercial spheres of life—could help the naive, ignorant masses open their eyes and see the truth behind the disingenuous propaganda constantly piled on them by the radio stations and the press.

In order to break down this Great Wall, we must create the tools and the means as this fortification of hatred and animosity will not be broken in one day. We must strive to do that every day and in any way possible so that we could uproot one stone at a time from underneath the fortified wall around us—until one day we will succeed in destroying it altogether.

We are surely right in emphasizing the strengthening of the Israel Defense Forces in all of its branches. As a consequence of the strength and bravery of the Israel Defense Forces, the enemies who want to destroy and remove us from the world recoil from a collision and [from] deciding the conflict by military confrontation with us and also accept our existence and presence in this region.

The Sinai Operation, in which Nasser's arrogant and overconfident army was defeated,[1] sobered up the Arab nations and gave boastful Nasser a lifelong lesson. He now knows that any attempt to win the struggle against us by military means will lead to his fall from power. We should not underestimate these successes. Were it not for the Sinai Operation, we would not be sitting quietly within the vast ocean around us; an ocean so stormy and blustery that it threatens to devour all the ships in it.

The present calm and silence do not stop us from remaining alert—with our eyes wide open, watching everything around us. But within this storm, glimmers of light and hope for change and a transformation of the situation begin to surface. Nasser's rule—like a captain struggling to navigate his ship in stormy water—is not eternal. Other tyrannies were not eternal, not only in undeveloped countries like the Arab states, but also in the enlightened countries of Europe. As is the case with any tyranny, Nasser jumps from one adventure to another. The more he goes through, the more he risks his position and rule. The chain of events in this region since the revolution of July 14, 1958, in Baghdad[2] introduces many dangers for Egyptian tyranny. Nasser, who pumped his flock full of pompous slogans against foreign agents and internal traitors, is losing the most important weapon he had precisely because of the Baghdadi revolution. His slogans are losing their value, and the influence of his speeches and declarations is slowly waning. What does he have now to come to his flock with: the gang wars between Yemen and Aden? Pronouncements of solidarity with

1. [Sitton is referring here to the 1956 Suez War, in which Israel, Britain, and France fought against Egypt, beginning with Israel's invasion of Egypt on July 26, 1956. Gamal Abdel Nasser was president of Egypt from 1956 to 1970.]

2. [The coup led by Major General Abdul Karim el Qasim that overthrew the Hashemite monarchy in Iraq.]

the people of China? The masses in Egypt are increasing by the thousands each year; they need bread and want answers. When will they be relieved from this tyranny, pressure, and oppression? This day will come; it is not far off.

B

Yet besides threatening with the power we created in the IDF's [Israel Defense Forces'] navy, air force, and platoons, we must also prepare other tools that are no less important than the weapons of war and destruction. We need to create manpower to pave the way and use its spirit to have an impact on our surroundings. We need to train this manpower to be able to communicate with our neighbors and provide us with great achievements so that the day of peace will be closer to our state. Although we have seen major developments and achievements in the military realm, there is effectively zero activity in the domain of training the manpower capable of both engaging the Afro-Asian region and dealing with the [non-Jewish] minorities within our [Israeli] society—a situation that poses major problems for which we find no solution.

Worse still, as days go by and our state develops, it appears that we are losing the required ground for training people for these emerging new tasks. By now we face a severe shortage in suitable people to fill these jobs and fulfill these missions. Such people must have the knowledge, and the necessary qualities, required for interacting and communicating with the region's rulers and state representatives in order to explain our nature, status, and position in the region. It seems that we have a major problem in interacting with the peoples around us, forging connections with them, and explaining who we are. The envoys and diplomats that the Israeli government and other state institutions send to Asian and African states are deployed on their missions and jobs without the required skills because they were not properly trained.

The late David Remez [1886–1951], who was Israel's first minister of transportation and communication, was able to answer his critics [by saying] that he was new to the position since neither his father nor his grandfather had ever been a minister. Yet after the first decade of existence, no one in Israel has been able to use the same line of argumentation and say that we have never had a diplomatic corps in Japan or do not know the African continent. At this point, one should criticize the lack of use of the human capital we do have for missions and positions in the regions of Asia and Africa. We want and must make the colored nations understand that we are not foreign in this environment.[3] We must explain that even if an exile of thousands of years separated us from our homeland—the land of the Hebrews—we never ceased being connected to the Oriental people's cradle of civilization in terms of our culture, features, and spiritual and moral values.

The diverse Jewish cultural treasures were acquired only when we were dwelling in the land of the Hebrews, the Middle Eastern diasporas, and medieval Sefarad [the Iberian peninsula]. The Bible that influenced—and still influences—the Oriental and Western nations, the Talmud and rabbinic literature, as well as the literary, scientific, and philosophical masterpieces of the sages of Sefarad, were all created while we were linked to the cultural treasures of the Orient. It is these cultural treasures that nourished and affected all the generations of the sages of Israel; it is the spirit of these treasures that gave rise to the giants of Israel during the time of revival prior to the founding of the State of Israel.

These spiritual and cultural treasures likewise kept our nation from total assimilation and disappearance in the Diaspora. This is true not only with regards to the European Diaspora, but also in relation to the Jews of the Islamic world. Over the generations, the Jews of Yemen and North Africa, notwithstanding living among undeveloped gentiles, absorbed the Torah from the books of the sages of Israel. Their mass *aliya* to Israel—when the sound of the shofar of redemption and the news of the revival of the Third Temple were heard—is the fruit of the longing and the yearning for Zion that they preserved over the generations by adhering to the literature and creations of the sages of Sefarad and their subsequent authors.

And those young and old brothers who came to Israel and now comprise half of the people of Zion—what is their weight and status regarding the managing of our country's interests? Almost zero. Is it true that all the people skilled at running the state's institutions, capable of fulfilling the diplomatic tasks on behalf of Israel and the Zionist movement—not just in missions to the West and to the United States, but also to Asia and Africa—are only of, say, German descent? Is it really true that the German Jews are familiar with the Oriental nations—their ways of life, customs, and modes of thinking—more than those who came to Israel from the Middle East and Asia? It is argued that so far there are no youth from Asia and Africa suitable for carrying out the diplomatic mis-

3. [By "colored nations," Sitton refers to the non-European nations, specifically those in Asia and Africa.]

sions and political tasks of the state. Yet this cannot but raise the question: why during Israel's ten years of existence were no efforts made in order to recruit and train young people from the Oriental countries so that they would be able fulfill this important national task?

In his book *Travels in Asia*, where he discusses his important journey to the Far East, Moshe Sharett[4] tells us about the important and significant roles and positions played and held by Jews. Jews from Iraq and other Oriental countries played major roles in creating commercial and cultural relations between Europe and the Far East in past centuries. These Jews have laid the foundations for commercial and economic life across the huge region of the Asian continent, and it is clear that they had a decisive impact on the local authorities. The Sassoons, Ezras, and Kedouries have all written glorious chapters in the histories of the Asian continents in this century.[5] Similarly, the role played by the Jews of Iraq, Syria, Lebanon, Egypt, Algeria, Morocco, and Tunisia in the governments of these countries was also quite significant, both before and after European colonization.

Thus, if we have politicians and financial and economic entrepreneurs hailing from the families of Ezra, Kedourie, and Sassoon in the Far East—and Farhi, Qattawi, and many more in the Near East—why can't their younger generations come and receive the proper training and go on missions that will be a blessing to Israel? Moshe Sharett brought back another important surprise from his travels in Asia. Since he was on a mission on behalf of the Israeli State, he tried in every way possible to convince the heads of state and spiritual leaders whom he met that the Jewish people are an Oriental people who were physically forced to leave their homeland by enemies and foes and who have now returned to restore their lives and land.

His efforts notwithstanding, Sharett failed to be persuasive, no matter how hard he tried to convince his interlocutors—who received these ideas with suspicion. They were at the same time influenced by pan-Arab and pan-Islamic propagandists who claimed that we are a "white" people just like all colonialist nations that have conquered and enslaved the Oriental peoples in Asia and Africa since the fifteenth century. Luckily, among Sharet's entourage, the

---

4. [Sharett (1894–1965) was minister of foreign affairs (1949–56) and the second prime minister of Israel (1954–55).]

5. [These families, and others, were all part of a Baghdadi Jewish migration to India, China, and several other Asian countries, and they indeed have played such roles.]

lovely brown-skinned member of the Knesset, Rachel Tzabari[6]—who is from Yemen—managed to resolve many doubts and problems. As a consequence, politicians in those countries came to realize that there are dark-skinned [Jewish] citizens in Israel; that is, people of the "colored" races just like the rest of the peoples in Asia and Africa. Shouldn't such a reaction on the part of the Asian nations teach those responsible for Israel's foreign policy a lesson? Is it not the time to go and train tens of our best young men and women from the East for positions and missions in Asia and Africa so that they can bring blessings to our country and draw these nations and countries nearer?

C

As mentioned above, the Israeli government's propaganda campaign has been weak. The world's hostile attitude toward us in the wake of the Sinai Operation was sufficient to reveal this flaw in our system. This attitude of alienation and misunderstanding on the part of other nations and states—not only in Asia and Africa, but also in the Americas and especially in the United States—revealed just how much the propaganda machines of both the Zionist movement and the Israeli government are failing in their tasks. Only after great efforts did we manage to drive away the clouds that hovered above our skies. Yet our weakness is not just vis-à-vis the distant world. The same weakness is also evident in the propaganda attempts in our own region. Even the [non-Jewish] minorities among us are informed and fed by the horror propaganda constantly broadcasted by the media and press of our enemies.

To this day, ten years after the establishment of the state, we have not managed to establish a daily newspaper in Arabic of an acceptable literary level capable of providing comprehensive information about Israel and its citizens to the minorities and the citizens of the neighboring countries. The daily El-Yawm [Today], which was established after 1948 and is edited by Michael Assaf, is shrinking on a daily basis [in terms of readership and circulation], and its level is poor. It makes a mockery of us in the eyes of [native Arab] minority readers. We have among us journalists from Iraq and Egypt who were very respected, famous, and hugely

6. [Rachel Tzabari (1909–95), of Yemeni origins, was a member of the Knesset representing the Mapai Party between 1952 and 1965. One of her sisters, Dr. Simha Tzabari (1913–2004), was one of the leaders of the Palestinian Communist Party during the Mandate.]

influential in the Arabic press in those countries both as writers and editors. Why don't we utilize these talents so they can be a blessing to us by establishing a respected [Arabic-language] media to educate the younger minority generations who [now] feed off of Nasser's venomous propaganda?

Only in one domain can we see any progress. That is the propaganda activity carried out by the Arabic radio broadcast of *Kol Israel* [Voice of Israel]. Those responsible for this important propaganda tool were written off for years and suffered from isolation and a lack of appreciation. Only thanks to the persistence of several young educated people who came to us from Iraq, Syria, and Egypt did *Kol Israel* in Arabic manage to overcome many obstacles and become the powerful tool it is now. In fact, it is the only medium through which we transfer comprehensive information to the thousands of listeners in the Arab world, not only about Israel but also about the Arab states themselves. In the wake of the Sinai Operation, our propaganda chiefs opened their eyes and saw the impact of the transmitted word from *Kol Israel* in Arabic on our enemies around us. Thanks to it we were able to publicize the news of the arrogant Egyptian tyrant's defeat to the masses that are under the influence of the false propaganda of Cairo and Damascus.

If there is one person who runs Arab policy among us it is Sha'ul Bar Haim,[7] who manages the Israeli broadcast in Arabic and who turned the radio transmitter into a powerful tool of unimagined impact. His broadcast is not only equal to [those of] other larger and more experienced radio stations in other nations, it is better. Yet these accomplishments are not enough. We can still expand and increase further the scope and the impact of this Arabic broadcast so it can fulfill the greater job of bringing the word of our existence not only to our Arabic-speaking neighbors but also to any nation in Asia and Africa that is either becoming closer to us or with whom we seek closer ties.

[…]

D

It is the duty of all nations and countries to have trained cadres to carry out the missions that the state assigns to them. Diplomats, propagandists, and en-

7. [Sha'ul Bar-Hayyim was the founder and first manager of the Voice of Israel in Arabic Radio Station. He was born in Iraq and emigrated to Palestine shortly before 1948. The station's staff included then, and still does today, many Iraqi Jews.]

voys do not grow like truffles and mushrooms in a field. In order to train such manpower, we must pay more attention to the problems related to the forging and training of that force. In Israel's first decade of existence, we did not pay any attention to the need to research and publish history and ethnography books or any other material that could expand the knowledge of the nations around us. It is doubtful if there were in this entire decade more than six books published in Hebrew by Israeli scholars about the Arab nations and the Orient. Does it make sense that our younger generations will grow up without understanding the region and its citizens—its peoples and their conditions, cultures, and aspirations? During this first decade, we failed to instill among our high-school students the will and importance of teaching the Arabic language. The number of those studying Arabic in Israeli high schools is decreasing yearly. Faced with this dangerous phenomenon, the initiative was made to establish "the Orientalist track"[8] in high schools. The curriculum of this "Orientalist Department" is carried out in three stages: (1) preliminary studies in the seventh and eighth grades; (2) additional training in the Israel Defense Forces; and (3) advanced studies in the Department of Middle Eastern Studies at the [Hebrew] University. The total duration of this study is therefore eight years.

Graduates of the Orientalist track are meant to take their place in the governmental structure in Israel—in the education system, the military government,[9] and other governmental institutions. Indeed, if we had had the brains to train the necessary manpower, we would have definitely saved ourselves a great deal of trouble. It is worth mentioning that the Ratner Committee—which dealt with the problems related to the military government—demanded, even after justifying its existence and mandating its prolongation, an improvement in the level and training of its personnel as a prerequisite for guaranteeing a fair and desirable regime. The curriculum in the Orientalist track includes classical Arabic, spoken Arabic, history of the Arabs during the Golden Age, and lectures on Middle Eastern problems and geography. There still remains a problem in car-

8. [This track in Israeli high schools focused mostly on teaching Arabic as preparation for service in the Israeli intelligence forces following graduation.]

9. [Following the 1948 war, Israel granted citizenship to Palestinians who managed to stay and who comprised 15 percent of Israel's population. At the same time, Israel imposed a military rule on this community, which was cancelled only in 1966. The military governors were chiefly in charge of monitoring and controlling the internal affairs of Israel's Arab-Palestinian citizens. As of 2011, Palestinian-Arabs comprised 20 percent of Israel's citizens.]

rying out the Orientalist track due to a lack of highly trained and academic-level teachers. In the entire Tel Aviv area, there are only three teachers of Arabic with academic training. The kibbutz movement was willing to open an Orientalist track. When they tried to recruit teachers, they failed to find them. So far the number of graduates of the Orientalist track does not exceed twenty, and this number signifies the lack of willingness among high-school students to join it.

In this area too we must create the right atmosphere in order to attract the young generation to receive this training. The youth are willing to serve in the air force and in the navy; they recently expressed much enthusiasm about serving in the new submarines purchased by the IDF, despite the difficult conditions such service entails. This Israeli youth will surely take up jobs related to administration and government. But until now the youth—with its various strands and ethnic backgrounds—has not been exposed to any proper clarification about the great benefit to the country that such services would provide if the young people were to dedicate themselves to them. Even in the area of the Orientalist track, we must strive to integrate the Oriental Jews. These teenagers are able to train themselves and study the material included in the Orientalist track's curriculum and fill in the shortage in academic teachers [of Arabic] and other related jobs in the government.

It is time to correct past errors. The sooner we do it, the greater the benefit will be to our country and to the next generation that grows up among us.

Avraham Abbas

Avraham Abbas (1912–58) was born in Damascus and was one of the founders of the Zionist Ha-Halutz movement in Syria. In 1929 he led the first group of migrants from Syria to Palestine, where he became a member of Kibbutz Kfar Giladi. Between 1931 and 1934 he served there as a Histadrut emissary to Syria. During this period, he organized Jewish emigration to Palestine from Syria and Lebanon. After his return to Palestine, he was a construction worker until, in 1941, he was once again sent to Syria to organize what was then illegal emigration from there. This time he served as an undercover emissary of the Mossad. Between 1941 and 1944, about 15,000 Jews emigrated from Syria to Palestine through this channel. Abbas represented the Ahdut Ha-'avoda (Labor unity) Party in the Knesset from the time of his election in 1955 until his death, three years later.

From a young age, Abbas was very active in the Sephardic community in Palestine (and later Israel), mostly among workers. In 1949 he was elected a member of the Executive Committee of the Histadrut and was in charge of its relationship with workers of Middle Eastern origins (Abbas headed the "Mizrahi wing" of the organization). In 1951 he was elected a delegate to the World Sephardic Congress and was a member of the Executive Committee of the Sephardic Communities Union—an organization that later became the World Federation of Sephardi Jews. He was one of the founding editors of the Sephardic journal *Shevet ve-'Am* (Tribe and People). Abbas contributed regularly to the journal, writing on cultural as well as social issues. His unique position as both a member of the Knesset and its Absorption Committee and head of the Mizrahi Department of the Histadrut gave him access to the most accurate data concerning the Mizrahim in Israel during the state's first decade. From this position he was able to compose one of the earliest comprehensive reports on the social conditions of the Mizrahim in Israel, which he published in *Shevet ve-'Am*.

33

From Ingathering to Integration:
The Communal Problem in Israel

Excerpt from Abraham Abbas, *From Ingathering to Integration:
The Communal Problem in Israel* (Jerusalem: Achva, 1959).

Abbas produced this lengthy and detailed report in Hebrew in 1958. Most notably, it was not written by a member of the Hebrew University's Department of Sociology, one of whose tasks was dealing with questions of Mizrahi "integration," nor did it appear in an official governmental publication. It is striking to see how many of Abbas's insights at the time were later reflected in the findings and conclusions of Israeli sociologists who criticized the government's policies from the mid-1970s onwards. This report is also probably one of the first times that the term "Second Israel" — often used in the 1970s and 1980s in reference to Mizrahim — appeared in print, either in Hebrew or English. In this regard, the report marks a turning point, a shift toward the discourse on Mizrahi Jews as a social problem within Israel. Furthermore, most of the authors presented in this volume — those who wrote before 1948, in particular — spoke of the Jews of the Middle East in nonconcrete terms. Middle Eastern Jewry was a collectivity that they imagined as a single whole. In contrast, this report discusses Mizrahi Jews from all countries as one whole community in concrete terms. Abbas was not the first to do that, but his report was probably the most comprehensive treatment at the time of what would become the "question of the Mizrahim" in Israel. Considering that Israel had existed only ten years when Abbas wrote the report, and given that he represented a party that was part of the government, the report's critical tone is quite remarkable.

A year after Abbas's death, and shortly after the violent clashes of 1959 known as the Wadi Salib Events, the Sephardic Council reproduced the report in English as a special publication of the World Sephardi Federation. It is not clear who made the translation, but its awkward, sometimes inconsistent, style makes it clear that it was done in some haste. It is clear that the Sephardi or Mizrahi organizations felt an urgent need to send a message in English — probably to Jewish and Zionist organizations abroad — about the tensions within Israel. In this respect, the publication of the report in English turns it into a different document from the Hebrew original. The English translation is another turning point. It tries to convey, probably for the first time, the Mizrahi perspective on Israel's internal social problems and ethnic divisions to an English-speaking audience — American and other Western Jewish philanthropist organizations and Jewish supporters of such Zionist organizations as the Jewish Agency. Attempts like this one to speak to world Jewry, as it were, about the social and ethnic divisions within Israel's Jewish population would intensify during the 1960s and 1970s. The translation is reproduced here almost in its entirety, with the original foreword by the federation. We chose not to interfere with its awkward style except in a few cases.

Foreword

The author of this survey, the late Abraham Abbas M.K. [member of the Knesset] whose untimely death in 1958 was mourned by wide sections of the community, was an extraordinary phenomenon in the public life of Israel. A self-educated man who came from Syria with the Youth Aliyah, he quickly advanced to a position of leadership in the large community of Syrian and other oriental Jews, most of whom were either totally disorganized, or could evince meagre understanding for the organizational patterns of the Israel community. All recognized in him a single-minded and dedicated public worker and accepted him all the more willingly as one of their accredited leaders because he eschewed the strictly communal approach. The pressing need for the quick up-building of the land was always uppermost in his mind. The value of the present survey and its conclusions is considerably enhanced by the fact, known to all who followed the late Mr. Abbas's public career, that for a long time he was opposed to any sort of separate organization by Sephardi and oriental Jews. It was his direct contact with the problems of the masses of immigrants who came since the establishment of Israel, both as party leader (member of the Executive of the Ahdut Ha-'avoda Party) and as a well-known and reelected Sephardi leader (member of the Executive [Committee] of the World Federation of Sephardi Jews), which moved him to change his mind, and sound in this survey an alarm call to the leaders of Israel to take immediate measures for full integration before it is too late.

We believe, therefore, that the posthumous publication of a full and unabridged English version of his survey will serve a useful public purpose at this stage. It should bring home the full facts to wide sections of readers in the English-speaking world, and should focus public attention on the major issue of integration. Knowledge of the facts is an essential pre-requisite to constructive thinking on ways and means towards the solution of the problem.

As [t]his pamphlet goes to press, ugly inter-communal riots broke out in the

Wady Salib quarter of Haifa inhabited by immigrants of North African origin, and in other places which sounded an alarm call to the leaders of the state.

Without prejudging in any way the findings of a Committee of Enquiry investigating the immediate as well as the root causes of the riots, this Federation expresses the hope that it will be allowed to make its own constructive contribution towards the solution of one of the most pressing problems of the State of Israel.

In conclusion we wish to make it clear that in sponsoring the posthumous publication in the English language of this important study, we do not necessarily identify ourselves with all the conclusions reached by its author.

World Sephardi Federation
Jerusalem

From Ingathering to Integration, by (the Late) Abraham Abbas, M.K.

I shall bring thy seed from the east,
And gather thy seed from the west,
I will say to the north "give up"
to the south "keep not back"
Bring my sons from far
And my daughters from the ends of the earth.

ISAIAH, 43

It is not easy to discuss the—now universally acknowledged—duty of the community of Israel to fuse and integrate into the body politic of the land the masses of immigrants that have come to the country since the establishment of Israel. Now that the "ingathering of the exiles" has been in large part accomplished, or has reached at least a crystallized stage, it is the duty of all of us to survey the situation, and see what has been done and, more important still, what remains to be done, to affect the integration into the community of Israel of those who have come from Asian and North African countries. "Ingathering" was itself a long and tedious process full of hazards, but "integration" has proved to be much more complex, even painful.

The problem discussed in the survey can be approached from two—not necessarily mutually exclusive—angles: The surveyor might concern himself with the paramount cause of the welfare of the State of Israel as a whole, or he might concentrate on the pressing need for the betterment of the lot of the mass of these underprivileged people. Although these two ultimate goals are closely interwoven, I have preferred the strictly "national," not the "sectional" (or communal) approach.

The paramount concern of us all is for the welfare of the State we have established after thousands of years of dispersion. I beg the reader to bear in mind this paramount concern when he reads in what follows facts and figures that ostensibly reflect the grievances of only one specific section of the Jewish people, though one which now numbers more than half the population of Israel.

This survey will review what has been done to integrate into the community of Israel the immigrants from Asian and African lands; it will survey the facts and the figures as to immigration from these countries and the steps that have been taken for their absorption in useful and constructive employment (a very different thing from "integration"), and will draw conclusions as to the most effective measures that remain to be taken for their full integration into the community.

I approach my task not without diffidence, precisely because I profoundly believe that the full integration of these new settlers into the community of Israel is the key problem of this country, and on its just and equitable solution will depend the survival of the State.

The surveyor of the achievements of Israel in her first decade will be justified in a sense of pride and gratification over what has been achieved: The foundations of the State are being increasingly strengthened. A pattern of a Jewish sovereign society is in process of evolution. The economy is gaining in organic strength, and our frontiers are safer than they ever were. But when this has been said in justification of our sense of national pride, there still remains the nagging question we must all ask ourselves: Are we, all of us who are foregathered in the land of Israel, full partners and associates in this tremendous creative process of the reconstruction of our land?

The first ten years of Israel have also intensified the sense of solidarity of all parts of the diaspora with Israel and her fortunes. From near and far corners of the world came generous expressions of preparedness and offers to help the State consolidate itself. American Jewry and Jewish communities all over the world have contributed very large sums towards the strengthening and development of the State. All feel a sense of national pride over the State, and echoes of such national gratification have come even from Jewish communities behind the Iron Curtain, while many thousands of Jews from socialist lands, such as Bulgaria, Romania, Hungary and Poland, have actually managed to come and settle in the land during the first decade. After a brief pause, immigration has latterly been resumed. Over 160,000 immigrants arrived in 1956/57, a substantial portion of them from Eastern Europe. We have every reason to hope that these small (resumed) beginnings of immigration from Eastern countries will expand before long to a substantial stream. Some 15,000 Jews from Egypt, all refugees who escaped the Egyptian dictator's rule, have found their way into the country, and established their home in it, after the Sinai campaign.

Some 600,000 of the 900,000 immigrants who arrived in Israel during the first decade came from Moslem countries, North Africa and Arabia, and the great majority of them came during the first ten years of the State. The following table specifies the countries of origin (numbers are in round figures):

150,000 immigrants came from Algeria, Morocco and Tunis;
125,000 immigrants came from Iraq;
50,000 immigrants came from Yemen;
40,000 immigrants came from Bulgaria;
40,000 immigrants came from Turkey;
40,000 immigrants came from Libya;
35,000 immigrants came from Iran;
40,000 immigrants came from Egypt;
10,000 immigrants came from India and Aden;
10,000 immigrants came from Greece & Yugoslavia;
10,000 immigrants came from other Arab countries

Total: 550,000.

These figures show the substantial ratio of Jews from oriental countries in the demographic structure of Israel.

Until the establishment of the State of Israel immigrants from oriental countries were few and far between, and played no role in the demographic structure of the *Yishuv*. The Zionist Organization had virtually bypassed oriental Jewish communities, and its activity among them was meagre. There were many reasons for its relative inactivity among them, into [on] which we would not dwell here. But in spite of the unavoidable restrictions on Zionist activity in Arab countries, many thousands of Jews from Arab and Moslem countries found their way to the Promised Land through numerous hardships and vicissitudes. They crossed deserts, "smuggled" themselves through barriers and formidable frontiers, and literally "infiltrated" into Palestine, when they failed to get the coveted immigration certificates from the British Mandatory Administration.

To the category of those so-called "illicit immigrants" belong some 50,000 Jews from Syria and Lebanon who immigrated long before the State of Israel was established, and before a properly equipped organization for illegal immigration began to operate. In 1929 there had already been in operation a "Halutz" movement of Syrian and Lebanese Jews who launched their own illegal immigration machinery that operated all these years without interruption.

That movement accounted for the entry into Palestine of over thirty thousand Iraqi Jews, many of whom were trained by the emissaries of the KIBBUTZ ME'UHAD[1] movement in the Halutz Training Camps that were established in Iraq during the 1940s.

Syrian Jewry began to feel the beneficent impact of the Halutz movement in the 1930s, and there were also large waves of "illegal" immigrants from Greece, Bulgaria and Turkey. It is all the more regrettable, therefore, that those who wrote the history of illegal immigration virtually ignored these large waves of illegal immigrants from oriental countries: Works like *Porzey She'arim* by Bracha Habas offended against that historical truth.[2]

On the establishment of the State of Israel oriental Jews constituted 30% of the Jewish YISHUV. Long before the *Bilu* and *Hibbat Zion* immigration (mainly from Eastern Europe) they already resided in Jaffa, Tiberias, Haifa, Jerusalem and Saffed many thousands of Jews from oriental countries.[3] It is only since the proclamation of the State that immigration has become a mighty factor in the demographic structure of the community. In the thick of the fighting in the War of Liberation many communities of oriental Jews dislodged themselves completely from their temporary abodes in the diaspora and abandoned there all the fortunes they could build up in a lifetime of hard labour, including substantial assets in real estate.

Absorption

Many of these immigrants were absorbed in the various branches of the economy. The Jewish Agency and the Government of Israel [made] concerted efforts in large-scale housing projects to house them. While, however, some

1. [The Kubbutz Me'uchad (United kibbutz), founded in 1927, was the kibbutz movement associated with Mapai, the main labor party. The more left-leaning Kibbutz Artzi, founded in 1936, was associated with the Mapam Party.]
2. [Bracha Habas's 1957 book in Hebrew was translated by Ann Walinska Habas into English as *The Gate Breakers* (New York: T. Yoseloff, 1963).]
3. [Bilu and Hibbat Zion were two early Zionist organizations.]

success may be said to have attended such efforts for the *economic* absorption of the immigrants, I must say regretfully that to this day they have not yet been *socially* integrated. In the social and cultural spheres there is an almost unbridgeable chasm between the so-called "First Israel" and the so-called "Second Israel."

The surveyor of our demographic scene is in duty bound to expose frankly, almost brutally, the many causes for such deplorable disparity between the two. Oriental Jews have made a substantial contribution to the growth and development of the State. Theirs was the decisive share in the rehabilitation of our desert expanses and the repopulation of the Negev and the 'Aravah.[4] These erstwhile petty traders, brokers and peddlers have been transformed in the country into builders, farmers and road constructors. They underwent a process of almost complete occupational transformation. Masses of them are huddled in immigrant settlements and development centres.They are scattered through the length and breadth of the country. The hardships of integration in their new cities and villages did not deter them, and they were not at all "choosy" in their quest for employment. All they asked for was: employment at a fair wage to support their large families. Such was not, however, available to them; nevertheless, they hung on to their temporary barracks and shacks, and sought to strike roots in the land even under such impossible housing conditions.

I. AGRICULTURAL SETTLEMENT

In the absence of definitive statistical data on the share of oriental Jews in the agricultural re-settlement effort in the land, one can only assume (and this, on the evidence of experts) that they now constitute well over 25% of the agricultural population of Israel. Many of their youth were actively associated with youths of other sections of the Israel population in the building of Kibbutz nuclei. Thousands of boys and girls who came with the "Youth 'Aliyah" remained in the settlements in which they received their early training. Those who belonged to the Halutz movement in the diaspora went to *Kibbutzim* to work on the land. All of them are now integrated in the Kibbutz life in border settlements.

But the great majority of oriental Jews continue to live in the "immigrant settlements" which were established early in the days of the State of Israel. In response to the call of the Jewish national institutions they went to work on the land, and there established numerous villages and settlements. That effort

4. [The Negev and 'Aravah are desert regions in southern Israel.]

itself was of unprecedented scope and dimensions in the history of our own colonisation, and was all the more remarkable because few of these new settlers had any prior training, agricultural or social, for such large-scale settlement. The following is the demographic structure of the new immigrant settlements which were established under the auspices of the Histadrut:

25% of the settlers came from North Africa;
20% of the settlers came from Yemen and Aden;
22% of the settlers came from Iraq and Kurdistan;
30% of the settlers came from European countries;
3% of the settlers came from other countries.

100%

These figures reflect great credit on those who undertook, in the literal and physical meaning of the word, one of the major tasks of the State of Israel, namely the rehabilitation of the waste and derelict lands of the Negev, Galilee, the Jerusalem corridor and the Hill Country. They have proudly borne the brunt of the cooperative re-settlement effort, of which they knew little or nothing in the countries of their origin. It is only fair to add that there were occasional migrations from such new centres, which were due to recurrent hardships and crises, economic, social and vocational. Many of them still experience hardships in their efforts to strike roots. Not all new settlements have consolidated them-selves, and settlers still have to face formidable difficulties due to unemployment, lack of approach roads or inadequate lighting, inadequate technical training and instruction, insecurity, and difficulties in the marketing of their produce. But all such difficulties and hardships notwithstanding, the new settlers have on the whole held their own and the occupational structure of their communities has been completely transformed.

They have increased agricultural production, and thereby contributed to a large decrease in imports of food commodities. The food basket of the popula-tion has been enriched through their labour, and they were responsible for the expanded agricultural exports from the country (peanuts, cotton, citrus).

So stupendous an effort of colonisation could not proceed without its pitfalls. We must examine some of the negative facets of it dispassionately, and see what can be done to remedy them. The organization of an agricultural community on the basis of the geographical origin ("communal") of its members, whatever the reasons that may be adduced for it, presents a grave danger to the process of integration, indeed puts off integration and crystallizes present "communal" divisions. A "communal" settlement of which all members belong to the same community, sometimes to the same family group, is bound to perpetuate *Galuth* values and standards of organization. So that, while we may be gratified by the purely *agricultural* record of their achievement, we must say that on the social, cultural and educational fronts much work remains to be done before we could point to similar progress. The present organization rules out the so essential uprooting of *Galuth* habits and traditions. The young generation is being reared on the same habits of the *Galuth*. The wife and mother of the family has not really changed her mode of life, even if she has struck roots in her work on the land. Her status remains very much what it was before, and, like before, she remains subservient to a patriarchal mode of life.

This is the sad picture one obtains on looking at life in all those immigrant settlements of which the bulk of the population belongs to the oriental communities. It becomes all the more urgent for us to examine these grave dangers objectively. It is incumbent on the Zionist movement and on the Labour movement to leave no stone unturned and find the satisfactory solution that will restore the uniting bridge between all the different tribes and exiles in Israel.

Ma'abarot (Transit Camps)

The Transit Camp population, too, is homogeneous in communal composition. There can be no doubt as to the magnitude of the achievement of the State of Israel, in concerted effort with the Jewish Agency, in the absorption of immigration; and especially in the measures taken towards the solution of the housing crisis: Of the 900,000 new settlers since the establishment of the State, only some 100,000 remain who reside in the temporary Transit Camps. Yet with all due appreciation of what has been done to resolve the manifold problems connected with the full absorption of the immigrants, the surveyor of the communal scene of Israel cannot help recording the most deplorable fact that large masses of the settlers, who have been in the country for years, continue to live in the congested shacks of the Transit Camps and the British Army Camps. His perturbation will be all the greater when he remembers that practically the entire Transit Camp population is homogeneous in its social structure and its geographical origin. Over 90% of the Transit Camp population are oriental Jews. This is a phenomenon of utmost gravity, and one that will prove to be a grave stumbling block in the process of full integration.

The following figures (culled from a brochure on the subject presented by the Minister of Labour to the Knesset as material for a debate on the final solution of the housing problem for the Transit Camp population), shed light on the true situation:

Length of Residence in Transit Camp	Percentage
From 4 to 8 years (i.e., settlers who arrived in the years 1948/52)	56%
From 4 to 5 years (i.e., settlers who arrived in 1953/54)	17%
From 2 to 3 years (i.e., settlers who arrived in 1955/56)	22%
From 1 to 2 years (i.e., settlers who arrived in 1957)	5%

The inevitable—and most regrettable—deduction from these figures is that discriminatory policies were pursued in the process of the integration of immigrants. Against the paramount fact that the bulk of the Transit Camp population is oriental, all the magnificent work done since the establishment of the State shades into insignificance, if only because these new immigrants have been made to feel—and indeed say so in private conversations—that had they been Ashkenazi Jews, their suffering would have come to an end.

The government has now pledged itself to accelerate a solution for this painful problem. The Minister of Labour has formulated a 3-year plan for the housing of these 20,000 families. The span of time envisaged for such [a] final solution is all too long, and we must hope that the hardships of these people will impel a shortening of that period.

The fear is, however, prevalent that even if the housing projects are implemented according to the minister's plan, the houses will remain vacant, because the Transit Camp population belongs to the poorest section of the community. An analysis of its occupational and social structure will shed light on this precarious social phenomenon:

TABLE 1. FAMILY COMPOSITION

Families of 2–4 members (mostly nearer 4)	56%
Families of 5–6 members	25%
Families of 6–7 members	19%

TABLE 2. SOURCES OF LIVELIHOOD

45% have regular work
26% have part time employment, or are unemployed
10% are shopkeepers, have kiosks, or are members of liberal professions
19% are social welfare cases

In the light of the above figures the question arises whether a population of such social and economic structure could afford the comparatively high rentals they are charged for their new houses. The leases (or agreements) for such new flats stipulate regular payments of rentals over a period of thirty years by the tenants, the same people who have hitherto occupied free of charge their miserable shack-lodgings. It must be realized that a monthly payment of 30–40 Israeli Lira for the tenancy of such flats (including rates) is too high for a population 60% of whom have lived on the dole of the Ministry of Social Welfare. Little wonder that few of these settlers have found it possible to move to these new lodgings. I submit that the government must find the way for easy payments for these people of the Transit Camps, in a supreme effort to eliminate this scar from the Israeli landscape, and put an end to the Ma'abarot scandal.

II. EDUCATION

The State of Israel's record of achievement in education has been equally substantial. The Ministry of Education has overcome formidable obstacles in the pursuit of its policy to raise the general standard of education. Mass immigration to Israel brought to the country prospective citizens who were poles apart from one another in their cultural standards. They lacked, too, one common vernacular. The schools of Israel have served as the natural educational melting pot for all these disparate elements, and educational standards were evolved that suited people from such most divergent cultural origins.

Dwindling of Elementary School Population
The Minister of Education Mr. Aran[5] stated to a rally of schoolmasters inter alia, that only 3% of the elementary school population was "falling off" each year, and that 90% of those who left the schools before completing their education in

5. [Zalman Aran (1899–1970) was a Mapai politician and an educator. He was minister of education in 1955–60 and 1963–69.]

them were of the oriental communities. Among the causes listed for such flight from the school was inability to attain the standard of study set by the schools. Even at this comparatively low rate (I believe that the actual number of pupils leaving school before ending their study to be much greater), this means that there are each year more than 15,000 children who leave school without completing their education at the elementary school; multiplied by three (for the last three years), we obtain a total of about 50,000 children who have not completed their education at an elementary school.

It may be argued that this is normal, and there are similar phenomena in most countries. That may well be so in most other countries, which could possibly put up with this. Not so Israel, where the "quitter" is a real menace to the State, if only because the majority of those who quit school without completing their education in it are of the oriental Jewish communities. This means that a generation is growing in Israel without the benefit of even elementary school education, and that generation is of a homogeneous social and "communal" structure.

To these figures must be added the 50,000 boys and girls who (according to the survey of the Ministry of Labour) are working as apprentices, and have never had the benefit of an elementary school education. They add up to a total that is all the more frightening because of the extreme difficulty of integrating into society boys and girls who have not completed their elementary school [education].

The fact that the majority of quitters are oriental Jews presents an extraordinary, indeed abnormal, phenomenon. It is grave because it will make for the continuance of communal isolation and separation. All who are familiar with the true conditions will absolutely repudiate any argument that the falling off is due to inability of the pupils to live up to the standards of tuition set by the schools. The true reasons for such falling off are those set out in a survey prepared a few years ago by special investigators in the Beersheba district, namely:

1. The economic condition of the parents;
2. Housing conditions;
3. Undernourishment;
4. Inadequate school buildings;
5. Lack of suitable textbooks, and perhaps lack of books generally;
6. Large families, whose breadwinners cannot afford tuition costs;
7. Last, and most important, teachers of a low standard of proficiency.

Most of the teachers in development areas, immigrant settlements, slums and "abandoned" villages are either unqualified, or, if qualified, are young and inexperienced. Competent and able teachers do not rush to teaching posts in such areas.

I submit that a solution of these difficulties can definitely be found with due regard to the causes of the present unsatisfactory state of things. Our educational authorities must understand that boys and girls without the benefit of a school education, if dumped on the labour market, or, more correctly, doomed to a life of idleness, are actually exposed to a life of destitution, cruel, bitter and degrading, without a single redeeming feature that will light the darkness of their grey existence. They are most dangerous social "explosives." There are some who do not hesitate to dub these stepchildren of Israel "The Second Israel." They who do so render no service to the State. One does not contribute to a solution of a pressing problem by simply ignoring it. The problem is there for all to see: On the one side—there are children, almost all of whom [are] from oriental communities, who are almost completely deprived of the benefit of a secondary, vocational or agricultural training (even, in many cases, of education in forms 6, 7 and 8 of the primary schools); on the other side—there are the children of the Ashkenazi communities, the great majority of whom has completed its education in secondary schools or had the benefit of a vocational or agricultural training, and many of whom have even benefited from a higher education. Here are a few figures that illustrate the problem:

[TABLE 1]. [DISTRIBUTION OF SECONDARY SCHOOL POPULATION BY CLASSES (OF SCHOOLS AND COUNTRIES OF ORIGIN)]

Form	Oriental Jews
9	15.8% of all students are oriental Jews
10	13.5% of all students are oriental Jews
11	9.8% of all students are oriental Jews
12	7.8% of all students are oriental Jews

TABLE 2. DISTRIBUTION OF VOCATIONAL SCHOOL POPULATION BY CLASSES (OF SCHOOLS AND COUNTRIES OF ORIGIN)

Form	Total Number of Students	Students of Oriental Jewish Communities
Form 9	2,196	29.7%
Form 10	1,414	25.5%
Form 11	1,141	20.4%
Form 12	456	11.6%

TABLE 3. DISTRIBUTION OF AGRICULTURAL SCHOOL POPULATION

Form	Total Number of Students	Students of Oriental Jewish Communities
Form 9	1,285	33.9%
Form 10	968	26.4%
Form 11	694	22.3%
Form 12	380	11.6%

Distribution of school population in secondary, vocational and agricultural schools according to father's country of origin:

Country of Origin	Number	Percentage
Israel	1,904	8.5
Iraq	1,260	5.7
Syria and Lebanon	193	0.9
Turkey	371	1.7
Yemen and Aden	789	3.5
Other countries	457	2.0
Egypt	235	1.1
North Africa	619	2.8
Eastern Europe	13,892	62.3
Western Europe	2,147	9.3
America	76	0.3
Unknown [other, unidentifiable, countries]	355	1.6
Total	22,288 [22,298]	100.0

The above figures expose a very sad picture in the sphere of education. One cannot help asking: what hope have we for complete integration if the ever-widening chasm is of such dimensions?

The problem will yet [be] aggravated by reference to problems of vocational training and the general economic standard of students: Oriental Jewish students of the age group 14–17 constitute 55% of all age groups. They number 17% of the school population in all post-elementary schools—agricultural, secondary and vocational—a percentage likely to be considerably reduced if the continuation classes in the Kibbutzim are taken into consideration. According to figures adduced by the Working Youth movement there are 48,000 boys and girls of the age group 14–17 who do not continue their studies.

It is difficult to exaggerate the gravity of this social threat to the community as a whole resulting from the fact that masses of boys and girls are left without any primary education, and exposed to the hazards of the street, and the danger is aggravating, not lessening, from year to year. In 1956 there were 2,700 juvenile delinquents who came to grips with the law, apart from those whose offences could not be established.

Equally unsatisfactory and inadequate are the arrangements for rallying the youth of oriental Jews to the various organized youth movements: There are some 20,000 organized youths in the Working Youth Movement, and 16,000 of them are regular rate payers to labour organizations. Most of these have joined the movement in the hope of getting work through it. But half of the whole youth of oriental Jews is not at all organized within *any* movement. This means in effect that a generation of unorganized labourers is growing in Israel, who threaten to supplant organized labour from their social achievements. The cut-throat competition between organized and unorganized labour is bound to lead to low wages, the dumping of unskilled labour, ignorance and virtual illiteracy. A formidable wall between the various sections of youth makes for almost complete isolation, and the chasm is ever widening.

Boys and girls who arrived in Israel with their parents as children of 7 or 8 years now stand disillusioned and frustrated. The State of Israel has failed to find the organizational pattern which alone can impart to them the full extent of its social gains.

Distribution of University Students by Countries of Origin

The following two tables complete a sad picture. They show that higher education in Israel is almost wholly the patrimony of boys and girls of the Ashkenazi communities.

The composition of the student body of the Hebrew University (by faculties and countries of origin) in 1957/58 was as [shown in the following table].

(In 1956/57 the total number of University students was smaller by 86, whereas the total number of students of Asian and African origin rose by 28: this means that their relative ratio within the student body dropped from 1956 to 1957 from 6% to 5%.)

Country of origin	Humanities	Social sciences	Law	Natural sciences	Agriculture	Medicine	Total number	%
Israel	552	298	225	423	160	221	1,888	56.6
Syria and Lebanon	3	3	4	—	1	1	12	0.4
Iraq	27	11	20	19	6	13	96	2.8
Turkey	4	1	2	3	1	2	13	0.4
Yemen and Aden	3	—	1	1	—	1	6	0.2
Other Asian countries	6	3	—	4	1	2	16	0.5
Egypt	10	4	3	3	1	3	24	0.7
Eastern Europe	222	111	98	179	43	184	837	25.1
North Africa	4	2	—	3	—	—	9	0.2
Western Europe	128	50	24	72	27	49	350	10.5
America	40	11	3	16	7	6	83	2.5
Total	999	494	380	732	247	482	3,334	100
Percentage of oriental Jewish students	5.7	4.9	7.9	4.5	4.0	4.6	5.3	

FIRST YEAR STUDENTS IN HAIFA TECHNION (IN 1957/58)
ACCORDING TO COUNTRIES OF ORIGIN

Israel	277
Iraq	6
Syria and Lebanon	0
Turkey	2
Yemen and Aden	1
Other Asian countries	1
Egypt	2
North Africa	3
Eastern Europe	110
Western Europe	29
America and South America	6
Total	436 [437]

Even if we assume that a proportion of the Israelis included in the above figures is of oriental Jewish origin, the distressing picture will remain substantially unaltered, and will continue to expose the deplorable gap between the two sections of the population in the sphere of higher education.

Groups of Breadwinners in Israel

An analysis of some data on groups of breadwinners in Israel will be of interest in the pursuit of this theme:

Police: Although half of the total Police Force of 6,000 belongs to oriental Jewish communities, there are only 10% of the total of 600 officers and NCOS [noncommissioned officers] who are of oriental Jewish origin.

Teachers: Of a total of 13,927 teachers in the country, less than one quarter is of oriental Jewish origin, as the following figures (for 1955/56) show:

Eastern Europe	48.0%
Israel	24.2%
The Balkans	12.4%
Asian countries	9.5%
African countries	3.4%
Other countries	2.5%
Total	100.0%

Civil Service: Senior civil servants, judges, administrative officials and diplomatic envoys are decisive and major determining factors in the processes of Israel's development. Of a total of 2,083 such senior civil servants etc. there were 1,966 of Ashkenazi origin, and only 117 Sephardim and oriental Jews. (This is euphemistically termed "a policy of non-discrimination.")

Wage earners in agriculture: lowest 40,000 of a total of 50,000 such workers are oriental Jews, and their wages are among the lowest.

90% of the total 35,000 *building workers* are oriental Jews.

Metal Workers: 50% of a total of 35,000 such workers are Sephardim and oriental Jews.

Labour Exchange Applicants, Workers in Temporary and Emergency Jobs: 95% of all applicants for work to Labour Exchanges, and of those in partial or emergency employment and in receipt of the all too meagre relief dole, are Sephardim and oriental Jews. 50% of all unskilled labour are oriental Jews.

Many more illustrations from the Israel labour [force] could be adduced to prove that Sephardim and oriental Jews definitely belong to the underprivileged and submerged class of the community.

[...]

III. THE SHARE OF ORIENTAL JEWS IN PUBLIC INSTITUTIONS

I feel I must introduce this chapter with a few unequivocal personal remarks to avoid any possible impression (or suspicion) that my remarks on this subject are actuated by a sense of personal frustration. I must be permitted to say at the outset that I am totally immune from any such sense of personal frustration. The party to which I belong has entrusted me with several public tasks: I am a Member of Knesset and also serve as member of my party's central secretariat. Not only new immigrants and dwellers in the slums and Transit Camps suffer from the present oppressive atmosphere of discrimination and maltreatment, but also a number of old-established residents of the country. The facts and the figures set out in what follows speak for themselves. My remarks in what follows are mainly addressed to those who formulate policy in party caucuses in the hope that they will be prompted thereby to a true appreciation of the gravity of the problem which I will try to expose to them as objectively as possible.

Communal Ferment

As the day approaches for the election of the Knesset and the local and municipal authorities, Sephardi and oriental Jewish leaders evince increasing alertness to the problems before them. There are rallies of communal leaders in several places; several separate burial societies for Sephardim are being organized in a number of communities. Some of the leaders who lend their support to such separatist moves are undoubtedly driven by noble public considerations in joining such organizations; they hope thereby—to take one specific grievance of recent experience—to express their utter dissatisfaction with the discriminatory policies of the Ministry of Religions which sought to dislodge Sephardi public servants from positions they had long held. There are others, however, who embarked upon such separatist moves as a springboard for the forthcoming electoral campaign, in a vain attempt to exploit the frustration of oriental Jews for their own personal designs and ambitions. It is this psychological background which has rendered possible special separatist rallies of Sephardi engineers, lawyers, rabbis etc., or groups like a federation of immigrants from all Asian and North African countries.

But when this has been said, it must be admitted that each such separatist move (or organization) feeds on a sense of general malaise and disaffection that derive from the cumulative effect of long bitter experience, namely, the overriding fact that after years of residence in the country large masses of people have not yet been integrated into the social economic, educational and cultural life of the country (the strictly educational aspect of the problem has been laboured [dealt with] above in my remarks on education). Again, the leaders of several political parties of the country have indirectly contributed to such separatist organization, for they have always viewed oriental Jewish communities as little more than *suppliers of votes in times of election*. Party leaders often accuse Sephardi, and oriental leaders of separatist and sectional trends, alleging also that the mass of the communities for whom they speak are simply unwilling to find their place within the framework of existing organization. Let us examine such charges dispassionately and see how much truth there is in them. Have the spokesmen for the State, *of all parties*, done their own soul searching without bias? Have they asked themselves whether it would be just and fair for them to pursue the path they pursued hitherto, and leave these naive and simple oriental Jews on the fringes and in the by-paths of the public institutions, without enabling them to have a say in the framing of their policies?

We will begin our survey in this sphere with an analysis of the Zionist movement and its institutions, and will then proceed to the Knesset, the Cabinet, the Histadrut and the political parties themselves. Do the composition and structure of these bodies and parties reflect the substantial demographic change which has occurred in the State?

Representation on the Executive of the Jewish Agency and the Zionist Council

For decades these important public bodies have been constituted on an absolutely communal basis, and none but Ashkenazi Jews served on them. To ignore or dismiss this overriding fact is to offend against the truth. Many hasten to draw facile and dangerous inferences from this fact. One of these is: that Sephardi Jews, that very section of the Jewish people which has literally realized the Zionist ideal by coming in the mass to settle in the country, was [were] not Zionist at all. Although the constituted bodies of the Zionist movement are there essentially to tackle the problem of these very Jews, they themselves are not represented on [in] the supreme organs of the movement. I refer not to a purely communal representation (I have always discountenanced any such course; on the contrary, in my many years in the country I have always fought for the affiliation of oriental Jews with existing political parties, through which—and through which alone—Sephardi claims and views should be pressed). But let us see whether even on the existing system of representation by parties, Sephardi and oriental Jews could be said to have received their just deserts. The blatant fact is that all political parties, represented on the Executive of the Jewish Agency, have virtually joined in a conspiracy of which the obvious effect is to dismiss Sephardi Jewry as an utterly insignificant factor, so that not a single oriental Jew of the respective parties was nominated for such representative public office. This charge could not perhaps be properly directed to parties with only one representative on the Executive. But there are parties with a fairly large number of representatives, yet all these are Ashkenazi Jews. The Zionist Council with a membership of 80 (apart from several dozen Deputy Members) continues to this day to be constituted, as it was originally constituted, of Ashkenazi members, with perhaps only one or two Sephardi members.

It is futile to argue—as some do—that this body is now stripped of any real influence. If it were so devoid of influence, it should have had no right to exist. But if it exists and functions, we [would] very much like to be associated with it. We would like to take an active part in its deliberations on immigration quotas; the measures it considers for integration; the question of whether the Zionist

Organization should be constituted as a unitary and uniform organization or as a federation of political parties. We whould like to take an active part in the framing of the policy of *selection* in immigration, particularly insofar as it applies to North African Jews, and all the more so because that policy was responsible for the denial of immigration facilities to scores of thousands of Jews in Morocco. We claim our share in the public missions sent to all parts of the world. We refuse to believe that there are not among us public leaders and speakers with vision, sympathy and understanding who can carry the message of the land to millions of their brethren abroad.

It is absurd to accuse us of separatism and sectional trends; the reverse is the truth. It is the bodies of the Zionist movement that are composed on an absolutely sectional basis. If political parties are anxious to avoid and preclude communal organization machineries, they must give adequate representation on the elected bodies of the Zionist Organization to Sephardi and oriental Jews, especially to those of them who have proved their loyalty and dedication to the national welfare. There are many such public-spirited leaders in all political parties, and only by enabling these to have a say in public affairs, will it be possible to rule out separatist organizational machineries. No power in the world can dismiss the sense of frustration that derives from the fact that *all* leaders in the Zionist movement are Ashkenazi Jews, without even a handful of competent Sephardi leaders who have been found worthy and suitable by their parties for the undertaking of public tasks.

I say without hesitation that oriental Jewish emissaries will discharge with loyalty and dedication the missions entrusted to them by the party. They will defend the interests and principles of the party just as competently as all other emissaries, and will gain experience in public affairs that will prove beneficent to all sections of the people.

Representation in the Knesset

Whatever else one may think of the wisdom of the course pursued by the government of Israel in its foreign policy, there can be no question that the State of Israel has definitely laid the foundations for Jewish self-government. By far the most important of all self-governing institutions is the Knesset, the House of the People's Representatives, who[se members] are elected once every four years. Israel's citizens vote freely and democratically. We have enacted basic laws of procedure in and for Israel's Parliament as well as a most extensive network of laws to govern all our affairs.

Since the establishment of Israel three Knessets have been elected, but in neither [none] of them has there been a change in the numerical strength of the representation of oriental Jews. The third Knesset was elected about three years ago, yet it failed to reflect the substantial change that has occurred in the demographic structure of the population. Half of Israel's population is now of oriental Jewish origin. The first question that presents itself is: Have the leaders of the parties who draw up and compose the lists of candidates nominated for election to the Knesset made any variation in these lists to the end of making them a true reflex of the immense demographic change, and giving a voice in parliamentary affairs to one half of the population? We all remember the abundance of promises that were showered upon the electorate in the thick of the electoral campaign for the Knesset. Let us examine these in retrospect, and see what has been done: The General Zionist party has sustained two separate lists of communal candidates—one Sephardi, and the other Yemenite. The Herut party, which was vociferous in its promises, won large numbers of votes from among the masses. Leftist parties too, were equally generous in promises. It must be admitted that in the grey and prosaic pre-election days some parties make perhaps greater efforts than others to integrate oriental and Sephardi leaders into their day-to-day party work. Nevertheless, the overall picture as reflected in the composition of the Knesset is most gloomy. Of the 113 Jewish Knesset Members there were, in all parties, no more than 11 Sephardi or oriental Jewish Members of Knesset. [. . .]

In the second Knesset there were two more Sephardi Members on the Mapai list than in the third. The Herut party allotted to a Sephardi Candidate, Mr. Arditi, 14th place in the list, a precarious and uncertain place, but he got elected.[6] The first oriental candidate on this list was given the eleventh place. An analysis of these figures shows that each party adds, more or less for decorative purposes, a single candidate, and no more, of the Sephardi and oriental communities. Often such a candidate is allotted a place so far down in the list as to make his election most unlikely.

I venture to say that candidates' lists composed on this basis constitute a distortion, rather than an affirmation, of true democracy. The State of Israel does pursue true democracy, but party caucuses, I regret to say, abuse it and distort it. There must be a radical departure from these methods in the elections for

6. [Herut was the right-wing party headed by Menachem Begin that later became the Likud Party. Binamin Arditi, a Bulgarian Sephardi, served in the Knesset from 1955 to 1965. He was also member of the Sephardic Council in Jerusalem.]

the 4th Knesset if democracy is to survive. Party leaders must do their utmost to make it possible for all sections of the people to be represented in the Knesset. If grave social upheavals are to be avoided, if disaffection is to be forestalled not only within their own ranks, but also among the mass of the people who have ceased to have any faith in their promises, they must all draw the correct deductions from this unhealthy state of things. The mass of the oriental Jewish section of the population is at heart non-partisan. Most of the oriental Jews have been cruelly and bitterly disappointed, and they have ceased to have any faith in the public declarations of party leaders and in their professions of true equality for all the citizens of Israel. These slogans have been largely discredited, and the Sephardi electorate are bound to draw far-reaching conclusions from their frustration.

I address my appeal particularly to the leaders of the labour parties, several of whom have expressed themselves in the past in favour of such a change. They must see to it that oriental Jewish leaders are invited to join their representative delegations on the national institutions, and on all missions abroad. If they do so, other parties will follow their example. Mere opposition to "communal" candidates lists will not do. I have no doubt that had the Knesset included representatives of these communities, the painful problem of the Ma'abarot would long [ago] have been solved. These people seek a say not alone in the foreign and defence policy of the land, but also in its home policies—lighter tax burden, larger support for large families, free education at all levels, full employment, and unemployment insurance.

[...]

To sum up: what can be done by the leaders of Israel to accelerate the process of full integration?

Planning Authority

At the second Sephardi Congress which was held in Jerusalem in 1954 I stressed the need for the immediate constitution of a supreme Planning Authority vested with sufficient powers and equipped with the necessary financial resources to pull down the inter-communal barriers and remove the root causes that perpetuate the Galuth. Four years have since elapsed. The analysis in this study proves beyond doubt the urgent need for such a Planning Authority. The proposed Authority must be an effective and strong body provided with adequate financial resources that will enable it to enlist in its service the best talent, experts who should prepare periodical surveys of the situation and should be able to make recommendations for methodical action designed to accelerate the process of complete integration. There must be full co-ordination between Ministers and Ministries in this vital work, and unmethodical and piecemeal action must cease. There must be a definite plan for the regulation of all action in this sphere. Above all, there must be a plan for the pressing educational problems and difficulties. Nothing but a planned and methodical action will yield tangible results in this tremendous job, which must be tackled by all of us with sympathy and understanding, indeed with enthusiasm, so that at the end of the second decade of the State we might be able jubilantly to proclaim that the vision of the integration of all exiles has become a reality.

Further Readings

Bernstein, Deborah. "Immigrants and Society—A Critical View of the Dominant School of Israeli Sociology." *British Journal of Sociology* 31, no. 2 (1980): 246–64.

Bernstein, Deborah, and Shlomo Swirski. "The Rapid Economic Development of Israel and the Emergence of the Ethnic Division of Labour." *British Journal of Sociology* 33, no. 1 (1982): 64–85.

Dahan, Yossi, and Gal Levy. "Multicultural Education in the Zionist State—The Mizrahi Challenge." *Studies in Philosophies and Education* 19, nos. 5–6 (November 2000): 423–44.

Ram, Uri. *The Changing Agenda of Israeli Sociology: Theory, Ideology and Identity*. Albany, NY: State University of New York Press, 1995.

Saporta, Ishak, and Yossi Yonah. "Pre-Vocational Education: The Making of Israel's Ethno-Working Class." *Race, Ethnicity and Education* 7, no. 3 (2004): 251–75.

Swirski, Shlomo. *Israel, the Oriental Majority*. London: Zed, 1989.

———. *Politics and Education in Israel*. New York: Falmer, 1999.

Publication Credits

Selection 25: Sasson Shalom Dallal, "Last Letter," in Yūsuf Rizq-Allāh Ghanīmah, *A Nostalgic Trip into the History of the Jews of Iraq*, trans. Reading A. Dallal (Lanham, MD: University Press of America, 1998), 175–76. Reprinted with permission of Rowman & Littlefield Publishing Group, Lanham MD.

Index

218; Mizrahi-to-Ashkenazi assimilation, xxii; old Jewish community and, 98–101; Zionism as response to, 215

Avisar, David, 114

'Azza, Khuthayyir, 33, 33n7

Balfour, Lord Arthur, 149–150

Balfour Declaration, 102, 117, 123–27, 132, 149–151, 153

Bar-Hayyim, Sha'ul, 221, 221n7

Benison, Ariel, 111–12, 111n1

Ben-Kiki, Hayyim, 87, 102–3

Ben Mordechai, Alexander, 203

Bevin, Ernest, 149–150

Bivas, Rahamin, 65

Boer War, 14–17

Buber, Martin, 131

Bulgaria, 44, 44n20, 229t

capitalism, 145, 148, 150–55, 156. See also economy

Cattaui Pacha, Joseph Aslan, 80

Cazès, David, 5, 5n3

Christianity: Christian anti-Zionism, 62, 98; Christian Arabs, 62, 91; Egyptian Jewish-Christian relations, 49–53; European cultural dominance and, 89–92; Middle Eastern Christian education, 92–94; missionaries in Jewish areas, 64

class: Arab-Israeli conflict and, 181–88, 191–92; Egyptian social democracy movement, 194–96; Jewish Question and, 143–45; Mizrahim "Second Israel" class status, 209, 225, 231, 237; persecution of Jews and, 155–56

colonialism/imperialism: British intervention in Egypt and, 176–78; colonization of Palestine, 39–40, 40n14; exploitation of Arab-Israeli relations, 180–88, 191–92; imperialist "divide and rule" strategy, 11, 38, 150, 153–54; overview of Western imperialism, 38,

88–92; Zionist movement and, 147–155, 159–160, 168–69, 191

communism. See socialism/Marxism/ communism

Confino, Michael, xxviii

Coughlin, Father Charles, 154, 154n3

Curiel, Henry, 174–75

Dahan, Yitzhak, xxii

Dallal, Sasson Shalom, 141–42, 162

Daniel, Menahem Salih, 109

Danon, Abraham, 5, 5n3

Darwish, Yusuf, 195n10

democracy: democracy movement in Lebanon, 188; Egyptian social democracy movement, 194–96; European Jews in post-World War II democracies, 161; independent Palestine as, 160–61, 169–170; Mizrahi representation in Israeli elections, 246–47; as solution to Jewish Question, 160–61, 166–67

diaspora: assimilation and, 98–101, 215, 218; Israel as homeland for, 74, 116–17, 122–23, 132n10, 133, 215; Jewish commercial traditions and, 156; Middle Eastern Jewish diaspora, xxvi–xxvii, 5–6, 138–39; origin of Jewish Question and, 143–45; persecution as experience in, 123–25, 132n10, 139, 144; post-World War II refugees, 138, 167, 170–71; retention of Galuth values from, 233, 247; Uganda as proposed homeland, 148; unified diaspora nationalism, 156–59, 157n7

Dinar, al-Sayyid Ali, 16

diversity: Balfour Declaration guarantees for, 150–51; in Egypt, 83–85; Israeli non-Jewish minorities, 217–220; Mizrahim isolation in Israel and, 206–12, 214, 226, 230–31, 242; non-discrimination in Iraq, 138–39, 142; Sephardim communal identity, 8–9, 243. See also nationalism

Douek, Ramond, 195n10

economy: Arab economic blockade of Israel, 182–83, 190; British political/economic interests in Palestine, 125–27, 130; economic self-reliance, 42–44; economic status of Mizrahim in Israel, 225, 236–37, 241–42; origin of Jewish Question and, 143–45; Palestinian Arab and Jewish labor, 128–29. *See also* capitalism; class

education: Arab and Jewish education in Palestine, 129; Arab women's education, 31–37; cultural nationalism and, 42–43, 45; development of Hebrew education, xxxi; history of the people of Israel, 117–18; Middle Eastern Europeanized education, 92–94, 100; of Mizrahim in Israel, xxix, 235–242; Ottoman education, 21–22

Effendi, Haim Nahum, 80

Effendi, Sasson Heskel, 80

Egypt: antifascism in, 164, 174; anti-Zionism in, 166; Arab-Israeli War of 1948, 177–78, 180–81, 222n9; Cattaui as government official, 80; colonialist antisemitism in, 155, 155n4; constitutional initiative, 55–57, 59–61, 80; Esther Azhari Moyal work in, 30; Gaza Strip and, 178, 181–84, 181n4, 189–190; immigrants to Palestine, 229t, 238t, 240t, 241t; independence movement, 15, 24–26, 176–78, 186n6; inter-religious relations in, 49–53, 58–59; Marxist movement in, 164–65, 174, 176–78, 180–87, 191–96, 216–17; nationalist newspapers, 49, 58–59; Palestine relationship with, 177, 183–87; Sannu' exile from, 23–26; Suez War of 1956, 216, 220–21; women's movement in, 99, 99n7; Ya'qub Sannu' contributions in, 10–11; Zionist activism in, 171–72

Eliachar, Elie (Eliyahu), xxxiii, 119, 213

Elkabir, A. S. (Ibrahim al-Kabir), 137

Elmaleh, Avraham, 1, 78

English language, 36, 65, 225–26

Epstein, Yitzhac, 102–6

European Jews: assimilation of, 98–101; persecution of, 124–25, 144–45, 154, 156, 207; post-Balfour settlement influence, 133; post-World War II democracies and, 161; post-World War II refugees, 138, 167, 170–71; religious and cultural dominance of, xxii–xxiii, xxv–xxvi, 62–63, 89; views of Islamic tolerance, 58–59. *See also* Ashkenazim

Ezra, Ibn, 8

Fahmi, Ziad, 23n8

Farag, Murād, **48**

Fascism, 145–46, 154–55, 159, 168–69

feminism, 30–37, 72–73, 99, 99n7

Fishman Maimon, Yehouda Leib, 78, 78n3

Ford, Henry, 154

France, 11, 148–49

Franco, Moise, 5, 5n3

French language, 36, 65

Gaza Strip, 178, 181–84, 181n4, 189–190

Germany, 39–40, 124–25, 139, 145, 148–49, 154, 156, 166–67

Golding, Louis, 151

Gramsci, Antonio, 145n1

Great Britain: antisemitism in, 154–55; Boer War, 14–17; "divide and rule" strategy, 11, 150, 153–54; Egyptian independence and, 15, 24–26, 176–78, 186n6; formation of Jordan and, 182; Jewish migration to Palestine from, 158; Peel Commission, 120; political/economic interests in Palestine, 125–27, 130, 148–155

Greece, 229t

Gromyko, Andrei, 177, 177n2

Habas, Bracha, 230

Ha-Ichud (Union), 131–32

Halevi, Yehuda, 8, 69

Halutse Ha-Mizrah (Pioneers of the East), 114

Ha-Mizrah, xxxiii
haskala, xxix
Hatata, Sharif, 195n11
Hebrew language: adoption by Mizrahi
    writers, xxxi, 198; Hebrew advocacy
    movement, 1; Israeli Hebrew literary
    culture, 199; as liturgical language,
    91–92; Palestine traditional Hebrew
    language/culture, 75–76; as proposed
    Eretz Yisrael co-official language,
    116; role in Zionist Palestine, 64–66;
    scholarship on Arab nations in, 222;
    as Sephardic language, 1, 8
Hussein bin Ali, Sharif, 149, 153

imperialism. See colonialism/imperialism
India, 15, 229t
integration (of Mizrahim into Israeli
    society), xxvii–xxviii, 103, 114, 137, 168,
    225–26, 236–244. See also assimilation;
    Mizrahim
Iran, 229t
Iraq: Effendi as government official, 80;
    immigrants to Palestine, 229t, 230,
    232t, 238t, 240t, 241t; Iraqi Jewish
    Arabic-language writing, xxxiii, 142;
    Iraqi Orientation integration initiative,
    137; Jewish population in, xxix,
    110–13, 138–39; Mizrahi intellectuals in,
    xxxiii; persecution of Jews in, 162–63;
    Revolution of 1958, 216; theosophical
    movement in, xxxvii n26; views on
    Palestine in, 140, 141–43; Zionist
    movement in, xxxvi n17, 110–13
Islam: Christian imperialism and,
    89; difficulty of assimilating into,
    100; European influence on, 94, 96;
    Jewish views of, xxix, 12–13; Koranic
    writings on tolerance, 18–20; Muslim
    Brotherhood (Egypt), 184, 186;
    nationalist education and, 94–95;
    Sannu' regarded as Muslim, 28; women's
    movement in, 99, 99n7

Islamic-Jewish relations: Arab-Jewish
    cultural revival, xxxiii–xxxiv; as East and
    West theme, 7; in Egypt, 49–53; Koran as
    paradigm for, 18–20, 27; Sannu' regarded
    as Muslim, 28. See also Arab-Israeli
    relations; Arab-Jewish relations
Israel: Arab-Israeli War of 1948, 177–78,
    180–81, 222n9; Arab nationalist
    movements and, 187–88; Eurocentric
    culture in, 201–2, 205–8, 214, 219–220;
    impact on Mizrahim, xxvi–xxvii, xxx;
    Israeli Communist Party, 180–81, 186–88;
    Israeli nationalism, 200–203; as Jewish
    homeland, 74, 116–17, 122–23, 132n10,
    133; literary culture in, 199; Mizrahi
    immigrants in, xxxii, 198, 206–12,
    218–19, 226–29; "Mizrahi problem"
    issue, xxii, xxvii, xxxvi n16; non-Jewish
    minorities in, 217–220; overview of
    first-decade immigration, 228–29;
    political representation of Jewish groups
    in, 244–48; social discrimination against
    Israeli Mizrahim, 207–12, 214, 219–220,
    230–31; statehood proposal, 115–16; Suez
    War of 1956, 216, 220–21; traditional
    Hebrew language/culture in, 75–76.
    See also Arab-Israeli relations; Arab-
    Jewish relations; Palestine/Eretz-Yisrael;
    Yishuv; Zionism

Jabotinsky, Ze'ev, 125
Jewish Question, xxv, 143–45, 153–55,
    159–161, 166–69
Jordan/Transjordan, 129, 182, 190

al-Kabir, Ibrahim, 137
Kahanoff, Jacqueline Shohet, xxxi, xxxiii–
    xxxiv, 205
Karaite Judaism, 48
Kibbutz movement, xix, 153, 223, 230–32
Kook, Avraham Yitzhak Ha-Kohen,
    72–73
Kurdistan, 16